SC⬭FFERS

Responding to Those Who Deliberately Overlook Creation and the Flood

SIMON TURPIN

First printing: August 2021

Master Books®, P.O. Box 726, Green Forest, AR 72638
Master Books® is a division of the New Leaf Publishing Group, Inc.

ISBN: 978-1-68344-267-7
ISBN digital: 978-1-61458-783-5
Library of Congress Number: 2021941589

Cover by Diana Bogardus

Please consider requesting that a copy of this volume be purchased by your local library system.

Printed in the United States of America

Please visit our website for other great titles:
www.masterbooks.com

For information regarding author interviews,
please contact the publicity department at (870) 438-5288.

Master
Books®
A Division of New Leaf Publishing Group
www.masterbooks.com

Contents

Too many church leaders have wittingly or unwittingly undermined the authority of God's Word in Genesis, which has contributed to considerable damage generationally to the church and its effectiveness in the culture. In his book *Scoffers*, Simon Turpin uses his theological training, in-depth biblical research, and vast experience in the creation apologetic ministry to challenge those who would reject the Genesis account of creation and the Flood as literal history. A fresh approach to give needed understanding to God's revelation in Genesis, the age of the earth, and the promise of the final glorious redemption of creation. Another unique publication all Christians should devour.

Ken Ham, CEO, Answers in Genesis, The Creation Museum and The Ark Encounter

In this book Simon shows why the events of creation and the global Flood are crucial to understanding the message of the Bible, especially the Gospel of salvation. The warnings given in the second letter of Peter are very relevant for today.

Professor Stuart Burgess (BSc(Eng), PhD, CEng, FIMechE). Professor of Engineering Design at the University of Bristol (UK).

This book shows in crystal clear reasoning that if we accept the authority of God's Word as believers, and in particular the second epistle of Peter, then we must accept the supernatural creation of the world followed by the historical global, catastrophic Flood which is taught clearly in this epistle. Simon Turpin shows first the canonicity of 2 Peter and then using 2 Peter itself argues that the growing heresy within the church of believing Genesis to be a non-historical myth is precisely what Peter is warning would happen in the last days. Turpin rightly argues that these very days of apostasy are marked by many in the evangelical community not accepting the authority of Genesis, and that this is linked with an unbelief in the coming judgement upon the world and the Return of Christ. All Christian leaders need to read this excellent book, written by one who is a well-trained theologian.

Professor Andy C. McIntosh (DSc, FIMA, C.Math, FEI, C.Eng, FInstP, MIGEM, FRAeS). Emeritus Professor of Thermodynamics, School of Chemical and Process Engineering, University of Leeds, Leeds, UK.

Adjunct Professor, Faculty of Engineering, Liberty University, Lynchburg, VA, USA. Adjunct Professor, Crown Seminary, Knoxville, Tennessee, USA.

INTRODUCTION

"Scoffer" is the name of the arrogant, haughty man who acts with arrogant pride (Proverbs 21:24).

For at least the last two hundred years, the Western world has openly scoffed (mocked) at Christians and at their beliefs about the Bible. Scoffing is basically argument by ridicule, an approach that the religious leaders of Jesus' day often took to His teaching (Luke 16:14, 23:35). Much of the scoffing, or ridicule, Christians receive today comes from those who have rejected the Bible's history, especially in Genesis 1–11. Those who scoff at Christianity, such as atheistic evolutionists or skeptics, often ridicule Christians who accept the belief in the supernatural creation of the world and a global Flood by calling them "fundamentalists," "anti-intellectuals," "extremists," and "literalists." Or they use other disparaging remarks like "dishonest," "ignorant," or "stupid" to describe those who argue for the biblical creation position. These sorts of arguments are known as epithet fallacies. Rather than using sound logical argumentation, they use biased emotional language to support a conclusion that is logically unproven in order to capitalize on people's emotions. Logical fallacies are often seductive and tend to be persuasive for many people because they are very subtle. The news media, internet, and evolutionary literature are full of these emotionally charged arguments (often without making a logical case for their argument) against Christians and the Bible. You may have come across some of the following "arguments" and statements against the biblical creation position:

- "Evolution vs. Creationism." This is a common way to frame the evolution vs. creation debate. By attaching "ism" to creation and not evolution, it subtly implies creation is a belief whereas evolution is science.

- "The six-day creation position is misleading, as it teaches people to believe nonsense and lies." This is simply using emotional language to try to persuade. It is also arbitrary, as the same can be said of the evolution position.

- "To be a creationist, you'd have to ignore tons of scientific evidence." This remark is the fallacy of the question-begging epithet because it uses biased language (and not logic) to suggest that scientific evidence supports evolution.

- "Genesis teaches that God created the world in six days, but the best scientists tell us that the universe is billions of years old." How do you know who are the best scientists? There are many PhD Christian scientists who believe in a young age for the universe.[1]

Because evolutionary scientists view creation as religion veiled as *pseudoscience* and are generally unfamiliar with creationist arguments, they deliberately choose a strategy of scoffing when engaging with them. In his book *Replacing Darwin: The New Origin of Species*,[2] Dr. Nathaniel Jeanson gave critics of biblical creation the means by which to potentially tear down scientific models: he gave them testable predictions that future experiments could reveal to be true or false. Unfortunately, rather than engage his testable predictions, his critics prefer ignorance to his claims. Dr. Jeanson has witnessed the strategy firsthand in public debates on his genetic research. He notes:

> …not only are professional scientists raised in a bubble and practice their careers in a bubble; they also deliberately choose to live in a bubble, ridiculing any opposition as outrageous and unworthy of serious consideration.[3]

Not only do evolutionists ignore the claims of biblical creationists, but they also argue creation is unscientific because it is not falsifiable, but then they appeal to scientific evidence to try and refute it. This just shows

1. See Dr. Jason Lisle, "The Fallacy of the Question-Begging Epithet," August 24, 2009, https://answersingenesis.org/logic/the-fallacy-of-the-question-begging-epithet/.
2. In his book *Replacing Darwin*, Dr. Nathaniel Jeanson shows that creation science meets the golden standard of science, falsification, as he made several testable predictions, ranging from field studies to DNA mutation rates. See Dr. Nathaniel Jeanson, *Replacing Darwin: The New Origin of Species* (Green Forest, AR: Master Books, 2017).
3. Dr. Jeanson gives a specific example from an evolutionary scientist that he debated who admitted in a blog post years before the debate to employing a strategy of ridicule when it comes to dealing with creationists. See Dr. Nathaniel T. Jeanson, *Replacing Darwin Made Simple* (Petersburg, KY: Answers in Genesis, 2019), 79.

the contradictory claims of evolutionists. If biblical creation is not falsifiable, then you cannot use evidence to try and refute it, and if it is testable (as Dr. Jeanson and others have shown), then it is scientific.

All the above arguments, however, are not based upon logic but are driven by pure emotion, and the Apostle Peter warned believers about being exploited through the "false words" of scoffers (2 Peter 2:3). The same "ignorant" and "unstable" people distort the meaning of Scripture to their own destruction (2 Peter 3:16). We need to remember that "false words" from scoffers, which call into question the truth of God's Word, have the power to deceive people, as they are meant to distract us from the truth. This was the approach the serpent (Satan, Revelation 12:9, 20:2) used when he came to Eve in the Garden, by taking God's Word and reshaping it, saying: "Did God actually say?" (Genesis 3:1). Satan's words, which were designed to get Eve to debate God's Word, entertained the possibility that God did not know what was best. While God had commanded Adam not to eat from one tree, Satan told Eve it was "… any tree in the garden." In other words, Satan presents God as the cosmic killjoy, someone who comes along and likes saying "no" to everything and everyone. In his temptation, Satan did not just point to the tree and simply say, "Go on, eat it," but he re-describes reality in a way that is *false*.

This first step by Satan, that deceived Eve, began by distorting the truthfulness of God's Word. As Adam and Eve found out, there are only tragic consequences when we reject God's Word as the sole authority for our lives. Although once naked and without shame, after they disobeyed God, Adam and Eve realized they were naked and became ashamed. In that shame, they were alienated from God (Genesis 3:7). Eve gave in to temptation because she saw that the tree was 1) good for food, 2) pleasing to the eye, and 3) desirable for gaining wisdom (Genesis 3:6). These temptations correspond to John's description of the things of this world: "The desires of the flesh and the desires of the eyes and the pride of life" (1 John 2:16). This is a pattern of temptation that runs through Scripture: 1) start listening to the creature instead of the Creator; 2) follow our own impressions instead of God's instructions; 3) make self-fulfilment the goal.

The prospect of these things seems good to life when, in fact, it leads to death. If you rebel against the God who gives life, what else is there but death? As Scripture states: "There is a way that seems right to a man, but its end is the way to death" (Proverbs 14:12). In the Garden in Eden, Eve rejected the truth of God's Word and instead chose to believe a falsehood about Him. In this act of disobedience, Eve chose to follow Satan's "false words" over the truth of God's Word, and it resulted in death (see Genesis 3:1–5, 8, 19; cf. 2:17).

The way to deal with "false words" from those who scoff at God's Word is by standing on and proclaiming the truth and authority of God's Word and not by conceding it. Jesus is our example here in that when He was tempted in the wilderness, He relied on the truth of God's Word to defeat Satan (Matthew 4:1–10). Jesus overcame Satan's temptations by quoting Scripture, saying to him, "It is written," which has the force of or is equivalent to "that settles it," and Jesus understood that the Word of God was sufficient for this. In fact, Jesus quoted Scripture, in context, to refute the "false words" of the religious teachers (scoffers) of His day in His many debates with them (see Matthew 15:1–9, 22:23–33).

Relevant to this book, however, are the scoffers and their teaching described in 2 Peter 3:

> This is now the second letter that I am writing to you, beloved. In both of them I am stirring up your sincere mind by way of reminder, that you should remember the predictions of the holy prophets and the commandment of the Lord and Savior through your apostles, knowing this first of all, that scoffers will come in the last days with scoffing, following their own sinful desires. They will say, "Where is the promise of his coming? For ever since the fathers fell asleep, all things are continuing as they were from the beginning of creation." For they deliberately overlook this fact, *that the heavens existed long ago, and the earth was formed out of water and through water by the word of God*, and that by means of these *the world that then existed was deluged with water and perished*. But by the same word the heavens and earth that now exist are stored up for fire, being kept until the day of judgment and destruction of the ungodly. But do not overlook this one fact, beloved, that with the Lord one day is as a thousand years, and a thousand years as one day. The Lord is not slow to fulfill his promise as some count slowness, but is patient toward you, not wishing that any should perish, but that all should reach repentance. But the day of the Lord will come like a thief, and

then the heavens will pass away with a roar, and the heavenly bodies will be burned up and dissolved, and the earth and the works that are done on it will be exposed. Since all these things are thus to be dissolved, what sort of people ought you to be in lives of holiness and godliness, waiting for and hastening the coming of the day of God, because of which the heavens will be set on fire and dissolved, and the heavenly bodies will melt as they burn! But according to his promise we are waiting for new heavens and a new earth in which righteousness dwells (2 Peter 3:1–13; emphasis mine).

Peter tells us that in the last days (the era from Christ's first coming until His return; cf. Acts 2:17), scoffers will come scoffing at the belief that Christ will come again. They will base their ideas upon the assumption that the world has not changed, deliberately ignoring two major events in the history of the world:

1. God's supernatural creation of the world, and

2. God's judgment of the world by the historical, global, catastrophic Flood in the days of Noah.

Does this sound familiar? It should, because today's secular Western world is characterized by people who scoff at and ridicule the second coming of Christ and Christianity because they have already rejected the historicity of the accounts of supernatural creation of the world and the cataclysmic global Flood in Genesis, as they reason "scientific" knowledge (i.e., evolution and millions of years) makes it impossible to believe such things. For example, in an article in the English newspaper the *Independent*, the author, James Williams, an agnostic, scoffs at the Bible because of its supernatural content and believes that this is one of the reasons why the current generation of British young people are rejecting Christianity and becoming increasingly secular. Williams argues:

The problem for religion [Christianity] is that it can be very illogical. Take, for example, the idea of a talking snake, or people turning into salt, or a 600-year-old man building a boat to house every species of animal. This is what Darwin realised: such stories were just stories. Not fact, not truth. . . . As an agnostic and researcher into creationism, I encounter many ultra-evangelical Christians who believe the Bible from first word to last, including the talking snake and story of Noah. These people show, in extremis, that belief and faith can be irrational and without evidence. . . .[4]

As a "researcher" into creationism, Mr. Williams should have known better than to say that Noah built a boat to house every species (*genus*) of animal, as creationists teach that Noah took two of every kind (*family*) of animal onto the Ark (see Genesis 6:20). This article, like many others, was not about research or truth but simply about scoffing at the Christian faith. There can be no doubt that the current generation of young people in the Western world, who have been indoctrinated in a secular worldview, find the content of the Bible illogical. This is not because of logic or reason, but it is due to their secular worldview. It is important to realize that the secular worldview separates the heart and mind, whereas the Bible brings them together (Matthew 22:37). The secular worldview regularly confuses emotion with truth, and feelings with logic. The secular worldview is based upon human autonomy, the belief that man determines what is right and wrong and that morality must be judged by the values of this present age. The worldview behind secularism is evolutionary naturalism, the belief that nature is all there is, and man is just the end result of a cosmic accident. In this worldview, reality is what we make it because there is no God (or even purpose) that created it, maintains it, or declares any absolutes; therefore, we can construct the world around us through our thought, language, and autonomous human reason. The reason secular thought finds Christianity illogical is not because it is illogical or irrational (as logic and reason only make sense if the God of the Bible exists) but because of its supernatural content (i.e., supernatural creation, a talking snake, a global Flood, the virgin birth, miracles of Jesus, the Resurrection, etc.). The point of ultimate conflict between secularism and Christianity is in their basic presuppositions. The foundational presupposition for secularists is autonomous human reason as the only way to understand human opinions and actions. For Christians it is divine revelation, the truth of God's Word, that is the foundation for all truth.

---

4. See James Williams, "How Better Education Has Built a More Secular Britain," *Independent*, September 14, 2017, http://www.independent.co.uk/news/education/how-better-education-has-built-a-more-secular-britain-a7947091.html.

Nevertheless, although secularists say they reject the Bible because of its illogical claims, for some reason, they have no problem with believing the universe came from nowhere and no reason and believing in the miracle that a single cell produced all the variations of species that we now see today. Or that dinosaurs evolved into birds or even the belief that people evolved from ape-like creatures. All of these things are very illogical and are without evidence and are believed upon because of a particular worldview (i.e., evolutionary naturalism).

Sadly, it's not just unbelievers who scoff at what the Bible says about the creation of the heavens and earth in six consecutive 24-hour days, the global Flood, and the age of the earth. Today there are many influential Christian leaders who, because they have accepted the secular assumptions of naturalism and uniformitarianism, are helping to scoff (maybe unwittingly) at the fact that God created everything supernaturally in six days just a few thousand years ago. One of the leading Christian apologists in the world today, William Lane Craig, professor of philosophy at Houston Baptist University and research professor of philosophy at Talbot School of Theology (Biola University), is one of these people:

> ...I've seen a comparable statistic that says that over 50% of evangelical pastors think that the world is less than ten thousand years old. Now, when you think about that ... that is just hugely embarrassing; that over half of our ministers really believe that the universe is only around ten thousand years old. This is just scientifically nonsense, and yet this is the view that the majority of our pastors hold. It's really quite shocking when you think about it.[5]

The reason Dr. Craig finds it "embarrassing" and "shocking" that Christians would believe what the Bible says about the creation of the world in the Book of Genesis is because he has already been convinced by the arguments for millions of years of geological history and the big bang. Because of the influence of the secular view of the origins of the world, Dr. Craig has also had to alter his view on the inerrancy of Scripture (believing in limited inerrancy[6]), has rejected Adam and Eve as the first

---

5. See William Lane Craig, "Dr. Craig on Collins vs Dawkins on Design of Universe," January 20, 2013, https://www.reasonablefaith.org/media/reasonable-faith-podcast/dr.-craig-on-collins-vs-dawkins-on-design-of-universe/.
6. See William Lane Craig, "What Price Biblical Inerrancy?" Reasonable Faith, July 1, 2007, http://www.reasonablefaith.org/what-price-biblical-errancy.

humans who were supernaturally created by God,[7] believes that the
Flood mentioned in Genesis 6–8 was only a local flood, is only reason-
ably confident of the virgin birth,[8] and even suggests Jesus in His humanity held false beliefs (e.g., on creation and the Flood).[9] Dr. Craig's doubt
over these vital doctrines flows out of his rejection of the sufficiency and
inerrancy of Scripture in order to defend the Christian faith. Instead, he
argues for what he calls "Mere Christianity."[10] The problem with "Mere
Christianity" is not only does it narrowly defend the nature of the Christian worldview, but most importantly, it leaves out the gospel. A Bible
that is not sufficient to define the gospel or is only limited in its inerrancy
is not enough for the claim that Jesus Christ is Creator of all things,
that He lived a perfect life, died a substitutionary death on the Cross,
and rose again on the third day, conquering sin and death (see Hebrews
1:1–3, 4:15, 9:28; 1 Corinthians 15:4).[11] These are supernatural claims,
and they must be grounded in supernatural revelation. We need to realize
that there are consequences to ideas. Many Christians are often unaware
of (or simply do not care about) the devastating consequences for synthesizing the belief in millions of years with the Bible. Christians, like Dr.
Craig, who accept the idea of millions of years are unwittingly helping to
erode belief in other vital doctrines of the Christian faith (i.e., inerrancy
and sufficiency of Scripture, historicity of Genesis 1–11, etc.).

When the Apostle Peter wrote to believers in his second letter, he
was trying to stir up their minds by way of reminder so that they would
be ready for the coming attacks of the scoffers of his day. Just as with
every generation, Christians today again need that reminder, as there
are scoffers still around! For the last two hundred years, the scoffers have
been mounting a particular attack on the foundation of Scripture (Gen-

7. See W.L. Craig, "Focus on Adam and Eve," Podcast transcript, reasonablefaith.org, September 9, 2018.
8. See Nicholas Kristof, Professor, "Was Jesus Really Born to a Virgin? I question William
Lane Craig of Talbot School of Theology and Houston Baptist University about Christianity," December 21, 2018, nytimes.com.
9. See William Lane Craig, "Should OT Difficulties Be an Obstacle to Christian Belief?"
Reasonable Faith, April 16, 2017, http://www.reasonablefaith.org/should-ot-difficulties-be-
an-obstacle-to-christian-belief.
10. The "Mere Christianity" apologetic solely defends the cardinal doctrines of the Christian
faith (Trinity, Deity of Christ, etc.) affirmed by all the Christian confessions, whether
Catholic, Orthodox, Protestant, or Coptic.
11. The words in this sentence are not original to me; I heard apologist Dr. James White say
something similar to this.

esis 1–11) and helping to erode confidence in it and other parts of the Bible connected to it. This is why, when it comes to the discussion over the supernatural creation of the world in six days and the global Flood, many people mistakenly think that the issue only involves the interpretation of the early chapters of Genesis. It is important to remember that the teachings of the New Testament are also significant to this debate. Peter's understanding of these two events is key, as it helps us see how the Apostle read Genesis. This in turn informs our understanding of the issue of the earth's age. Unfortunately, many Christians today reject the idea of the supernatural creation of the world in six days and the global Flood of Noah's day. This rejection has nothing to do with what the Bible teaches but is an implication of accepting the idea that the earth is millions of years old. The Apostle Peter clearly understood that the early chapters of Genesis refer to a supernatural creation and global Flood, and he used that understanding to counter the arguments of the scoffers in his time. These biblical events in the Book of Genesis are so important to understand, as they are foundational for:

- Understanding Scriptures, authority, clarity, and inerrancy
- Understanding God's goodness in creation
- Understanding the origin of death and suffering
- Understanding the origin and nature of sin
- Understanding the reality of salvation from sin
- Understanding God's purpose and patience in judgment
- Understanding how the global Flood is key to understanding the age of the earth
- Understanding God's roles as Judge and Saviour in redemptive history
- Understanding the final redemption of creation with the new heavens and earth

The purpose of this book is to show that while there are those, both inside and outside the Church, who choose to scoff at what the Bible says about the supernatural creation of the world (chapter 6) and the cataclysmic global Flood (chapter 7), they do so not based upon any evidence but upon philosophical (uniformitarian) presuppositions (chapters 4 and 5). Due to the effects of uniformitarian thinking in the Western world, many pastors and teachers today no longer exhort or instruct their congregations correctly when it comes to understanding Genesis 1–11 as actual events that took place in space-time history. Because of this compromise with evolution and millions of years, many evangelical theologians today are beginning to interpret the creation and Flood accounts as myth rather than history (chapter 2) and redefine vital biblical doctrines like inerrancy so that it takes into account human error (chapter 3). God's judgment of the whole world in the past by the Flood (and Sodom and Gomorrah) also helps us understand the purpose of this judgment and why He continues to wait patiently to once again judge the world in righteousness (chapters 8 and 9). It is also important to understand that it is not just the beginning of the Bible that is affected by compromise with evolution and millions of years, as it also affects how we view the redemption of creation with the new heavens and earth (chapter 10).

The teaching of evolution and millions of years has had, and is continuing to have, a devastating effect on the body of Christ worldwide. I hope this book shows why the events of biblical history, specifically creation and the global Flood, are important to the coherence of the whole of the narrative of the biblical narrative which culminates in the restoration of creation in the new heavens and earth. We must realize that any attempt to synthesize theistic evolution or old-earth creation with the Bible will just not work, and it only helps erode the redemptive history (creation-fall, redemption, and consummation) set forth in Scripture.

CHAPTER ONE

PETER'S SECOND EPISTLE?

2 Peter 3:1

This is now the second letter that I am writing to you, beloved
(2 Peter 3:1a).

In order to have a proper understanding of any book or letter, it is
helpful to know who wrote it, why they wrote it, the people they were
writing to, and when it was written. This is especially important with 2
Peter, as it is one of the most-attacked books of the New Testament. The
letter of 2 Peter is probably one of the most neglected and criticized in
all the New Testament. It seems it is one of the least preached, studied,
and referenced by Christians in the Church today. There may well be
reasons for this, such as the issues to do with authorship, its date, the
complex passages on the future judgment of the world, and its condemnation of false teachers (scoffers). In a post-modern world, which says
there is no wrong thinking (orthodoxy or heresy), to have a book that
says there is wrong thinking (false teaching) may be a reason that it does
not make it first on a preacher's list for a new sermon series. However,
this is the very reason 2 Peter should be top of our preaching list, as
false teachers are very real, and they will wreak havoc in the life of the
Church. Second Peter then is a well-timed corrective to our post-modern way of thinking.

One of the issues that may not be known to many Christians about 2
Peter is that it is one of the most-disputed books in the canon of the New
Testament. This is because critical scholars would argue that Peter did not
write this letter, as he had died long before it was written. These critical

scholars would claim, along with some who would consider themselves evangelical scholars, that 2 Peter is pseudonymous, written sometime in the late 1st century or early 2nd century (A.D. 80–150). A pseudonymous letter is one that has been written by a person who writes a book under a false name. These scholars would offer a number of reasons for this:

1. The supposed historical inconsistencies (i.e., the reference to Paul's letters as Scripture).[1]
2. The letter's relationship with 1 Peter and how to resolve the language and style of 2 Peter with the New Testament portrait of the Apostle.
3. The similarities between 2 Peter and Jude indicate Peter copied from Jude.
4. Its struggle for canonical status in the Early Church.

The suggestion that 2 Peter is a pseudonymous work is a serious challenge to the authenticity of the letter. The problem with the idea that 2 Peter is pseudonymous would mean it's a forgery and not compatible with the inspiration of Scripture. Despite these claims, the internal evidence of the letter confirms that the Apostle Peter is the author. The Lord has placed 2 Peter in the canon of the New Testament for a reason, and therefore we must pay close attention to what it teaches, as it has much relevancy for the Church today.

Authorship

The author of 2 Peter is the Apostle Peter, Simon Bar-Jonah (Matthew 16:17), the fisherman who grew up in Bethsaida (John 1:44) along the coast of the Sea of Galilee. This is the claim of the letter, that it is written by "Simeon Peter," with the form Simeon being used — Συμεών *Symeōn* (2 Peter 1:1) — which is used of Peter only in Acts 15:14. If the author was pseudonymous, then why not use the form of address in 1 Peter or another title used for Peter in the New Testament? The claim that the letter was written by Peter also appears in 3:1: "This is now the second letter that I am writing to you, beloved." It's not just that the name "Peter" appears in the letter but that it also makes positive

---

1. Many critical scholars assume that the New Testament canon had not developed that early, but this has been shown not to be the case. For a refutation of the late date for the New Testament canon, see Michael Kruger, *The Question of Canon: Challenging the Status Quo in the New Testament Debate* (Nottingham: InterVarsity Press, 2013).

claims to be the person that bears that name and recounts events that took place in Jesus' life. The author presents himself as someone who was actually an eyewitness of the event of the transfiguration of Jesus Christ (1:16–18); he mentions that the Lord had shown him that His death was close (1:14; cf. John 21:15–19) and identifies himself as a close associate of the Apostle Paul (2 Peter 3:15). Given the personal nature of these statements, it is difficult to see how a pseudepigraphal author could write such words with any authority.

Peter was called into ministry by Jesus (Mark 1:16–18) and was one of His original 12 disciples (Mark 3:13–16). A man of great boldness, courage, and self-confidence, Peter would not only physically defend Jesus (John 18:10) but also deny that he knew Him (Mark 14:66–72), though he was later restored to fellowship by Jesus after His resurrection (John 21:15–19). Peter was a key leader in the Early Church and preached the very first sermon, at Pentecost, when three thousand people were saved on that day (Acts 2:14–41). He not only continually defended the faith by boldly preaching the gospel, but he also suffered greatly for it (Acts 4:8–12, 5:17–18, 40–41, 12:1–5). As one of the leaders in the Early Church, he was, according to the Apostle Paul, called to minister to his fellow Jewish people (Galatians 2:8). Nevertheless, God also used him to minister to people from the nations (*ethnos*, Acts 10, 15:7; cf. 1 Peter 1:1).

Is 2 Peter pseudonymous? As we have already seen, the personal statements in the letter suggest not, but there are also other reasons to reject pseudonymity. Second Peter's emphasis on truth (2 Peter 1:12, 2:12) and warning about false teachers who "will exploit you with false words" (2 Peter 2:3) is hard to reconcile with someone who is writing falsely about who he is. Also, the words, concerning the transfiguration, "we were eyewitnesses" and "we heard" (2 Peter 1:16, 18), cannot be easily said by someone writing in a pseudepigraphal way. Moreover, would this be a principle early Christians would be fine with? Not at all! We need to remember that authorship was very important for early Christians.[2] They believed in apostolic authority. The Apostle Paul cautions against pseudonymous writing in 2 Thessalonians 2:2: ". . . not to be quickly

---

2. People may argue that if authorship was so important for early Christians, then why was the letter to the Hebrews accepted into the canon, as we don't know who wrote it? Even though we don't know definitively who the author of Hebrews was, we do know he was part of the apostolic circle (Hebrews 2:3, 13:23).

shaken in mind or alarmed, either by a spirit or a spoken word, or a letter seeming to be from us, to the effect that the day of the Lord has come."[3] The idea that Peter did not write 2 Peter but it is still Scripture is an incoherent statement; it's like saying falsehood is inspired.

There is another reason why 2 Peter is not pseudonymous. When books or letters are written in different time periods, they obviously reflect the time period in which they are written. For example, if Peter was written in the 2nd century, then we would expect it to address some of the key concerns of the 2nd century Church, such as: the fading hope of the *parousia* (second coming of Jesus),[4] discussion of the institutional structure of the church (i.e., bishops, hierarchy of leadership structure), or creedal language (i.e., new ways of expressing doctrine). If 2 Peter was a 2nd-century document written by a pseudonymous author, then what was his motive for writing it? Second Peter lacks the concerns of the state of the Church in the 2nd century.[5]

The difference in style of writing between 1 and 2 Peter may be explained by the use of secretaries (1 Peter 5:12). Peter may have written one letter himself and used a secretary for the other or even for both. It is also important to recognize that there are lots of problems with stylistic objections between the two letters, as they are often very subjective and overlook obvious reasons why an author would use different vocabulary and style (i.e., setting, context, and audience). The stylistic differences reflect different pastoral situations. For example, 1 Peter is written to encourage believers who are facing suffering for their faith (1 Peter 1:6, 3:14). On the other hand, 2 Peter is written to warn believers about false teachers. Furthermore, writing in his second epistle, Peter is at a different stage in his life, although only a few years apart from 1 Peter, as he knows that he is near death and so is leaving a farewell address (2 Peter 1:12–15). Even though there are differences in the style of writing, we should not overlook the many thematic links between epistles:[6]

---

3. The irony of this is that critical scholars argue that 2 Thessalonians is pseudonymous.
4. Peter reminds believers that the *parousia* is something that is very real and a factor in the life of the believer.
5. See Thomas Schreiner, *The New American Commentary: 1, 2 Peter, Jude,* Vol. 37 (Nashville, TN: B&H Publishing Group, 2003), 268–270.
6. Simon J. Kistemaker, "2 Peter," in *A Biblical-Theological Introduction to the New Testament: The Gospel Realized,* ed. Michael J. Kruger (Wheaton, IL: Crossway, 2016), 473.

1 Peter	Theme	2 Peter
1:10–12	inspiration of the Old Testament	1:19–21
1:2	doctrine of election	1:10
1:23	doctrine of the new birth	1:4
2:11–12	need for holiness	1:5–9
3:20	Noah and his family protected	2:5
4:2–4	immorality and judgment	2:10–22
4:7–11	exhortation to Christian living	3:14–18
4:11	doxology	3:18

The question of 2 Peter's literary relationship to the letter of Jude is brought up because there are at least 19 of the 25 verses in Jude that have a parallel in 2 Peter, some of which are:

2 Peter	Jude
denying the Master, 2:1	denying the Master, v. 4
condemnation of false teachers, 2:3	condemnation of false teachers, v. 4
angels kept in darkness, 2:4	angels kept in darkness, v. 6
Sodom and Gomorrah, 2:6	Sodom and Gomorrah, v. 7
slander of celestial beings, 2:11	slander of celestial beings, v. 8
blaspheme about matters of which they are ignorant, 2:12	blaspheme all that they do not understand, v. 10
followed the way of Balaam, 2:15	Balaam's error, v. 11
blackest darkness reserved for false teachers, 2:17	blackest darkness reserved for false teachers, v. 13
scoffers in the last days, 3:3	scoffers in the last days, v. 18

How then should we understand this literary relationship? There are at least three options suggested by scholars:

1. Second Peter copied from Jude.
2. Jude copied from 2 Peter.
3. Both copied from a common source.

The first option is the most popular view among scholars (although not all believe this), but this is largely because of the assumed pseudonymity of 2 Peter. The third option seems unnecessary because why appeal to hypothetical sources when we can appeal to Jude and 2 Peter? While there is no easy solution, as it is a complicated question, my preferred option is that Jude used 2 Peter as his source.[7] The only clue we have to this is that verses 17–18 of Jude seem to be quoting another apostolic source: "But you must remember, beloved, the predictions of the apostles of our Lord Jesus Christ. They said to you, 'In the last time there will be scoffers, following their own ungodly passions.' " The words "the apostles . . . said to you" could well point to Jude using Peter's writing as his source. Given that the author of 2 Peter is Peter, then there is no reason to think Jude was not dependent on Peter.[8]

Destination and Date

Because Peter was the author of the letter, it must have been written before his death, which was imminent at the time of writing (2 Peter 1:14). According to tradition, Peter was martyred in Rome under the Roman Emperor Nero, who died in A.D. 68; therefore, it must have been written before then. Also, because Peter mentions Paul's letters (plural, 3:16), it cannot have been written until at least most of his letters were penned; therefore, it cannot come before the mid-60s. So, it was probably written somewhere around A.D. 64–68.

There is not a lot to go on for the origin of the letter, but if written by Peter, then it was probably written in Rome (cf. 1 Peter 5:13),[9] as this is where tradition tells us he was before his death. The letter's destination, like its origin, is hard to know, as again, there is so little information to go on. The fact that 2 Peter seems to be writing to the same people as 1 Peter gives us a clue (2 Peter 3:1). It is therefore likely that he is writing to ". . . those who are elect exiles of the Dispersion in Pontus, Galatia, Cappadocia, Asia, and Bithynia. . ." (1 Peter 1:1).

Canonicity

Second Peter was not accepted into the canon of Scripture without a struggle. One of the reasons for this is that there were other letters that

---

7. Literary dependence does not call into question the inspiration of Scripture (see Luke 1:1–4).
8. See Simon J. Kistemaker, "Jude," in *A Biblical – Theological Introduction to the New Testament – The Gospel Realized*, ed. Michael J. Kruger (Wheaton, IL: Crossway, 2016), 510.
9. The reference to Babylon in 1 Peter suggests that Peter wrote from Rome. Babylon was a code name for Rome (the enemy of God; cf. Isaiah 13–14, 46–47; Jeremiah 50–51).

were forgeries (e.g., *The Gospel of Peter, The Acts of Peter, The Apocalypse of Peter*) around the second century claiming to be written by Peter. Again, the irony of the claim that 2 Peter is pseudonymous is that some Early Church fathers objected to its being in the canon because they did not think Peter wrote it. The Early Church did not accept books that were pseudonymous, as they cared about whether the author was really who he claimed he was. The Early Church father and historian of Christianity Eusebius (A.D. 263–339), in his compilation on Early Church history, tells his readers that although 2 Peter was disputed, it was not unknown but recognized by many (*Hist. eccl.* 3.25). Irenaeus (A.D. 130–202), bishop of Lyon, seems to have had access to 2 Peter as the wording of 3:8, "with the Lord one day is as a thousand years, and a thousand years as one day," is very close to what he wrote (*Haer.* 5.23.2). Other Early Church fathers, such as Clement of Alexandria (A.D. 150–215), also appear to accept 2 Peter as Scripture (*Hist. eccl.* 6.14.1):

> Eventually the church coalesced around 2 Peter, and it was received as authentic by such figures as Jerome, Athanasius, and Augustine, as well as the councils of Laodicea (ca. 360) and Carthage (ca. 397).[10]

Although there were doubts originally, there is no valid reason to doubt that 2 Peter is a part of the canon of Scripture.

Purpose

As has already been mentioned, 2 Peter includes a "last testament" or "farewell speech" in the form of a letter, as Peter acknowledges that his death is close at hand (2 Peter 1:12–15).[11] Last testaments generally include two things: 1) moral exhortation and 2) discussion on the future (eschatology). There are a number of reasons for Peter's writing, but the main thrust that dominates throughout the letter is that of dealing with false teachers (2 Peter 1:16, 2:1–22, 3:3). Peter knew he was coming to

---

10. Kistemaker, "2 Peter," 475.
11. Kistemaker notes: "Since most known examples of testamentary texts are forgeries, scholars have suggested that 2 Peter must therefore be a forgery. However, such a conclusion does not necessarily follow. Although, 2 Peter certainly shares certain features with the testamentary genre, it lacks others. For instance, it does not record a 'heavenly journey' of Peter — something often found in other testamentary literature. But the most important difference is that 2 Peter is in the form of a *letter* — a feature lacking in all testamentary literature up to this period." Kistemaker, "2 Peter," 475.

the end of his earthly life, and so he sought to warn of the danger of these false teachers and encourage believers to live holy lives (2 Peter 1:14, 3:11). These false teachers were trying to influence Peter's readers in a certain moral direction. The reason for this rejection of moral boundaries by the false teachers was the idea that the second coming (*parousia*) of Jesus in final judgment would not happen (2 Peter 3:4).

What is the philosophy behind the false teaching? Well, there is no consensus among scholars as to what the philosophy is. Some say it was Gnosticism, but if 2 Peter was written in the mid-60s, this would be too early for the emergence of Gnosticism. Others have identified Epicureanism as a possibility, but scholars have raised doubts about this as well.[12] It may be that the false teachers had ". . . a philosophy that is otherwise not attested in the New Testament or extant extrabiblical literature, similar to the 'Colossian heresy,' which likewise appears to have been unique and local."[13] Although we cannot be exactly certain as to the philosophy behind the false teachers, we do know that these false teachers are basically stating four things:

1. that there has been no divine intervention since the beginning of creation
2. that there is no reward for good or punishment for evil
3. that Jesus had not returned within the time frame of the first generation of the original Apostles
4. that Jesus would therefore not return and bring a final divine judgment

This thinking that is advocated by Peter's opponents is very similar to the things being denied in our world today by naturalistic evolutionists. The message of 2 Peter is immensely relevant to our modern world. The false teachers (scoffers) that Peter had to deal with were eschatological skeptics teaching that Christ is not coming back and that God will judge sin, which results in moral freedom (I can live how I want). False teachers are not a thing of the past; they come about at every stage of the Church. There were false teachers in the Old and New Testaments; they contin-

12. See Peter H. Davids, *The Letters of 2 Peter and Jude: PNTC* (Grand Rapids, MI: W.B. Eerdmans Publishing Company, 2006), 133–136.
13. Andreas J. Kostenberger and Michael J. Kruger, *The Heresy of Orthodoxy: How Contemporary Culture's Fascination with Diversity Has Reshaped our Understanding of Early Christianity* (Wheaton, IL: Crossway, 2010), 96.

ued after the Apostles died out, and they continue until this day. In light of the false teaching, Peter sums up his message to believers in the final verses:

> You therefore, beloved, knowing this beforehand, take care that you are not carried away with the error of lawless people and lose your own stability. But grow in the grace and knowledge of our Lord and Savior Jesus Christ. To him be the glory both now and to the day of eternity. Amen (2 Peter 3:17–18).

Whereas false teachers have an external association with God (2 Peter 2:1), Peter wants his readers to continually grow in a personal knowledge of God — the Lord Jesus (2 Peter 1:1).

CHAPTER TWO

WE DID NOT FOLLOW CLEVERLY DEVISED MYTHS

2 Peter 1:16–18

For we did not follow cleverly devised myths when we made known to you the power and coming of our Lord Jesus Christ, but we were eyewitnesses of his majesty. For when he received honor and glory from God the Father, and the voice was borne to him by the Majestic Glory, "This is my beloved Son, with whom I am well pleased," we ourselves heard this very voice borne from heaven, for we were with him on the holy mountain (2 Peter 1:16–18).

It is not uncommon today to hear those who would scoff at the Bible say that "Genesis is just another myth written by Bronze Age goat herders." Of course, this claim is without evidence, as the historicity and accuracy of Genesis and the rest of Old Testament is well attested to. For example, recent evidence suggests that the world's oldest alphabet was developed by the Hebrews, and not by the Phoenicians as previously believed. In his book *The World's Oldest Alphabet*, archaeologist Dr. Douglas Petrovich argues that it is the Hebrew language that is represented in the original proto-consonantal script.[1] In his book, Petrovich also confirms the biblical account of the Israelites in Egypt. Petrovich studied an inscription

---

1. See Dr. Douglas Petrovich, *The World's Oldest Alphabet — Hebrew as the Language of the Proto-Consonantal Script* (Jerusalem: Carata, 2016).

on a stele known as Sinai 115 (Year 18 of Amenemhat III ca. 1842 B.C.) that speaks of an expedition including a group that has connection to the early Israelites and reads: "Six Levantines, Hebrews of Bethel the beloved" (Bethel was the home of Jacob, see Genesis 35:1). This places Joseph's son Manasseh in Egypt in 1842 B.C.[2] This would make it world's oldest extrabiblical reference to the Hebrews (Israelites). Petrovich's discovery has some important implications, one of which is that it confirms that the Hebrew people were present in Egypt during the time period of Joseph to Moses (1876–1446 B.C.; Genesis 45–Exodus 12).

Here is the point: The Church didn't have this archaeological find for nearly 2,000 years. Yet, did it stop them believing in the truthfulness of historical accounts in Genesis and Exodus? No. Not at all. Does having these archeological discoveries help to further our understanding? Yes! What we need to realize is that there are lots of theories that contradict the Bible, but the facts, when rightly understood, never do. Even though archaeology cannot prove or disprove the message of the Bible, Alan Millard, Rankin Professor Emeritus of Hebrew and Ancient Semitic Languages at the University of Liverpool, reminds us it does "provide a good basis for a positive approach to the biblical records" and therefore "enable[s] its distinctive religious message to stand out more boldly."[3]

The attack on the Bible's history has led churches in the West to fail to emphasize the history of the Bible in preaching and teaching, which has led to many seeing the Bible as a myth. The consequences of this are that, if we do not emphasize the historicity of the Bible, there will be a divide between the Church and the world around us and preaching will become less effective. The Bible becomes a fanciful myth, and faith is seen as simply a matter of opinion. Therefore, it is important in our teaching and preaching that we emphasize the Bible's historical reliability.

The assertion that the events of Scripture are not unique but are just like other ancient "myths" is not a recent claim; the Apostle Peter also had to argue against this with the false teachers of his own day. The context of the Apostles not following "cleverly devised myths" is "when we made known to you the power and *coming* of our Lord Jesus Christ," which is what the scoffers, whom Peter was arguing against, rejected: "Where is the promise of his *coming*?" (2 Peter 3:4; emphasis mine). The false teachers of Peter's day "scoffed" at the future coming of the Lord Jesus, as they

2. Ibid., 15–29.
3. Alan Millard, *Treasures from Bible Times* (Lion, 1985), 14.

saw it as just another "myth" (*mythos*). Peter's apologetic against this is necessary because in the Greek worldview, the stories about the gods and great heroes were considered "myths."[4] The Greeks, who valued reason and wisdom above all things (1 Corinthians 1:22), believed these stories were simply untrue. Just as the Greeks were philosophically opposed to the resurrection of the body (Acts 17:32) because it did not fit their worldview (the Greeks saw the body [matter] as corrupt and not worthy of any form of immortality), so they were with the idea that Jesus would return physically. Peter defends his case against the accusation from the false teachers by stating, "…we were eyewitnesses of his majesty." It was at the transfiguration where Peter saw the glory and majesty of the Lord Jesus and heard God (the Father) pronounce Jesus as his Son (see Matthew 16:27–17:13). For Peter, then, the transfiguration anticipates the second *coming* of Jesus as it unveils the power and majesty that He will come in. The term "coming" (*parousia*) is associated in the New Testament with the return of Jesus (Matthew 24:3, 27, 37, 39; 1 Corinthians 15:23; 1 Thessalonians 3:13, 4:15; 2 Peter 3:12).

Peter is arguing that this view of Jesus' second *coming* as being a "myth" is wrong because the Apostles were "eyewitnesses of his majesty"; in other words, these claims are based in history. The uniqueness of Christianity is that it is grounded in history. The gospel is based upon the historicity of the life, death, and Resurrection of Jesus Christ. This is why whenever the history of the Christian faith is under attack from false teaching, then eyewitness testimony is appealed to (see 1 Corinthians 15:1–8; 1 John 1:1–3). It is to the "eyewitness" testimony of history that Peter appeals to in order to refute the scoffers. The reason for this is that God has given us history as a vehicle to communicate truth, as theologian Abner Chou argues:

> *The biblical writers do not see history as merely a means of communicating theology; rather, they see history as the means of actualizing theology.* History is the vehicle by which theological truth comes into our world and impacts our lives. Far from separating history from theology, the Bible seems to tie them inextricably together.[5]

4. See Davids, *The Letters of 2 Peter and Jude*, 200.
5. Abner Chou, " 'Did God Really Say..?'— Hermeneutics and History in Genesis 3," in *What Really Happened in the Garden: The Reality and Ramifications of the Creation and Fall of Man* (Grand Rapids, MI: Kregel Academic, 2016), 27.

The Bible's theological claims cannot be separated from its historical claims (cf. Exodus 20:1–2). Because of the impact of the idea of evolution and millions of years, many evangelical scholars see the account of the supernatural creation of the world and the cataclysmic Flood in Genesis as "myth." In an interview with Nicholas Kristof in the *New York Times*, Christian apologist William Lane Craig identified Genesis as "mytho-history":

> **Nicholas Kristof:** You don't believe the Genesis account that the world was created in six days, or that Eve was made from Adam's rib, do you? If the Hebrew Bible's stories need not be taken literally, why not also accept that the New Testament writers took liberties?
>
> **William Lane Craig:** Because the Gospels are a different type of literature than the primeval history of Genesis 1–11. The eminent Assyriologist Thorkild Jacobsen described Genesis 1–11 as history clothed in the figurative language of mythology, a genre he dubbed "mytho-history." By contrast, the consensus among historians is that the Gospels belong to the genre of ancient biography, like the 'Lives of Greeks and Romans' written by Plutarch. As such, they aim to provide a historically reliable account.[6]

It is interesting that Craig looks to a secular Assyriologist to determine the genre of Genesis and yet rejects the reliable New Testament authors and Jesus' affirmation that Genesis was history (as well as the testimony of believing archeologists who see Genesis as history). As we will see, Genesis is neither myth nor clothed in the figurative language of myth. Rather, as true history, it confronts and challenges the myths of the ancient world. It is important, therefore, like Peter, that we defend the events of creation and the Flood as they are presented to us in Genesis: as history.

Genesis and Modern-day Myth Claims

Just as Charles Darwin's *Origin of Species* has helped define the worldview of the Western world, so there were ancient Near East (ANE) accounts of creation and a flood (i.e., *Enuma Elish, Atrahasis Epic, Gilgamesh Epic*) that were seen as the intellectual framework of the ANE. When biblical scholars talk about the ANE, they are basically thinking of the nations

---

6. Nicholas Kristof, Professor, "Was Jesus Really Born to a Virgin? I question William Lane Craig of Talbot School of Theology and Houston Baptist University about Christianity," December 21, 2018, nytimes.com.

that surrounded Israel from Egypt all the way over to Babylon, the area that we today call the Middle East. These nations include Assyria, Babylon, Egypt, the Hittites, and Persia. This period of history stretches from the patriarchal period until the Babylonian exile (2000–587 B.C.).

It is in this polytheistic ANE context that we find other creation and flood accounts that have similarities with the accounts in Genesis. These other texts parallel the biblical accounts of creation and the Flood, and the existence of similarities between Genesis and ANE literature led critical scholars in the early 20th century to conclude that all of the material of Genesis 1–11 was borrowed by the Jews, from a single land understood to be Mesopotamia, who then filled it with Hebrew monotheism. In his commentary on the Book of Genesis in 1907, Old Testament scholar Samuel Driver argued this, but he also believed that the Hebrew writers had not just borrowed from the Mesopotamian accounts but removed the paganism from them:

> . . . that we have in the first chapter of Genesis the Hebrew version of an originally Babylonian legend respecting the beginning of all things . . . no archaeologist questions that the Biblical cosmogony, however altered and stripped of its original polytheism is, in its main outlines, derived from Babylonia.[7]

In the 20th century, critical scholars rejected the traditional view of the Mosaic authorship of the Pentateuch (Genesis to Deuteronomy) in the second millennium B.C. (1446–1406 B.C.[8]), looking instead to the Babylonian captivity (post-exile, 587 B.C.) as a key time of its composition. Critical scholars argued that Genesis was made up of multiple sources, known as the Documentary Hypothesis (J.E.D.P), that were written centuries after Moses died, and a redactor (editor) pieced together multiple strands. In the early 20th century, critical scholars had almost exclusively defined the early chapters of Genesis as myth. The influence of these ANE texts brought about the end to the debate, for critical scholars, over the historicity of the Book of Genesis, opening up the new perspective that it was myth. Of course, along with this, scholars rejected the unique worldview on the part of the Hebrews and therefore the idea of divine revelation and inspiration of Scripture.

7. S.R. Driver, *The Book of Genesis* (London: Methuen, 1907), 30.

8. This is based on an early date for the Israelite Exodus from Egypt (see 1 Kings 6:1; Judges 11:26).

In recent years, several influential evangelical scholars have also begun to argue that the early chapters of Genesis were influenced by ANE concepts of existence.[9] Probably the most notable of these scholars is John Walton, an Old Testament scholar at Wheaton College who is a specialist in ANE studies. Walton has proposed a novel interpretation for Genesis 1–11 and has argued for this position in several recent works.[10] Walton's proposal is that when Genesis 1 is read against its ANE background, it does not speak about the material origins of the world; rather, its concern is functional origins. More specifically, in Genesis 1, the days of creation are not about the material creation of the heavens and earth in six days but are speaking about the inauguration of a "Cosmic Temple."[11] Regarding the Flood in Genesis 6–8, Walton rejects the idea that the Flood account was borrowed from Babylonian myth and maintains that it is depicted literarily as a global event, but this is intentionally hyperbolic to highlight the Flood's significance.[12] So, for Walton, although the Flood was a historical event, it was not a global Flood.

In order to understand and interpret Genesis correctly, in Walton's own words: "The key then is to be found in the literature from the rest of the ancient world."[13] The points of similarity between Genesis 1–11 and other ANE accounts have led Walton and other evangelical scholars to conclude that Genesis is not historical but "is an ancient Near Eastern form of science."[14] In other words, the role of these texts in the ANE was, as Walton explains, ". . . like science in our modern world — it was their explanation of how the world came into being and how it worked. . . . Mythology is thus a window to culture."[15] The connection then, for these

---

9. See Tremper Longman III, "What Genesis 1–2 Teaches (and What It Doesn't)," in *Reading Genesis 1–2: An Evangelical Conversation*, ed. J. Daryl Charles (Peabody, MA: Hendrickson Publishers, 2013), 106–108; Denis O. Lamoureux, *Evolution: Scripture and Nature Say Yes!* (Grand Rapids, MI: Zondervan, 2016).

10. See John Walton, *The Lost World of Genesis One: Ancient Cosmology and the Origins Debate* (Downers Grove, IL: InterVarsity Press, 2009); John Walton, *The Lost World of Adam and Eve: Genesis 2-3 and the Human Origins Debate* (Downers Grove, IL: InterVarsity Press, 2015). John Walton and Tremper Longman III, *The Lost World of the Flood: Mythology, Theology, and the Deluge Debate* (Downers Grove, IL: InterVarsity Press, 2018).

11. Walton, *The Lost World of Genesis One*, 87–88.

12. Walton and Longman, *The Lost World of the Flood*, 45–49, 80.

13. Walton, *The Lost World of Genesis One*, 10.

14. Dennis R. Venema and Scot McKnight, *Adam and the Genome: Reading Scripture After Genetic Science* (Grand Rapids, MI: Brazos Press, 2017), 111.

15. John Walton, *The NIV Application Commentary: Genesis* (Grand Rapids, MI: Zondervan, 2001), 27.

scholars, between the biblical and the ANE worlds is that, just as with ANE literature, so Genesis 1–11 helps us "see how Israelites thought about themselves, their world, and their God."[16] The similarities then are associated with the fact that the biblical and ANE accounts are seen as "ancient cosmology" (e.g., Walton believes the Israelites believed in a flat earth and solid sky).[17] These scholars, while not rejecting the divine inspiration of Scripture, like the critical scholars, believe their view is based on careful analysis of the ANE context of Genesis 1–11. This, however, is just another way of "scoffing" at the biblical accounts of creation and the Flood because it means the Hebrew worldview is not uniquely revealed but belongs to the mythical worldview of its time. Sadly, many of these evangelical scholars today do not question the standard liberal historical-critical readings of Genesis (such as the discredited Documentary Hypothesis), which are highly speculative and debatable but are simply accepted to be true.

Before we go on, we need to understand what scholars mean by "epic" and "myth." An epic is essentially an extended poem that narrates acts of cultural human heroes who go on quests and adventures (e.g., Gilgamesh). Myths are stories in which the gods are the main characters (*Enuma Elish:* Apsu, Tiamat, and Marduk). In popular culture, a myth is generally equated with untruth, but when scholars use the term myth, this does not by definition preclude that some of its elements are true. Old Testament scholar and theistic evolutionist Peter Enns defines "myth" as:

> . . . an ancient, premodern, prescientific way of addressing questions of ultimate origins and meaning in the form of stories: Who are we? Where do we come from?[18]

This definition of myth, however, avoids the question of whether these stories narrate real history. It also has more to do with the arrogance of speaking out of modernity, as it seems to be implying that the Israelites were less intelligent than modern man, an example of what C.S. Lewis called "chronological snobbery." This is the idea that only recent and modern ideas can be right. Enns is implying that "pre-modern" and "pre-scientific" men are unable to tell the difference between myth and history, which, of course, is utter nonsense (cf. 2 Timothy 4:4). Enns is also guilty

---

16. Ibid., 27.
17. Walton, *The Lost World of Genesis One, 14–16; The Lost World of Adam and Eve*, 18–19.
18. Peter Enns, *Inspiration and Incarnation: Evangelicals and the Problem of the Old Testament* Second Edition (Grand Rapids, MI: Baker Academic, 2015), 39.

of isolating Genesis 1–11 from the rest of Scripture, especially when it comes to how the New Testament authors interpreted and understood these chapters, as they saw them as history (Matthew 19:4–6; Luke 17:26–27; Romans 5:12–19; 1 Timothy 2:13–14).

The purpose of this chapter is to see what the relationship is between the biblical accounts of creation and the Flood and the ANE parallels such as *Enuma Elish*, the *Atrahasis Epic*, and the *Epic of Gilgamesh*. Should we read them as the background to the creation account? Are the creation and Flood accounts rooted in the mythological worldview of their time? Why do the texts have similarities, and what about the differences? These are important questions to ask.

When and Why Was Genesis Written?

Before we look at the similarities and differences between Genesis and these ANE myths, it is important to ask the question, "When and why was Genesis written?" One reason critical scholars believe that Genesis was impacted by these ANE texts is the date of its composition. Critical scholars, as well as a number of evangelical scholars, still view the composition of the Torah (Pentateuch) as being the result of centuries of literary evolution, with its final composition in the Babylonian captivity, thereby ruling out its composition in the second millennium.[19] Despite the argument for the authorship of Genesis in the post-exilic period (587 B.C.), there is very good internal and external evidence to see the final form of Genesis as being "fundamentally from Moses"[20] in the second millennium (1446–1406 B.C.).[21]

---

19. Peter Enns states, "The Pentateuch was not authored out of whole cloth by a second-millennium Moses but is the end product of a complex literary process-written, oral, or both — that did not come to a close until the postexilic period." Enns, *The Evolution of Adam*, 23. The objections Enns raises for rejecting the Mosaic authorship of the Pentateuch have long been answered. See Gleason L. Archer, Jr., *A Survey of Old Testament: Introduction*, rev. ed. (Chicago, IL: Moody Press, 1985), 109–146; and also, Umberto Cassuto, *The Documentary Hypothesis and the Composition of the Pentateuch*, rev. ed., trans. Israel Abrahams (Jerusalem: Shalem Press, 2006).

20. The question of Mosaic authorship is not a straightforward issue, as what do we mean by it? Did Moses use oral and written sources? For example, there is good evidence that Moses likely used written sources in the composition of the Torah (this would explain many of the stylistic differences that occur in various sections), as sometimes these are clearly identified (e.g., Genesis 5:1; Numbers 21:14). Did Moses pen every single word himself (did he write about his own death in Deuteronomy 34?), or did he use scribes to record the accounts and laws of the Torah? Leaders in the ancient world seldom wrote books themselves.

21. It is important to remember that Jesus clearly believed in the Mosaic authorship of the Torah (John 5:45–47), as did the Apostle Paul (Romans 10:5, 19).

Moses was educated in the royal courts of Egypt, and his writings indicate that he knew the ancient world (Exodus 17:14, 24:4, 34:27; Acts 7:22). Many of the details of the Torah reflect eyewitness accounts and show that the person who wrote it was there (see Exodus 15:27; Numbers 11:7–9). The likeliest possible date for the writing of Genesis (the Torah) would be when Moses was at Sinai or in the plains of Moab across from Jericho, (Numbers 22:1, 26:63) when the Israelites were about to enter into Canaan. The scenario of Israel about to enter Canaan helps explain the reason for God giving Israel Genesis 1–11, as Old Testament scholar Douglas Petrovich explains:

> Therefore, he gave them Genesis 1–11 as a vaccination against the adverse effects that would be created by constant exposure to a poisonous worldview, to allow them to live skillfully and successfully among peoples with a lifestyle that was antithetical to a God-centered worldview. God himself expressly warned his people in reference to the wicked Canaanites, "For they will turn your sons away from following me to serve other gods; then the anger of Yahweh will be kindled against you." (Deut 7:4). Thus God, out of kindness and the desire to prevent his people from falling away from him and being subject to his fury, provided them with a God-centered worldview, in order to enable them to thrive among the godless peoples of Canaan.[22]

Because the people of Israel would have been influenced by the traditions of the surrounding nations (i.e., Egyptians, Canaanites, and later the Babylonians), God wanted to teach Israel the truth about the past and what He had done in the world. The purpose of the Torah, then, is to explain who the Israelites were, what God's plan for them was, and to teach them that He was not only their Creator (Genesis) but also their Redeemer (Exodus), who provides standards of holiness (Leviticus), protects and provides for them (Numbers), and keeps His covenantal promises (Deuteronomy). This background of Genesis 1–11 (Torah), having been written to give Israel a worldview to stand against godless peoples of the ANE, helps in understanding the similarities and differences between the accounts.

---

22. Douglas Petrovich, "Identifying Nimrod of Genesis 10 with Sargon of Akkad By Exegetical and Archeological Means," JETS 56/2 (2013), 274.

Creation: Myth or History?

Possibly the most well-known parallel to the account of creation in Genesis 1 is the Babylonian myth *Enuma Elish*. The *Enuma Elish* was recovered in 1849 by Austin Henry Layard, who worked for the British Museum, from Ashur at Koujunjik, Iraq. It was found in the ruined library of King Ashurbanipal (668–627 B.C.) in Nineveh and is written in Akkadian cuneiform on baked clay tablets and is dated between 1800–1600 B.C. It is probably the most complete Mesopotamian account of creation. The account describes creation as starting as a result of a cosmic struggle between order and chaos. The beginning of *Enuma Elish* (I: 1–9), which is said to resemble Genesis 1:1–2, begins this way:

> When on high, heaven had been named,
> When no earth had been called,
> When there was no divine elders . . .
> When there was nothing. . . . Nothing but
> Godfather Apsu and Mummu-Tiamat, God mother of All
>   living,
> Two bodies of water become one,
> When no reed hut was erected,
> When no marsh land was drained,
> When there were no divine warriors.
> When no names had been called,
> When no tasks had been assigned.[23]

The two deities mentioned in the text, Aspu and Tiamat, create other gods through sexual procreation. A great cosmic battle then erupts between Tiamat, a goddess of chaos, and Marduk, a god of order, and Marduk slays Tiamat and uses her remains to form the cosmos. It is in light of the similarities between Genesis and *Enuma Elish* that has caused scholars like Peter Enns to argue that "Genesis cries out to be read as something other than a historical description of events."[24] Enns' position unfortunately denies the uniqueness of the Scriptures in their ANE context since he believes the creation account is rooted in the mythological worldview, and therefore they "share a conceptual

23. Victor H. Matthews and Don C. Benjamin, *Old Testament Parallels: Laws and Stories from the Ancient Near East* (New York: Paulist Press, 2006), 12.
24. Enns, *The Evolution of Adam*, 58.

worldview."[25] Because of the connection between Genesis and the ANE, Enns writes that

> . . . any thought of Genesis 1 providing a scientifically or historically accurate account of cosmic origins, and therefore being wholly distinct from the "fanciful" story in *Enuma Elish*, cannot be seriously entertained.[26]

For scholars like Enns, the fact that Genesis 1 draws upon the worldview of the ANE is the reason that it does not portray actual events that took place in space and time but rather communicates theological truths about God, man, and the world. The purpose of Genesis, then, is not to show *how* the world was made but rather the *purpose* and *function* of its existence. To read Genesis 1 as actual history, at least for them, is to misrepresent the passage.

This leap from the ANE accounts to the biblical account of creation by Enns (and others), however, is very questionable. The gods in ANE literature are coexistent with nature, that is, pre-existing matter (in Genesis 1, God creates matter). The distinct character of the mythical worldview can be seen in Ba'al, the Canaanite storm god. The rain and storms were not just there to keep the land fertile but were worshiped as a god (1 Kings 17:1–7). However, the God of Israel was not a part of the material world and was before its existence, as He brought it into existence (Isaiah 43:10, 44:24). Unfortunately, too many Old Testament scholars today have an unwarranted dependence on ANE literature to interpret Genesis 1. While the worldview of the ANE can inform the background to our understanding of the text of the Bible, it should not dictate its meaning. Although the ANE myths do have similarities with Genesis 1, when they are read together, one should reach different conclusions:

Superficial Similarities

- The Hebrew word deep in Genesis 1:2 sounds like the word for the goddess Tiamat of the ancient Near Eastern creation myths.
- Both have waters above and beneath separated by a firmament.
- Both have light before sun, moon, and stars.
- Both describe mankind's failure to please deity.
- Both refer to plants that confer immortality.
- Both mention a serpent.

25. Ibid., 50.
26. Ibid., 40–41.

Profound Differences

- Battle elements. Genesis does not envision creation as a war of the gods.
- Pantheistic elements. Genesis does not talk about natural elements as gods.
- Creative activity as sexual activity. Genesis does not describe God's creation in this way.
- Poetic language. Genesis does not have "synonymous parallelism" (restating the same idea in two ways) in every description.
- Reference to time. Genesis speaks of creation "in the beginning" and "days," contrary to myths, which speak more about seasons.[27]

There are also many other differences between the accounts, such as man in the ANE myths is created to be a slave for the gods, yet in Genesis 1, God made man in His image to rule over His creation (Genesis 1:26–28). Also, in the ANE myths, the finished world is imperfect, but when God finished creating, He declared his creation to be "very good" (Genesis 1:31). Reading these texts in their original context, we would never come to the conclusion that Genesis is like the ANE myths. They are totally different in description and in purpose. While scholars have made much of the similarities between Genesis 1 and ANE myths, the dissimilarities are often downplayed when, in fact, they are significant. Analyzing these differences helps identify the precise relationship between Genesis 1 and the ANE myths. Although, some argue that the differences can be explained by the fact that the biblical writers used a process of demythologizing so that the author of Genesis removed the polytheism and filled it with monotheism. However, "the differences are monumental and are so striking that they cannot be explained by a simple Hebrew cleansing of myth."[28] These differences have led to the suggestion that one of the purposes of Genesis is that of a polemical account used to refute the false ideas of the pagan nations. Moses was countering myth with history. For example, in Genesis 1, God creates light on Day One before the sun, moon, and stars on Day Four. In the Egyptian ANE myths, the sun, moon, and stars were considered deities. In Genesis 1, however, God

---

27. See Abner Chou, "Genesis — The Original Myth Buster," April 1, 2013, https://answersin-genesis.org/creationism/creation-myths/genesis-the-original-myth-buster/.

28. See John Currid, *Against the Gods: The Polemical Theology of the Old Testament* (Wheaton, IL: Crossway, 2013), 44.

names the gathering of the waters seas, and the dry land earth, but He does not name the sun and the moon; they are known as the greater light and the lesser light (Genesis 1:17). Why? Because He is communicating to His audience that you may have heard that they (sun, moon, and stars) are gods parading in their victory in the heavens, but you are not to worship or fear them. Moses warned the people of Israel not to think that the heavenly bodies are deities. Why? Because he is rejecting and countering myth with history (Deuteronomy 4:19). In the ANE myths, the gods descend from the heavens and the earth, but in the Bible, it is God who creates the heaven and the earth (Isaiah 42:5).

The biblical creation view of Genesis 1 is that the Hebrew text is not written as myth but as a chronological historical narrative recording God's divine acts of creation that took place in six 24-hour days that occurred in space-time history. Genesis 1 contains a Hebrew verb form (*wayyiqtol*), which is a standard marker of historical narrative in the Old Testament.[29] This verb form is characteristic of other historical narratives, such as Genesis 12–50 and Exodus. Hebraist Dr. Stephen Boyd points out that Genesis 1:1–2:3 "should be read as other Hebrew narratives are intended to be read — as a concise report of actual events in time-space history."[30] And "narrative genre in the Old Testament . . . does not communicate myth."[31] This is the natural exegesis of the text, and the one that is meant by the author.[32] When it is read this way, it is clear what the author is asserting, namely that God created everything in one week. Using other passages that speak to the same topic assists in determining the proper interpretation, since Scripture will never contradict itself. Exodus 20:11 and 31:17 make it clear that the events of Genesis 1:1–2:3 occurred in six days, just as the text plainly reads.[33] Additionally, Genesis

---

29. Dr. Steven Boyd has undertaken a statistical study on the frequency of the *wayyiqtol* in narrative and poetical accounts and shows, based upon the distribution of verb forms, that Genesis 1 is definitely a narrative and not poetry. Steven W. Boyd, "The Genre of Genesis 1:1–2:3: What Means This Text?" in Terry Mortenson and Thane H. Ury, eds., *Coming to Grips with Genesis: Biblical Authority and the Age of the Earth* (Green Forest, AR: Master Books, 2008), 163–192.

30. Boyd, "The Genre of Genesis 1:1–2:3: What Means This Text?" 191.

31. See Chou, "Did God Really Say. . . ?" 36.

32. Though choosing not to believe that Genesis 1 was real history, James Barr understood that it was indeed the intent of the author. James Barr, *Fundamentalism* (Philadelphia, PA: Westminster, 1978), 42.

33. The creation account in Genesis 1:1–2:3 may have been a revelation given to Moses by God on Mount Sinai (see Exodus 24:16–18).

informs us that mankind was created on Day Six (Genesis 1:26–31), and Jesus confirmed this (Mark 10:6).[34]

Genesis 1, unlike the ANE creation myths, does not use mythical poetic language. While there is debate over artistic features in Genesis 1, there are convincing textual indicators that it is not poetic. Genesis 1 contains little or no figurative language, and there is no symbolism or metaphors.[35] What is more, one of the main characteristics of Hebrew poetry is missing, namely parallelism.[36] This is seen in the Psalms, for example, where a statement is made and then the same idea or its opposite is said in different words. So Psalm 19:1–2, an example of synonymous parallelism, says,

> The heavens declare the glory of God, and the sky above
>   proclaims his handiwork.
> Day to day pours out speech, and night to night reveals
>   knowledge.

Such construction is not found in Genesis 1. Nevertheless, even if it were demonstrated that Genesis 1 is a poetic text, this would not mean that it cannot also be an accurate revelation of details of actual history. For example, Psalms 78 and 136 recite some of the key events of the history of Israel in poetic form.

Others have argued that because Genesis 1 contains symmetry, it is not a normal historical narrative but rather is an "artistic arrangement" whereby its emphasis is theological, not historical.[37] The literary theorists, however, propose a false dichotomy between history and theology. Why can't the text be addressing both? The Bible's historical claims cannot be separated from its theological claims. Even if Genesis 1 does contain symmetry, "Why, then, must we conclude that, merely because of symmetry arrangement, Moses has disposed of chronology?"[38] The symmetry that has persuaded many scholars of the literary arrangement in Genesis is the supposed parallels between the days:

34. See Terry Mortenson, "Jesus, Evangelical Scholars, and the Age of the Earth," Answers in Depth 2 (August 1, 2007), https://answersingenesis.org/age-of-the-earth/jesus-evangelical-scholars-and-the-age-of-the-earth/.
35. See Currid, *Genesis 1:1–25:18*, 39.
36. See E.J. Young, *Studies in Genesis One* (Philadelphia, PA: Presbyterian and Reformed Publishing, 1964), 82–83.
37. See Henri Blocher, *In the Beginning: The Opening Chapters of Genesis* (Leicester, England: InterVarsity Press, 1984), 50.
38. Young, *Studies in Genesis One*, 66.

Environment	Contents
Day 1, Light	Day 4, Luminaries
Day 2, Water and Sky	Day 5, Birds and Sea Creatures
Day 3, Land and Plants	Day 6, Land Animals and Man
Day 7, Sabbath	

However, when examined carefully, the supposed parallels between Day One through Day Three, and Day Four through Day Six are not there:

- Light on Day One is not dependent on the sun, as it was created on Day Four. Secondly, the waters existed on Day One and not only on Day Two.

- Water was made on Day One, but the seas were not made until Day Three. The sea creatures of Day Five were to fill the "waters in the seas," which were created on Day Three, not Day Two.

- On Day Four, we are told that God made the sun, moon, and stars and placed them in the expanse, *rāqîaʿ* (Genesis 1:17), created on Day Two, not on Day One.

- Man was created on Day Six, not to rule over the land and vegetation (Day Three) but over the land animals created on Day Six and the sea creatures and flying creatures created on Day Five.

The literary theory is simply a more "sophisticated" approach to Genesis 1 that seeks to de-historicize the text. Furthermore, it has to be asked "whether the Israelites thought of this text in only literary/theological terms. This view risks reductionism and oversimplification."[39] Reformed theologian Herman Bavinck sums up how Scripture speaks of the creation account:

> When it speaks about the genesis of heaven and earth, it does not present saga or myth or poetic fantasy but offers, in accordance with its own clear intent, history, the history that deserves credence and trust. And for that reason Christian theology, with only a few exceptions, continued to hold onto the literal historical view of the creation story.[40]

---

39. Walton, *The Lost World of Genesis One*, 111.
40. Herman Bavinck, *Reformed Dogmatics: God and Creation Volume Two*, ed. John Bolt (Grand Rapids, MI: Baker Academic, 2004), 495.

Genesis 1 is clearly a historical account that speaks of God's sovereign creation of the world in six consecutive 24-hour days.

The Flood: Myth or History?

Just as with creation in Genesis 1, there exist other accounts of a great flood in the ANE, as well as other cultures all over the world. While there are some that are very little like the biblical account (Chinese and Fijians) and others bear some resemblance (Greek and Indians), the ones that look most like the biblical account come from the region of Mesopotamia. From here we have flood accounts such as the *Gilgamesh Epic*, the *Atrahasis Epic*, and possibly the oldest reference to a great flood is found on the Sumerian King List.

The *Gilgamesh Epic* is an epic poem containing an expanded version of a great deluge (Tablet XI) and was also recovered by Austin Henry Layard from the library of Ashurbanipal in Nineveh, Iraq, between 1848–49. It is written on baked clay tablets, about six inches high, in Akkadian cuneiform. The significance of this find was that scholars began to look upon the Genesis account of the Flood as having been dependent upon these Mesopotamian texts. The earliest copies date back to 2000–1600 B.C. and recount the adventures of Gilgamesh, the Sumerian king of Uruk. In the *Epic*, Gilgamesh is a powerful tyrant, which is why his subjects call out to the gods for relief from his control. The gods answer by creating Enkidu to be his companion in the hope that Enkidu will keep Gilgamesh from oppressing the people by taking him on adventures. However, the death of Enkidu causes Gilgamesh to search for immortality. It is while searching for immortality that he meets Utnapishtim and his wife, who have been granted eternal life by the gods after surviving a great flood. Gilgamesh fails in his attempt to gain immortality and so returns to Uruk to reign as king. In the *Gilgamesh Epic*, the boat is shaped like a cube (204 feet in length, width, and height), containing seven stories, and after the flood, which lasts seven days and nights, it comes to land on Mt. Nisir. Utnapishtim then sends out a dove, then a swallow, and then a raven. The raven doesn't return, so Utnapishtim makes a sacrifice to the gods, who in turn bless him.

The *Atrahasis Epic* comes from Mesopotamia and exists in the Babylonian and Assyrian dialects of Akkadian, written in cuneiform. It is the oldest of the ANE myths, dating back to the early second millennium B.C. The III tablet of the *Atrahasis Epic* contains a flood account where Enlil, head of the pantheon, is angry at humanity for making too much noise and so convinces the divine assembly to send a flood to destroy them. Another god, Ea-Enki, warns the hero Atrahasis, a king, to build a boat to save him, his family, and friends. The *Atrahasis Epic* contains parallels both to the Genesis account of creation and the Flood.

How then do we account for the similarities between the ANE and the biblical account of creation and the Flood? There are several suggestions that have been made for how to understand the common elements between the accounts:

1. The Hebrew account is dependent on the Babylonian account.
2. Both accounts are descended from a common original.
3. Babylonians borrowed from the Hebrew account.

The view that the Flood in Genesis 6 was influenced by the different flood accounts from the ANE is standard among unbelieving critical scholars and common in our culture, as can be seen from popular atheist books criticizing Christianity. The assumption that the biblical Flood account was dependent on ANE myths can be seen by the displays in many natural history museums around the world. For instance, the Ashmolean Museum of Art and History in Oxford (England) has a copy of the Sumerian King List (on a clay prism) that speaks of a flood in the region of Mesopotamia. Part of the museum's commentary about the King List states:

> This is the first side of the Sumerian King List, written around 1800 B.C. It mentions a legendary flood in Mesopotamia. Multiple or single flood events in prehistory may have inspired this story, in turn inspiring the Biblical Flood story in the Book of Genesis.

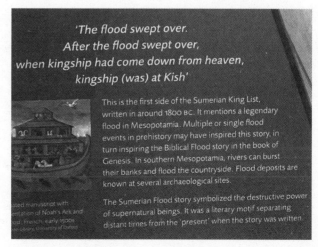

'The flood swept over.
After the flood swept over,
when kingship had come down from heaven,
kingship (was) at Kish'

This is the first side of the Sumerian King List, written in around 1800 BC. It mentions a legendary flood in Mesopotamia. Multiple or single flood events in prehistory may have inspired this story, in turn inspiring the Biblical Flood story in the book of Genesis. In southern Mesopotamia, rivers can burst their banks and flood the countryside. Flood deposits are known at several archaeological sites.

The Sumerian Flood story symbolized the destructive power of supernatural beings. It was a literary motif separating distant times from the 'present' when the story was written.

The question that needs to be asked is: Is the biblical account of the Flood dependent on these other texts in the ANE? Scholars who see Genesis as sharing a conceptual worldview with these accounts would raise the objection: How can we say the Mesopotamian texts are false and the biblical account of the Flood is true when they are both so similar? But is it that those ANE texts are false or that they make false claims?

The argument that similarities indicate borrowing is based on the common fallacy that if B resembles A, therefore B has borrowed from A. The dependency fallacy occurs when scholars believe that the Genesis account was borrowed from or was dependent upon the ANE accounts. This fallacy has dominated comparative mythology and religion studies for many years. The fact that two documents have similarities does not mean that the younger is dependent on the older. There are other explanations; for example, they could have come from a common source[41] or a common universal memory.[42]

The reason many scholars today accept that the biblical account is dependent upon these other ANE accounts is because they believe these other accounts are a prototype to Genesis. This is because it is believed the ANE accounts pre-date the writings of the Torah.[43] This assumes, however, that the record of creation and the Flood initially started with Moses (1446–1406 B.C.). But if we are thinking with biblical history in mind, even with the final composition of the Torah in 1406 B.C., then is it not possible that Moses could have used older written records that were not reliant on those myths?[44] The text of Genesis 5:1 specifically claims to be dependent on a written "scroll" (*sēper*),[45] so it "is reasonable to surmise that

41. See Jeffrey J. Niehaus, *Ancient Near Eastern Themes in Biblical Theology* (Grand Rapids, MI: Kregel Publications, 2008), 21–23.

42. See Kenneth Mathews, *Genesis 1–11:26*, vol. 1A of *The New American Commentary* (Nashville, TN: Broadman & Holman Publishing, 1996), 87.

43. Assyriologist Alexander Heidel dates the Babylonian accounts to the end of third to the beginning of the second millennium B.C. and recognizes that the earliest account of the Torah, if one accepts Mosaic authorship, is around 1400–1200 B.C. Alexander Heidel, *The Gilgamesh Epic and Old Testament Parallels* (Chicago, IL: University of Chicago Press, 1949), 260–261.

44. The Hebrew Scriptures were written on perishable material (leather, papyrus), which tend to dry out, crack, and eventually crumble away, whereas the ANE accounts are inscribed upon clay tablets and are more durable. Therefore, we would probably not expect to find a copy of the original account of creation and the Flood from the second millennium. However, the written accounts of those events have been reliably transmitted and preserved in the text of Scripture.

45. Jewish scholar Nahum Saran believes it is possible that the author of Genesis used written records. Nahum Sarna, *Genesis: JPS Torah Commentary* (Philadelphia, PA: Jewish Publication Society, 1989), 41.

the other genealogies occurring in Genesis were also recorded resources available to the author, especially the similar Shemite line (Genesis 11:10–26)."[46] Given that the Bible tells us that Adam and his descendants were intelligent to begin with (e.g., Adam names the animals, and his descendants create musicals instruments of bronze and iron and are involved in agriculture, Genesis 2:19, 4:22), then it is also not too difficult to believe they could have kept a record of their history at this time. The genealogical account of the Flood (Genesis 6:9ff.) reflects actual history of an event that has been accurately recorded by people who were involved in it, as precise details and chronological reference points are given:

- Genesis 6:10, 7:13 record the number of individuals who went upon the Ark.
- Genesis 6:15 records the size of the Ark.
- Genesis 6:19–20 and 7:2–3 record the pairs and sevens of animals that went into the Ark.
- Genesis 7:6 records Noah's age at the start of the Flood.
- Genesis 7:11 records the year, month, and day of Noah's life that the Flood waters came upon the earth.
- Genesis 7:17, 24 records how long it rained.
- Genesis 7:20 records that the mountains were covered by 15 cubits of water.
- Genesis 8:4 records the month and day the Ark came to rest.
- Genesis 8:4 records the mountains the Ark rested upon.
- Genesis 8:4 records that the Ark landed specifically in the region of Ararat.
- Genesis 8:5 records that the tops of the mountains were seen on the first day of the tenth month.
- Genesis 8:6–12 records that Noah released particular birds in a particular order.
- Genesis 8:13 records the year, month, and day that the water dried up from the earth.
- Genesis 8:14–15 records the month and day that Noah and his family came out of the Ark.

Even Old Testament scholar John Walton at least recognizes that the Flood account recorded in Genesis 6:9 could be the original:

---

46. Mathews, *Genesis 1–11:26*, 306.

Yet the possibility cannot be ruled out that the Genesis account is a pristine record of the event as passed down from Noah, which suffered corruption when transmitted in the hands of other cultures.[47]

The fact of the event of the biblical Flood is the reason other mythical accounts exist. Think about it: If a global Flood truly occurred in antiquity, one should not be surprised to find some reference to it in and throughout ANE literature. The similarities may reveal that the different accounts are explanations of the same event. Since the events of creation, the Flood, and the dispersion at Babel occurred in history, we should expect to find some reference to these in and throughout the ANE. At the account of the Tower of Babel, roughly several hundred years after the global Flood, the whole earth had one language and one speech (Genesis 11:1). This meant that mankind was united in both its language and habitation. It is here that they decide to build "a city and a tower with its top in the heavens" (Genesis 11:4). But why did the people choose to build a tower, and what was its purpose? The text gives two reasons for the people's desire to build the tower: to make a name for themselves and to avoid being scattered (Genesis 11:4). The builders' desire to make a "name" for themselves also reveals mankind's common ideological purpose: usurping God. The building of the city and tower was an act of rebellion against God, as the people were resisting His command to "increase" and "fill the earth" (Genesis 9:1; cf. 1:28). There is an interesting text in Deuteronomy 32:8–9 that helps us understand some of the details of Babel, as it has its background in the Table of Nations of Genesis 10.[48]

When the Most High gave to the nations their inheritance, when he divided mankind, he fixed the borders of the peoples according to the number of the sons of God. But the LORD's portion is his people, Jacob his allotted heritage.[49]

47. Walton, *Genesis*, 319.
48. The dividing of the nations in Deuteronomy 32:8 is part of the background of Paul's speech to the Aeropagus, where he affirms that God "made from one man every nation of mankind to live on all the face of the earth, having determined allotted periods and the boundaries of their dwelling place" (Acts 17:26). Paul is telling the Greek philosophers on Mars Hill that God has providentially arranged the movements of the nations, which were disinherited at Babel, so that they may seek Him (Acts 17:27).
49. Deuteronomy 32:8 in the Masoretic text reads "sons of Israel" (*běnê yiśrā'ēl*), but the nation of Israel did not exist at Babel, so this reading makes no sense in context. However, the LXX and Qumran fragment 4Q read "sons of God" (*běnê hā' ĕlōhîm*).

The question is, when did God (Most High; cf. Genesis 14:19) divide mankind (i.e., the nations)? This is obviously a clear reference to the event of the Tower of Babel. The verb translated "divided" (*pārad*) is used in the division of the nations in Genesis 10:5, 32, and here it refers to the dividing out of mankind (*bĕnê ʾādām*, "the sons of Adam"; NKJV) over the earth. With the close connection between Genesis 10 and 11, this then gives us a behind-the-scene look at what happened at the Tower of Babel. The text speaks of God having divided "mankind," or "the sons of Adam," among "the sons of God" (*bĕnê hā ʾĕlōhîm*), heavenly beings (cf. Job 1:6, 2:1, 38:7).[50] Because the people at Babel had disobeyed God by staying in one place and desired to make a name for themselves, it resulted in Him judging them by dispersing them over the earth and by giving them over to idolatry by allocating these fallen heavenly beings to the nations, who became their objects of worship (Deuteronomy 4:19, 29:24–26; cf. Daniel 10:20).[51] After the dispersion of the different nations at the Tower of Babel, the biblical account of creation and the Flood would have been lost in the mythical worldview of the nations.[52] Old Testament scholar Jeffery Niehaus accounts for the similarities between Genesis and the ANE texts in terms of "revealed truth in the Old Testament and the Bible, and distorted truth in the ancient Near East."[53] Niehaus believes that the distortion came about through demonic revelation. He states,

> Passages such as Deuteronomy 32:16–19; 1 Corinthians 10:20; and 1 Timothy 4:1 tell us clearly enough that demonic powers

50. See Daniel Block, *The Gods of the Nations: Studies in Ancient Near Eastern National Theology*, 2nd Ed (Leicester: Apollos, 2000), 27.

51. Old Testament scholar Michael Heiser points out the significance of Deuteronomy 32:8: "The point of verses 8–9 is that sometime after God separated the people of the earth at Babel and established where on the earth they were to be located, He then assigned each of the seventy nations to the fallen sons of God (who were also seventy in number). After observing humanity's rebellion before the Flood and then again in the Babel incident, God decided to desist in His efforts to work directly with humanity. In an action reminiscent of Romans 1, God 'gave humanity up' to their persistent resistance to obeying Him. God's new approach was to create a unique nation, Israel, for Himself, as recorded in the very next chapter of Genesis with the call of Abraham (Gen. 12). Hence each pagan nation was overseen by a being of inferior status to Yahweh, but Israel would be tended to by the 'God of gods,' the 'lord of lords' (Deut. 10:17)." Michael S. Heiser, "Deuteronomy 32:8 and the Sons of God," BSac 158 (2001), 52–74 (71).

52. In the New Testament, we see the reversal of God's judgment at Babel as the gospel goes out to all the nations (Acts 2:3, 6). In Acts 2:3, the Greek the word "divided" (*diamerizō*) is the same word used in Deuteronomy 32:8 (LXX), and in Acts 2:6, the Greek word "bewildered" (*sugcheo*) is the same word in Genesis 11:7 (LXX).

53. Niehaus, *Ancient Near Eastern Themes in Biblical Theology*, 178.

and intelligences are behind false religion, and even behind false theology in the church. . . . Demonic inspiration of false religion . . . is one of the things that the Bible teaches quite clearly in the passages noted.[54]

These ANE texts from pagan, idolatrous nations are demonically distorted versions of the truth. Those nations would have taken with them the truth of what took place at creation and at the Flood but mixed it with the twisted and distorted truth of that revelation about those events. At Babel, monotheism degenerated into animism, sorcery, magic, and polytheism — though some still retained it (e.g., Melchizedek, Genesis 14). The pure revelation of God had been generally lost, corrupted, and perverted by sin, leading to religious idolatry and giving rise to religious pluralism (cf. Joshua 24:2). Old Testament scholar John Currid explains this well:

If the Biblical stories are true, one would be surprised not to find some references to these truths in extra-biblical literature. And indeed in ancient Near Eastern myth we do see some kernels of historical truth. However, pagan authors vulgarized . . . those truths — they distorted fact by dressing it up with polytheism, magic, violence, and paganism. Fact became myth. From this angle the common references would appear to support rather than deny the historicity of the biblical story.[55]

Because of the fallen nature of humanity, it is understandable why the ANE texts are corrupted and distorted (Romans 1:18–32). This does not mean that the ANE myths are untrue but rather that they make false statements, whereas the Scriptures give a true historical account of the event through the inspiration of the Holy Spirit (2 Peter 1:21). The similarities, then, are different accounts and explanations of the same event. It is also important to point out that, just as with Genesis 1, while there are many similarities and parallels between the accounts, there are also major differences. The significant differences between Genesis and the ANE accounts of the Flood should lead us to conclude that Genesis is not dependent on them. The many differences between ANE accounts and the Flood narrative make them stand apart in significant ways. Some of these are:

54. Ibid., 179.
55. John Currid, *Ancient Egypt and the Old Testament* (Grand Rapids, MI: Baker, 1997), 32.

1. In the Mesopotamian accounts, overpopulation or humanity's noise interrupts the sleep of the gods and causes the flood. In Genesis, it is a wicked, corrupt, and violent humanity that causes God to send the Flood upon the earth (Genesis 6:5–12).

2. In the *Gilgamesh Epic*, the gods were terrified at the flood and cowered like dogs. In Genesis, it is God who rends the earth in judgment (Genesis 6:7, 13).

3. In the Mesopotamian accounts, the gods' decisions were to be kept secret from man. In Genesis, God speaks directly to Noah seven times (Genesis 6:13; 7:1; 8:15; 9:1, 8, 12, 17).

4. In the Mesopotamian accounts, the builders of the vessel (the boatman, relatives, and friends) are passengers with the hero and his family. In Genesis, it is only Noah and his family that enter the Ark (Genesis 7:1, 13, 8:18; 1 Peter 3:20).

5. Possibly the biggest difference between the accounts is that the ANE texts do not mention a covenant, whereas in Genesis 9:8–17, the term "covenant" appears seven times. There, God makes an unconditional, everlasting covenant with all humanity, to never again destroy the earth.[56]

These differences present a very strong argument for the uniqueness of the biblical account rather than it being dependent on the other ANE texts. Moreover, the language used of the Flood account in Genesis 6–8 presents itself to us as history and not myth. The presence of the *tôlĕdōt* ("These are the generations of Noah") strongly indicates that it is a historical account, as it is used in other historical sections of the Book of Genesis (Genesis 6:9; cf. 10:1; 11:10, 27; 25:12, 19; 36:1, 9; 37:2). The text is written as a historical narrative, as it uses certain grammatical markers that represent that genre. For example, the *wav-consecutive-plus-imperfect*, often translated as "and it was," is used a number of times throughout the narrative to present historical sequence. Genesis 6–8 also frequently uses the Hebrew word *'et*, which serves as a sign of the coming direct object, and it almost never occurs in poetic texts.[57]

---

56. See Bruce Waltke, *An Old Testament Theology: An Exegetical, Canonical, and Thematic Approach* (Grand Rapids, MI: Zondervan, 2007), 291.
57. See Currid, *Against the Gods*, 58.

Biblical Worldview Versus ANE Worldview

In his book *The Bible Among the Myths*, Old Testament scholar John Oswalt has concluded, "there are only two world-views: the biblical one and the other one."[58] Not only do the differences between accounts of creation and the Flood rule out their being dependent on the ANE accounts but also the differences in worldviews. The ANE texts reflect a worldview that contains several fundamental elements that are completely contradictory to the biblical worldview.

ANE Worldview	Biblical Worldview
Polytheism	Monotheism
Eternity of chaotic matter	Matter created
A low view of the gods	The reliability of God
Conflict as the source of life	Absence of conflict in the creation process
Low view of humanity	A high view of humanity
No single standard of ethics	Ethical obedience
A cyclical concept of existence	Linear concept of existence

What these diametrically differing characteristics of the ANE and biblical worldviews[59] show us is that when they are compared together, they "are radically different ways of thinking about reality."[60] The polytheism, the Theogony (creation of the various gods), the cosmic wars, and the magic that is at the center of these ANE texts are not found in the Bible. The talking serpent in Genesis 3 is often seen as suggesting the presence of myth within the text. Other Scriptures (Revelation 12:9, 20:2), however, make it clear that the serpent was a guise by which Satan spoke. What is more, "it is not the presence of the fantastic [e.g., speaking serpent in Genesis 3] that makes a piece of literature myth; rather, it is the presence of the mythical worldview."[61] As we have seen, the presence of the mythological worldview is absent in Genesis 1–11. Remember, Israel was told not to be like the other nations (Exodus 23:20–33; Deuteronomy 18:9–14). If Israel

58. John Oswalt, *The Bible Among the Myths: Unique Revelation or Just Ancient Literature* (Grand Rapids, MI: Zondervan, 2009), 28.
59. Ibid., 57–62, 99.
60. Ibid., 63.
61. Ibid., 103.

were to reject the thinking of the other nations, then why would God give them an account of creation containing a worldview they were told to reject? The worldview God gave Israel was a revealed one, which would mean a revealed cosmology and a revealed account of creation (Exodus 20:11, 24:16–18, 31:17–18). This is why, when it comes to the literature from the ANE, we need to approach it through the lens of biblical authority.[62] As Christians, we do not need to apologize for having a worldview, as everyone (including critical scholars) has a worldview. The question we need to ask is, which is the correct worldview to have? Many of the scholars who argue that the ANE should dictate how we read Scripture also believe in evolution, so they do not see Scripture as their final authority.

When it comes to evaluating the evidence, we do not throw away our presuppositions, but we examine the evidence honestly. In light of our biblical presuppositions about the God of creation, it should be clear that the biblical account of creation and the Flood is unique and shows that it is in no way dependent on the other ANE accounts. These ANE accounts of creation and the Flood from pagan, idolatrous nations are distorted versions of the truth. Genesis is not a modified version of pagan myths. There is no biblical evidence that God ever uses myths as a basis for teaching truth. On the contrary, Scripture clearly distinguishes truth from myth (2 Timothy 4:4; 1 Timothy 1:4; Titus 1:14).

It should be no surprise that the attack on the trustworthiness of the Bible's history began on its opening chapters, Genesis 1–11. Because of the influence of texts from ANE, many evangelical Christians now deny or downplay the history of the early chapters of the Bible in Genesis 1–11. Unfortunately, to get anywhere even in Christian scholarship today, it is more than likely you have to uncritically accept the prior theological and philosophical convictions that are brought to the text of the Old Testament. The majority of evangelical scholars who embrace Genesis 1–11 as myth today do so by following the dominant views present in

---

62. Old Testament scholar Eugene Merrill offers wise advice when it comes to understanding these ancient documents: "Although sources of all kinds make important contributions to the reconstruction of the past, they are not of the same weight or value, particularly in terms of biblical research. The Bible occupies a place of unchallenged supremacy and authority, at least to readers who accept its truth claims at face value. . . . Christians who hold the Bible to be inerrant Scripture have no more need to apologize for their a priori conviction than do skeptics who, on the same philosophical grounds, view it as mere fable or insupportable religious tradition." See Eugene H. Merrill, *Kingdom of Priests: A History of Old Testament Israel*, 2nd edition (Grand Rapids, MI: Baker Academic, 2008), 31.

critical Old Testament scholarship rather than reading Scripture in light of Scripture. The arguments for adopting the ANE worldview to interpret Genesis 1–11 are seriously flawed in light of Scripture and, sadly, history has shown that compromise on Genesis undermines and erodes the authority of the Bible, which in turn undermines the proclamation and believability of the gospel. We need to realize that we cannot lose the historicity of the Bible without losing the theology, and we cannot lose the historicity without losing the salvation that comes from it. The Bible has linked them intimately together. It is important, therefore, that like the Apostle Peter, we proclaim that we do not follow a cleverly devised myth, but we have been given an eyewitness account of the creation of the world and its destruction by a global Flood.

CHAPTER THREE

CARRIED ALONG
BY THE HOLY SPIRIT

2 Peter 1:16–18

And we have the prophetic word more fully confirmed, to which you will do well to pay attention as to a lamp shining in a dark place, until the day dawns and the morning star rises in your hearts, knowing this first of all, that no prophecy of Scripture comes from someone's own interpretation. For no prophecy was ever produced by the will of man, but men spoke from God as they were carried along by the Holy Spirit (2 Peter 1:19–21).

In our secular age, it is not uncommon to encounter people who scoff at the belief that the Bible is God's Word, asserting that "the Bible is full of errors" or "the Bible contradicts itself." These objections are obviously meant to suggest God could not have been involved in the authorship of Scripture, as He surely would not err or contradict Himself. Behind those objections, however, is another common objection: "You can't trust the Bible because it was written by men." Well, Christians agree that the Bible was written by men (we don't believe the Bible was dropped down out of heaven on tablets or dictated by God to the Apostles), but we have to qualify that since we also believe, as Peter tells us, that the men who wrote Scripture spoke from God as they were carried along by the Holy Spirit.

The Apostle Peter dealt with the objection of the false teachers, who said that the second coming of Jesus was a "cleverly devised myth" (i.e., something that he was speculating about), by appealing to the divine origin of Scripture. Likewise, today, we have to deal with arguments not just from scoffers but, sadly, from theologians and pastors who say that the Bible cannot be trusted (for example, when it comes to creation and the Flood) because it was written by humans, by appealing to the divine inspiration of Scripture. Peter is telling us that the reason we can rely on Scripture is because, behind its human authorship, God spoke. The God who spoke on the mount of transfiguration (2 Peter 1:17–18) is the same God who spoke through the prophets and the Apostles. Whereas the false prophets get things wrong because they give visions coming from their own minds (Jeremiah 23:16; Ezekiel 13:3–9), the origin of true prophecy did not originate in the mind of men but rather came about through the Holy Spirit. In other words, the words of Scripture did not just come about through the desires of men, but they were inspired by the Holy Spirit. The point Peter is making is that just as there were false prophets within the nation of Israel (Jeremiah 2:8, 26; 5:31; 14:13–15; 23:9–40), so they are now in the Church and are secretly bringing in destructive heresies (2 Peter 2:1, 13, 17; 3:5). It is important to realize that not everyone who claims to be a prophet speaks God's Word.[1] False prophets can be summed up by three characteristics: 1) they lack divine authority, 2) they promise the people peace when God threatens judgment, and 3) they will certainly be judged by God.[2] The "prophetic word" that is more fully confirmed here is not the prediction of the future but is a reference to the Old Testament Scriptures.

The belief that God has uniquely revealed Himself in Scripture has led to the affirmation that the Bible is self-attesting, in that it carries within it all the authority of God Himself in the text.[3] The power of God resides in the Bible, as it attests to its own authority. It does not

---

1. The Bible gives three criteria for claiming to be a prophet: 1) Doctrinal orthodoxy: prophecy had to be in line with what God has previously revealed (Deuteronomy 13:1–5), 2) Moral integrity: the prophet has to live by the standards set out in God's Word; false prophets can be measured by their lifestyle (2 Peter 2), and 3) Predictive accuracy: if a prophet claims to be speaking from God, then he needs to speak with 100% accuracy (Deuteronomy 18:20–22; cf. Jeremiah 28:9; Ezekiel 12:25; Acts 11:27–28, 21:10–11, 28:17). If the prophecy doesn't come true, then it does not come from God. The measure in the Bible is not how many prophecies you get right, but how many you get wrong.
2. See Richard Bauckham, *Jude, 2 Peter: WBC 50* (Waco, TX: Word Books, 1983), 238.
3. See the Westminster Confession of Faith and the Baptist Confession of Faith 1.4; Dr. Scott Oliphant, The Boice Center Lecture Series: "Inerrancy & Apologetics," March 19, 2014, https://www.youtube.com/watch?v=9qLciqx-XkY.

need an authority outside of itself to attest to it (i.e., theologians, pastors, bishops, priests, or church councils). Scriptural authority is tied to its author, God Himself. For some people, however, the belief that the Bible is self-attesting is troublesome because it sounds as though we have no reason to believe the Bible is God's Word (which is not true; we just do not surrender our foundation to autonomous human reason). One of the reasons for this is that since the enlightenment (the age of reason, 1685–1815), there has been an emphasis on human reason as the only basis of knowledge (i.e., rationalism). Enlightenment thinking, which has even infiltrated the Church, basically stated that if the mind cannot contain it, then it should not be believed. The enlightenment brought about three centuries of intense criticism of the supernatural from a presupposition which says things happen purely according to natural processes where God does not speak or act in history. The enlightenment sought to get rid of the supernatural and explain things rationally.

Contrary to enlightenment thought, however, the Bible is the foundation of our thinking because it is the uniquely revealed Word of the living God. Because it is our foundation, there is nothing behind or under it to support that claim. But suppose there were some pieces of evidence behind Scripture to hold it up (i.e., historical evidence of some sort or a philosophical argument). In order to believe that evidence, you would need an argument in place to support it and then that argument becomes the foundation. However, to posit anything meaningfully, you have to have a foundation to stand upon or you will go on *ad infinitum* trying to prove the evidence by another piece of evidence. If you have to prove the Bible is the Word of God, then what is the status of that proof? It will carry ultimate authority. In defense of the claim that the Bible is the Word of God, we are not just saying this because the Bible says so, but that it evidences itself to be the Word of God by:

1. The heavenliness of the matter
2. The efficacy of the doctrine
3. The majesty of the style
4. The consent of all the parts
5. The scope of the whole (which is to give all glory to God)
6. The full discovery it makes of the only way of man's salvation[4]

---

4. See the Westminster Confession of Faith and the Baptist Confession of Faith 1.5.

These arguments are put forward to *explain* but not *establish* the authority of Scripture. It is important to understand that people's eyes are not opened through philosophy (rational arguments) but through the communication of the truth of God in the Word of God, as the Apostle Peter declared:

> . . . since you have been born again, not of perishable seed but of imperishable, through the living and abiding word of God. . . (1 Peter 1:23).

The Word of God is the means God uses to awaken life in the unbeliever (Romans 10:17; James 1:18; cf. Galatians 3:2, 5). There is a warning in the New Testament against using a philosophy that is based upon man's natural reasoning and not recognizing that all the treasures of wisdom and knowledge are hidden in Jesus (1 Corinthians 2:14; Colossians 2:3–4). It is important to remember that the worldview in which we operate is the Christian one. A Christian philosophy is based on what God has communicated to us through His revelation in Scripture. Apologetics is fundamentally a communication of the truth of God, standing on the Word of God moving toward the gospel of Jesus Christ. Philosophy based upon autonomous human reason is not needed to do apologetics, but what is needed is the Word of God (cf. 1 Peter 3:15).[5] The only philosophy we are to be taken captive by is the philosophy that is "according to Christ" (Colossians 2:8).

When it comes to the nature of Scripture, it is true that God used men like Moses, David, Paul, and Peter to write Scripture, but God is ultimately the author of all Scripture (2 Timothy 3:16; cf. Exodus 31:18, 32:16; Mark 12:36). This means that as God used these men, He was not bound by them in order to communicate His truth. God is not bound by the context or culture of the ANE (see 1 Peter 1:24–25). God can come in the midst of any culture and communicate His truth from Genesis to Revelation. Of course, it is going to have the earmarks of the different personalities of the people who are involved (see Luke 1:1–4; 2 Timothy 4:13), but at every point, God is the author. This is so necessary to understand today as the attacks are coming again over the clarity, sufficiency,

---

5. This is not to say we cannot use philosophical arguments, but even they needed to be founded upon Scripture. This is because philosophy does not justify itself, but is encapsulated in a worldview, and if that worldview is not founded upon Scripture, it is the wrong philosophy. See the appendix for an exposition of 1 Peter 3:15.

and inerrancy of Scripture. There is a growing attack on Scripture from within the Church, mainly because of the assumption that the human authors were limited by their cultural context and so it resulted in the presence of errors in Scripture. We need to realize that today there are critically influenced scholars who are using historical-critical ideologies to redefine the nature of Scripture. These men, some who even identify as evangelical theologians, have great influence in the Church. Among these scholars, there exists a strong position of doubt and skepticism as to the belief in the inerrancy of Scripture since it is seen to be committing intellectual irresponsibility.

The doctrine of inerrancy is not a side issue; it is about the trustworthiness of Scripture, which reflects on the character of God since He is responsible for the content of Scripture (Hebrews 1:1–2; cf. Numbers 23:19). The inerrancy of Scripture is related to what we believe about God, since it is He who is speaking to us. God's speech cannot be false since He is incapable of lying or deceiving (Titus 1:2; Hebrews 6:18). Since Scripture is His Word, and because He cannot lie, then it is right to conclude that it contains no error or untruthfulness. The Bible tells us that God's words are "pure" (Psalm 12:6) and that all His words "prove true" (Proverbs 30:5). This view of Scripture has been called the verbal plenary view of inspiration, as theologian Brian Edwards explains:

> "Plenary" comes from the Latin *plenus*, which means "full," and refers to the fact that the whole of Scripture in every part is God-given. "Verbal" comes from the Latin *verbum*, which means "word," and emphasizes that even the words of Scripture are God-given. Plenary and verbal inspiration means the Bible is God-given (and therefore without error) in every part (doctrine, history, geography, dates, names) and in every single word.[6]

This chapter will look at some of the ways critical and evangelical scholars are scoffing at the doctrine of inerrancy because of the human element of Scripture, as well as whether the Bible contains error because it was written by human authors who were limited by their context. Then it will look at how the Apostles Paul and Peter viewed and understood Scripture.

---

6. See Brian Edwards, "Why Should We Believe in the Inerrancy of Scripture?" July 5, 2011, https://answersingenesis.org/is-the-bible-true/why-should-we-believe-in-the-inerrancy-of-scripture/.

Scoffing at Inerrancy

Before we look at how the doctrine of inerrancy is being redefined to fit an evolutionary paradigm, we need to ask what we mean by "inerrancy," as a standard is often foisted on the term that Scripture itself does not try to maintain. Theologian Paul Feinberg offers this helpful description of inerrancy:

> Inerrancy means that when all facts are known, the Scriptures in their original autographs and properly interpreted will be shown to be wholly true in everything that they affirm whether that has to do with doctrine or morality or with social, physical, or life sciences.[7]

Someone may object to this by stating that "we no longer have the original manuscripts"! But even though we do not have the original manuscripts, we do have the original text of Scripture, which is important, as it is the text that is inspired and not the ink on the parchment. The original text can exist without the original manuscripts, as it can be preserved in other ways, i.e., through the science of textual criticism.[8]

The doctrine of inerrancy has and will always be scoffed at. What may be surprising, or not, is that there are a growing number of voices within the Church and theological colleges that openly ridicule the idea of the Bible being inerrant. In his book *Saving the Original Sinner*, which scoffs at the historicity of the first man Adam, theistic evolutionist Karl Giberson, who once professed belief but is now a liberal critic, offers a common caricature of inerrancy that is sadly rife among liberal critics:

> Most Christians consider that God, in some sense, is the coauthor of the Bible, making the Bible both human and divine, with no obvious way to adjudicate those contrasting sources. In the New Testament Paul claims that "all scripture is inspired by God." Although he was referring only to the Hebrew scriptures — the New Testament did not exist yet — his claim became the basis for the assertion that the entire Bible was divinely inspired. ... This viewpoint ... championed by Protestant fundamentalists at the beginning of the twentieth century, removes any genuinely

7. Paul D. Feinberg, "The Meaning of Inerrancy," in *Inerrancy*, ed. Norman L Geisler (Grand Rapids, MI: Zondervan, 1980), 294.
8. See Kostenberger and Kruger, *The Heresy of Orthodoxy*, 203–231.

human element in the Bible, suggesting that the biblical authors were little more than scribes writing things that they often did not understand.[9]

While Giberson is correct about Paul's claim that "all Scripture is inspired by God" (actually, it is *breathed out by God*), he is wrong about it only referring to the Hebrew Scriptures and about the Apostles not having a New Testament (see below). Also, the idea that this view removes any genuine human element in the Bible simply does not consider what Protestant "fundamentalists" (epithet fallacy) actually believe about Scripture or what Peter means when he says that "men spoke from God as they were carried along by the Holy Spirit." Giberson's caricature of inerrancy is due to his compromise on the Bible with higher-critical ideologies and a desire to synthesize the Bible with evolution and millions of years.

Many people are familiar with the old adage "to err is human." For instance, what person would ever claim to be without error! Does it therefore follow that Scripture contains errors because human nature was involved in the process? Theologian and theistic evolutionist Kenton Sparks, Professor of Biblical Studies at Eastern University, who has been influenced in his thinking by evolution and higher criticism, believes that although God is inerrant, because He spoke through human authors, their "finitude and fallenness" resulted in a flawed biblical text.[10] In classic postmodern language, Sparks states:

> Orthodoxy demands that God does not err, and this implies, of course, that God does not err in Scripture. But it is one thing to argue that God does not err in Scripture; it is quite another thing that the human authors of Scripture did not err. Perhaps what we need is a way of understanding Scripture that paradoxically affirms inerrancy while admitting the human errors in Scripture.[11]

Sparks' claim of an inerrant Scripture that is errant is founded in current postmodern hermeneutical theories that emphasize the errant role of the human authors as receivers and receptors of their message. For Sparks, an inerrant Bible is worthy of the charge of Docetism (i.e., the denial of the

9. Karl Giberson, *Saving the Original Sinner: How Christians Have Used the Bible's First Man to Oppress, Inspire, and Make Sense of the World* (Boston, MA: Beacon Press, 2015), 23.
10. Kenton Sparks, *God's Word in Human Words: An Evangelical Appropriation of Critical Biblical Scholarship* (Grand Rapids, MI: Baker Academic, 2008), 243–244.
11. Ibid., 139.

true humanity of Scripture).[12] One could argue, however, that Sparks' view of Scripture is, in fact, "Arian" (denial of the true divine inspiration of Scripture). Nevertheless, Sparks attributes the "errors" in Scripture to the fact that humans err: The Bible is written by humans; therefore, its statements often reflect "human limitations and foibles."[13] Sparks' reasoning regarding human error leads him to argue that because Jesus, as a human, operated within His finite human horizon, He would have made errors. He states:

> First, the Christological argument fails because, though Jesus was indeed sinless, he was also human and finite. He would have erred in the usual way that other people err because of their finite perspectives. He misremembered this event or that, and mistook this person for someone else, and thought — like everyone else — that the sun was literally rising. To err in these ways simply goes with the human territory.[14]

To believe our Lord was able to err — and did err in the things He taught — is a severe accusation and needs to be taken seriously. First of all, it should be noted that nowhere in the gospels is there any evidence that Jesus either misremembered any event or mistook any person for another, nor does Sparks provide evidence for this. Moreover, Sparks' objection overlooks whether the divinity of Christ meant anything in terms of an epistemological relevance to His humanity and raises the question of how the divine nature relates to the human nature in the one person. We are told on several occasions, for example, that Jesus knew what people were thinking (Matthew 9:4, 12:25), which is a clear reference to His divine attributes. There is a personal union between the divine and human nature with each nature entirely preserved in its distinctness, yet in and as one person. So, even though Jesus was fully human, He never made an error in what He taught. Secondly, the language used in Scripture to describe the sun's rising (for example, Psalm 104:22) and movement of the earth are literal only in a phenomenological sense, as it is described from the viewpoint of the observer. This is still done today in weather reports when the reporter uses terminology such as "sunrise tomorrow will be at 5 a.m." What we also need to realize

12. Ibid., 373.
13. Ibid., 226.
14. Ibid., 252–253.

is that the idea "to err is human" is simply assumed to be true. It may be true that humans err, but it is not true that it is intrinsic for humanity to necessarily always err. There are many things we can do as humans and not err (examinations for example), and we must remember God created humanity (Adam and Eve) at the beginning of creation as sinless and therefore with the capacity not to err. Also, the incarnation of Jesus Christ shows sin, and therefore error, not to be normal. Jesus "who is impeccable was made in the likeness of sinful flesh, but being in 'fashion as a man' still 'holy harmless and undefiled.' To err is human is a false statement."[15]

Kenton Sparks is not the only one arguing that Scripture was affected by the errant assumptions of human nature. Dr. Denis Lamoureux, associate Professor of Science and Religion at St. Joseph's College in the University of Alberta, is a leading theistic evolutionist who openly denies that there ever was a first man Adam. When it comes to interpreting Genesis 1–11, his primary emphasis is in light of the worldview of the ANE. Lamoureux describes Genesis 1–11 as being "ancient science" that God used as a vehicle to communicate spiritual truth, as he states: "Evolutionary creationists believe that God's main purpose in the creation accounts of the Bible is to reveal inerrant spiritual truths."[16] This approach to the inerrancy of Scripture, however, raises a serious question as to how we can know whether any of theological teaching in Scripture that deals with things beyond our verification (eternal life, forgiveness of sins, justification, etc.) can be accepted as trustworthy or authoritative. If we reject the Bible's history as being inerrant, why do we think we can accept its spiritual teaching as being inerrant? Lamoureux's belief that Genesis is "ancient science" leads him to interpret passages that deal with the physical world through what he calls the "message-incident principle." This means that the Bible's spiritual truths are inerrant, but it presents them in the appearance of incidental and errant "ancient science."[17] Lamoureux recognizes that referring to the Bible as "ancient science" brings with it the accusation that God lied; therefore, he is quick to point out that this is not the case, as God ". . . accommodated in the Bible and permitted

15. Robert Culver, *Systematic Theology: Biblical and Historical* (Fearn, Ross-Shire: Christian Focus Publications, 2006), 500.
16. Denis O. Lamoureux, *Evolution: Scripture and Nature Say Yes!* (Grand Rapids, MI: Zondervan, 2016), 119.
17. Ibid., 89–90.

SCOFFERS

the use of an ancient understanding of origins in the creation accounts."[18] For Lamoureux, the concept of accommodation means Genesis is ancient (i.e., false) historiography. He states:

> Yet, for the Lord to reveal himself to ancient people in the past, he came down to their intellectual level. In doing so, God used their understanding of nature (ancient science) and their writing techniques (ancient poetry) as vessels to deliver life-changing spiritual truths.[19]

This understanding of accommodation means that the human author of Genesis believed the events happened just as described, but because of evolution, we now know they did not happen that way. This does, however, imply that God is responsible for communicating a flawed worldview to His people. Lamoureux confuses the concept of accommodation with the idea of error in the Bible. Rather, the traditional understanding of accommodation means "that [God] speaks truth in such a way that we can understand it, insofar as it can be understood by human beings."[20] For example, parents often accommodate their children with the question "Where do babies come from?" by answering, "They grow in their mother's tummy." On the other hand, to answer, "A stork delivered the baby," would be a lie, not an accommodation. Lamoureux's view of inspiration directly impacts how he understands Genesis, as it makes room for the errant assumptions on the part of the human authors of Scripture.

It is significant that in order to redefine the meaning of Genesis 1–11, Lamoureux has had to redefine how the nature of Scripture has been understood by evangelicals. The outcome of this position is that the Bible's authority is not found in its history but only through its theology. This is the abandonment of a verbal plenary view of the inspiration of Scripture in favor of a conceptual view, as this view of inerrancy only applies to the author's intent rather than his words. The idea that only the spiritual things, the intention or the concepts of the authors of Scripture, are inerrant and not the words of Scripture themselves is contrary to the apostolic teaching of Scripture as we will now see.

---

18. Ibid., 86.
19. Ibid., 31.
20. John Frame, *Systematic Theology: An Introduction to Christian Belief* (Harmony Township, NJ: P&R Publishing Group, 2013), 601.

The Divine and Human Nature of Scripture

Before looking at these words from Peter on the nature of Scripture, it is important to consider another well-known biblical passage that also speaks to the issue of inerrancy, the Apostle Paul's words in 2 Timothy 3:14–17. In Paul's first letter to Timothy, he instructed him to remain in Ephesus so that he may "charge certain persons not to teach any different doctrine" (1 Timothy 1:3). At this time, many false teachers were teaching myth and human commandments (1 Timothy 1:4; cf. Titus 1:14), which have their origin in demons (1 Timothy 4:1). This false teaching in Ephesus was doctrinal, as it included a distorted view of the resurrection (2 Timothy 2:18), a false view of knowledge (1 Timothy 6:20), a prohibition against marriage, and the eating of certain foods (1 Timothy 4:3–5). Yet Paul reminded Timothy to be confident in his ministry to the Christians at Ephesus and in his dealings with false teaching because his message came from God and not from men:

> But as for you, continue in what you have learned and have firmly believed, knowing from whom you learned it and how from childhood you have been acquainted with the sacred writings, which are able to make you wise for salvation through faith in Christ Jesus. All Scripture is *breathed out by God* and profitable for teaching, for reproof, for correction, and for training in righteousness, that the man of God may be complete, equipped for every good work (2 Timothy 3:14–17; emphasis mine).

Paul called Timothy to be faithful in his preaching of the true gospel, in all seasons, as there would come a time when people would no longer listen to sound teaching (2 Timothy 4:3). The only way to deal with false teaching is by holding to the trustworthy Word of God so that you will be able to rebuke those who contradict it (see Titus 1:9). Scripture is "God-breathed" (*theopneustos*, θεόπνευστος). In other words, God did not "breathe into" (inspire) all Scripture, but it was "breathed out" by God. This passage is not about how the Bible came to us but where it came from. Because the Scriptures are the only God-breathed revelation given to the Church, it means: "Scripture alone is the sole infallible rule of faith for the Church."[21] God's Word has no higher or equal authority. It

---

21. James R. White, *Scripture Alone: Exploring the Bible's Accuracy, Authority, And Authenticity* (Minneapolis, MN: Bethany House, 2004), 27–28.

is the ultimate authority in all things, for God cannot refer to any higher authority than Himself to establish the truthfulness of what He says (Hebrews 6:13). Since Scripture alone is God-breathed, it provides us with the very voice of God. Jesus reminded the Sadducees (who denied the resurrection, Acts 23:8) of this in His own day after they had asked Him a trick question regarding the future resurrection:

> But Jesus answered them, "You are wrong, because you know nei-ther the Scriptures nor the power of God. For in the resurrection they neither marry nor are given in marriage, but are like angels in heaven. And as for the resurrection of the dead, *have you not read what was said to you by God:* 'I am the God of Abraham, and the God of Isaac, and the God of Jacob'? He is not God of the dead, but of the living" (Matthew 22:29–32; emphasis mine).

This text is important for a couple of reasons. First, those who make the charge that the Scriptures contain error find themselves in the same position as the Sadducees who were rebuked by Jesus ("you are wrong"). The implication by Jesus here is that the Scriptures themselves do not err, as they speak accurately concerning history and theology (in con-text, the Patriarchs and the resurrection). Second, Jesus understood the words from the Book of Exodus (3:6) concerning Abraham, Isaac, and Jacob not only as being the very words of God but also as being appli-cable even to correct the Sadducees' misunderstanding of the resurrec-tion in the first century. Jesus held the Sadducees accountable to the scriptural revelation that God had spoken 1,400 years earlier. The con-cept of Scripture being "God-breathed" was not invented by Paul, it was something Jesus believed. Scripture is not bound by time and culture but is living and active (cf. Hebrews 4:12). Jesus' own view of Scripture was that of verbal inspiration, which can be seen from His statement in Matthew 5:18:

> For truly, I say to you, until heaven and earth pass away, not an iota, not a dot, will pass from the Law until all is accomplished.

For Jesus, Scripture is not merely inspired in its general ideas or its broad claims or in its general meaning but is inspired down to its very words because those words come "from the mouth of God" (Matthew 4:4). Whereas Scripture provides us with the very voice of God, human tradition not founded upon Scripture, as Jesus reminded the Pharisees, makes "void the word of God" (Matthew 15:6). A text that is usually cited (by Roman Catholic apologists) to try to show that there is equal value between Scripture and tradition is Paul's statement in 2 Thessalonians 2:15:

> So then, brothers, stand firm and hold to the traditions that you were taught by us, either by our spoken word or by our letter.

Although the term "tradition" (*paradosis*) can carry negative connotations among Christians today, we must remember that in the time of the Apostles, when the New Testament was being revealed, the Word of God was still being communicated in spoken form. In Paul's letters, these traditions deal with a number of diverse issues: the institution of the Lord's Supper (1 Corinthians 11:2, 23), the Resurrection of Jesus (1 Corinthians 15:3), self-sufficient labor (2 Thessalonians 3:6), and the gospel message (1 Thessalonians 2:13). But what is the tradition that Paul is referring to here? He's referring to one truth (the gospel) that is communicated in two ways: 1) by spoken word (preaching, 2 Thessalonians 2:5) and 2) by letter (1 Thessalonians). Paul's reference to tradition here cannot contain some unknown body of traditions (such as purgatory or papal authority) which the Thessalonians knew nothing of. Moreover, Paul told the Thessalonians to "stand firm" (*steko*), which elsewhere refers to the gospel (1 Corinthians 16:13), in these things, a command that assumes they possessed or knew what to stand firm in.[22]

The only thing that we have today that is God-breathed is Scripture (66 books of the Old and New Testaments). This is why it has the highest authority. However, since Timothy only knew the "sacred writings" (Old Testament) from childhood, does this alone prove their inspiration (as Giberson argued above)? The phrase "sacred writings" are qualified by "through faith in Christ Jesus," which Paul used to expand the scope beyond the Old Testament and to the gospel of Jesus Christ, as New Testament scholar William Mounce points out:

> It may be concluded that the expression "sacred writings" is drawn solely from the vocabulary describing the Hebrew Scripture, but since Paul is thinking about the culmination of the scripture hope realized through faith in Christ Jesus, he chooses

---

22. For these points, see White, *Scripture Alone*, 169–177.

the anarthrous plural construction to develop his argument in the direction of joining the Hebrew Scripture and the gospel.[23]

Timothy would have learned the gospel along with the Old Testament. Paul told him to "preach the word" (2 Timothy 4:2), which is not just the Old Testament alone but the whole counsel of God including the apostolic message:

> Follow the pattern of the *sound words* that you have heard from me, in the faith and love that are in Christ Jesus. By the Holy Spirit who dwells within us, guard the good deposit entrusted to you (2 Timothy 1:13–14; emphasis mine; cf. 1 Timothy 4:6–16; 6:3).

Moreover, there is an interesting reference in 1 Timothy 5:18 revealing that Paul regarded New Testament books as Scripture (*graphe*):

> For the Scripture says, "You shall not muzzle an ox when it treads out the grain," and, "The laborer deserves his wages."

Paul's first quote comes from Deuteronomy 25:4, but his second quote is identical to Jesus' statement in Luke 10:7.[24] According to Dr. Michael Kruger in his book *The Questions of Canon*, there is good evidence to believe Paul is citing from Luke's gospel rather than just an oral tradition:

1. This citation cannot be explained by appealing to oral tradition because it is clearly referred to as ἡ γραφή [*hē graphē*, the Scripture].

2. While another written source is a possibility . . . it should be noted that the Greek text in 1 Timothy 5:18 is identical to Luke 10:7 (and *only* to Luke 10:7).

3. The known historical connections between Paul and Luke at least provide a plausible scenario for why a Pauline letter would cite Luke's Gospel. In addition to being Paul's traveling companion throughout the Book of Acts, Luke is mentioned a number of

---

23. William D. Mounce, *Pastoral Epistles: Word Biblical Commentary 46* (Nashville, TN: Thomas Nelson, 2000), 564.

24. Although some scholars date Luke's gospel to be in the 70s A.D., there are a number of scholars who place it in the 60s. See D.A. Carson and Douglas Moo, *An Introduction to the New Testament* (Grand Rapids, MI: Zondervan, 2005), 207–208.

CARRIED ALONG BY THE HOLY SPIRIT

times in other Pauline letters (Colossians 4:14; 2 Timothy 4:11; Philemon 1:24) and clearly has direct connections to the apostolic circle (Luke 1:2).[25]

This shows that early in the first century (A.D. 62–64), Paul understood the gospel of Luke to be Scripture, just as the Apostle Peter considered Paul's letters to be Scripture (see 2 Peter 3:15–16). There are a number of Paul's own letters in the New Testament, as well as the Book of Revelation, that include instructions for them to be read in the public gathering of the Church:

> And when this *letter has been read among you*, have it also read in the church of the Laodiceans; and see that you also read the letter from Laodicea (Colossians 4:16; emphasis mine).

> I put you under oath before the Lord to *have this letter read* to all the brothers (1 Thessalonians 5:27; emphasis mine).

> Blessed is the one who *reads aloud the words of this prophecy*, and blessed are those who hear, and who keep what is written in it ... (Revelation 1:3; emphasis mine).

The reading of Old Testament Scripture in public worship gatherings was already something that took place among Jewish believers (Luke 4:17–20; Acts 15:21). There is good reason to believe then that when these New Testament letters were read aloud, they would have been considered Scripture just as the Old Testament writings were. Paul himself indicates this: "Until I come, devote yourself to *the public reading of Scripture*, to exhortation, to teaching" (1 Timothy 4:13; emphasis mine). All this suggests that there is evidence within the New Testament itself concerning an emerging canon of Scripture in the first century.[26]

Paul reminded Timothy that the basis of Scripture being *God-breathed* is that it is profitable for his work in the Church. The Greek term for "profitable" (*ophelimos*) only occurs two other times in the New Testament, both in Paul's pastoral letters: bodily training is of some value (1 Timothy 4:8), and devotion to good works is profitable (Titus 3:8). Paul tells Timothy that Scripture is profitable for four things: teaching, reproof, correction, and training. Teaching (*didaskalia*) in Paul's pastoral

25. Kruger, *The Question of Canon*, 201.
26. See Kruger, *The Question of Canon*.

letters refers to the "doctrinal formulation of Scripture"[27] (see 1 Timothy 4:13). Doctrine, not myth, is the foundation for Timothy's ministry and the only basis for correcting ungodly behavior (1 Timothy 1:10). The limitation against a woman teaching in the local church is founded upon the doctrine of creation before the Fall:

> I do not permit a woman to teach or to exercise authority over a man; rather, she is to remain quiet. For Adam was formed first, then Eve; and Adam was not deceived, but the woman was deceived and became a transgressor (1 Timothy 2:12–14).

The teaching that Paul does not permit a woman to do is the regular public instruction of God's Word to the gathered church assembly (1 Timothy 3:15; 4:13, 16; 6:2; 2 Timothy 4:2). Paul makes it clear that those men who serve as overseers in the church must be able to teach (1 Timothy 3:2). Timothy is also called to reprove (*elegchos*) those who persist in sin (1 Timothy 5:20) by preaching the Word (2 Timothy 4:2). Paul knew that false teaching would one day come into the Church (see Acts 20:29–30), and the only basis for reproving people of their false doctrine was Scripture. The purpose of rebuking those that teach false doctrine is that they will become "sound in the faith" (Titus 1:13). Because Scripture is both the standard and pattern of truth, Timothy is called to guard it (1 Timothy 6:20; 2 Timothy 1:13–14). Paul then moves from doctrine to behavior and tells Timothy that Scripture is profitable to "correct" and "train." The Greek word for "correct" (*epanorthosis*) occurs only here in the New Testament and refers to correcting improper behavior. For example, Paul had to correct Peter when he saw that his "conduct was not in step with the truth of the gospel" (Galatians 2:14). One way of correcting mistakes is by using Scripture to be "trained" (*paideia*) in righteousness (cf. Titus 2:12). While training can have an "instructional" or "educational" purpose (see Ephesians 6:4), it can also be used for "discipline" (1 Timothy 1:20; 2 Timothy 2:25). The purpose of being trained in righteousness (*dikaiosune*) is for practical purposes in the life of the believer (1 Timothy 6:11; 2 Timothy 2:22). All four of these things are by necessity what the man of God must do in the Church.

Paul's words also teach us about the purpose of Scripture. In verse 17, the words "that the" (*hina*) tell us the purpose of Scripture being

---

27. Mounce, *Pastoral Epistles*, 570.

God-breathed. Since Scripture comes from God, and is therefore true, it provides that which Timothy needs to "be complete, equipped for every good work." The word "complete" (*artios*) occurs only here in the New Testament and may be best understood as "thoroughly equipped" (NIV). Equipped (*exartizo*) is the verbal cognate of artios and "the fact that it is in the perfect tense, and its connection to πᾶν, 'every,' all emphasize the completeness of Scripture's preparation."[28] To be equipped is "to make someone completely adequate or sufficient for something,"[29] and only that which is God-breathed is sufficient to equip the believer for every good work. If the man of God is made sufficient by that which is God-breathed for every good work, then this teaches the sufficiency of Scripture to function as the only infallible rule of faith for the Church.

While the Apostle Paul told us *where* Scripture came from (a God-breathed text) the Apostle Peter tells us *how* the Bible came to us (a Spirit-carried author). Peter's words in 2 Peter 1:19–21 are one of the many reasons why Christians have long viewed Scripture as being authoritative, infallible, and inerrant:

> And we have the prophetic word more fully confirmed, to which you will do well to pay attention as to a lamp shining in a dark place, until the day dawns and the morning star rises in your hearts, knowing this first of all, that no prophecy of Scripture comes from someone's own interpretation. For no prophecy was ever produced by the will of man, but men spoke from God as they were carried along by the Holy Spirit (2 Peter 1:19–21).

As part of his apologetic against the false teachers, Peter focuses on the power, reliability, and inspiration of God's Word. But why does he? Well, think about it — Peter focuses on these things because the context is one in which false teaching is being fought (cf. Jude 3). Peter realized that the false teachers would probably try and discredit his letter to his readers by claiming that he was just inventing myths for them to follow. So, his solution is to give his fellow believers in the faith a firm foundation to believe in the divine inspiration of Scripture. The way to refute false doctrine is both specific and general. What do I mean? Although you can deal with false doctrine by specifically annihilating them one by one as

---

28. Ibid., 571.
29. Louw-Nida, "ἐξαρτίζω," in Greek-English Lexicon of the New Testament. Second Tim. 3:17, BibleWorks.

they come up, it is easier to refute it in a general way, which is by giving everyone a firm scriptural foundation through which they can repel false doctrine when it comes up. In other words, we should be teaching people why specific false teachings are wrong, such as evolution, and not just that it is wrong. The grounds for evolution being false is that God's Word is true and can be trusted when it speaks to the doctrine of creation.

In the last chapter, we saw how the Apostle Peter had defended the second "coming" (*parousia*) of Jesus, from the arguments of the false teachers that it was a "cleverly devised myth," by showing that the Apostles "were eyewitnesses" to the transfiguration (a view of His second coming in glory). This is the reason why we can be confident Jesus is coming back. The "we" in verse 19 is in the first-person plural (*echomen*) and is not the apostolic "we" of verse 16, as Peter has broadened out his argument to include believers. So, it's not just the Apostles who have the prophetic word (Scripture) "more fully confirmed," but all believers have this certainty. Peter exhorts Christians that they "will do well to pay attention" to the prophetic word because it is "a lamp shining in a dark place" (cf. Psalm 119:105). The prophetic word concerning the "coming" of Jesus is to guide us "until the day dawns and the morning star rises in your hearts."[30] As we walk through this dark world, anticipating the coming of Jesus, God has graciously given us a lamp (Scripture) to guide us in it. After Peter establishes that "we have a prophetic word more fully confirmed," he goes deeper into the discussion of inspiration. The words of 1:20 have brought about a lot of confusion, as they have been translated very differently, which has led to two different competing interpretations: Is Peter focusing on the origin or the interpretation prophecy?

> But know this first of all, that no prophecy of Scripture becomes a matter of someone's own interpretation (2 Peter 1:20; NASB).

> Above all, you must understand that no prophecy of Scripture came about by the prophet's own interpretation of things (2 Peter 1:20; NIV).

Notice that the NASB reads as if this passage is to how to interpret prophecy (the present reader), whereas the NIV (and ESV) reads very

---

30. The dawning day probably refers to the eschatological age (Romans 13:12; 1 Thessalonians 5:4–9), which comes with the return of Jesus (bright morning star, Revelation 22:16).

differently, seeing it referring to the origins of prophecy. These are two very different ways of thinking about this text. How then should we understand the meaning of this verse? The contextual flow of the passage seems to suggest not the "interpretation of prophecy" is in view but the "origin of prophecy."[31] For example, in the Old Testament, ". . . the prophet is given a sign (e.g., Amos 7:1; Jer 1:11, 13), a dream (e.g., Zech 1:8; Dan 7:2) or a vision (e.g., Dan 8:1), and then its interpretation."[32] The point Peter is making is this: Nowhere in the Old Testament does a prophecy arise just based on the understanding of the prophet. It's not just something out of their own understanding when they prophesy. It is the "origin" rather than the "present interpretation" of prophecy that is in view, as Peter is appealing to Scripture as a way to refute the claims of the false teachers that they (the Apostles) are misinterpreting their revelations from God (i.e., making things up). Peter is giving a second reason to believe in the second "coming" of Jesus by appealing to Scripture, as it comes from God. In other words, Peter is saying if our "eyewitness" testimony is not enough to convince you to believe in the return of Jesus, then believe us because "we have the prophetic word more fully confirmed." This would be difficult to refute if the verse was speaking about interpretation. The issue is about the reliability of the origin of prophecy which confirms the authority of Scripture. Scripture is not based upon the prophet's own understanding of things, as nowhere in the Bible does prophecy arise on the understanding of the prophet. So Peter, in verse 20, is not dealing with "one's own interpretation of prophecy" but with the origin and the interpretation of the prophetic revelation because it comes from God.

The reliability of the origin of prophecy is again confirmed in verse 21 as Peter explains: "For prophecy never came by the will of man, but holy men of God spoke as they were moved by the Holy Spirit" (NKJV). Prophecy was not motivated by man's will, in that it did not come from human impulse. Peter tells us how the prophets were able to speak from God by the fact that they were being continually "moved" (*pheromenoi*, present passive participle) by the Holy Spirit as they spoke or wrote. The Holy Spirit moved the human authors of Scripture in such a way that they were moved not by their own "will" but by the Holy Spirit. Peter

---

31. See Michael Green, *2 Peter and Jude:* Tyndale New Testament Commentaries (Leicester, England: InterVarsity Press, 1987), 100–102; Baucham, Jude, 2 Peter, 229–233.
32. Bauckham, *Jude, 2 Peter*, 231.

"uses a fascinating maritime metaphor in verse 21 (cf. Acts 27:15, 17, where the same word, *pheromone*, is used of a ship carried along by the wind)."[33] In a similar fashion, the prophets and the Apostles were carried along by the Holy Spirit and taken in the direction He wanted them to go and preserved those words so what they said were not just their own words but God's. This does not mean that human authors of Scripture were automatons; they were active rather than passive in the process of writing Scripture, as can be seen in their style of writing and the vocabulary they used. The role of the Holy Spirit was to teach the authors of Scripture (John 14:26, 16:12–15).

In the New Testament, it was the Apostles or New Testament prophets whom the Spirit led to write truth and overcome their human tendency to err. The Apostles shared Jesus' view of Scripture, presenting His message as God's Word (1 Thessalonians 2:13) and proclaiming that it was "not in words which man's wisdom teaches but which the Holy Spirit teaches" (1 Corinthians 2:13). Paul taught that revelation comes from God in and through words. Revelation, then, did not come about within the Apostle or prophet, but it has its source in the triune God. Biblical Christianity does not deny the true humanity of Scripture; rather, it properly recognizes that to be human does not necessarily entail error and that the Holy Spirit kept the biblical writers from making errors they might otherwise have made. Biblical Christianity embraces a theory of organic inspiration. In other words, "God sanctifies the natural gifts, personalities, histories, languages, and cultural inheritance of the biblical writers."[34]

The biblical view of the inspiration of Scripture is that revelation comes from God in and through words. The relationship between the inspiration of the biblical text through the Holy Spirit and human authorship is too intimate to allow for human errors in the text. Therefore, in the same way that Jesus can assume our full humanity without sin (1 Peter 2:21–22), so it is that God can speak through the fully human words of prophets and Apostles without error.

Peter's view of Scripture comes not only in 1:19–21 but also in two other important passages in his second letter. Earlier in his letter Peter wrote:

---

33. Green, *2 Peter and Jude*, 102.
34. Michael Horton, *The Christian Faith: A Systematic Theology for Pilgrims on the Way* (Grand Rapids, MI: Zondervan, 2011), 163.

> His divine power has granted to us all things that pertain to life and godliness, through the knowledge of him who called us to his own glory and excellence, by which he has granted to us his precious and very great promises, so that through them you may become partakers of the divine nature, having escaped from the corruption that is in the world because of sinful desire (2 Peter 1:3–4).

Peter tells us that God has given His people all the things they need for life and godliness, and "his divine power" to do this comes through his "precious and great promises." Those promises in God's Word are able to sanctify us as they change us so that we can become "partakers in the divine nature" (sharing in the moral excellence that belongs to God, 2 Peter 1:3).[35] The place where we get those promises are in Scripture (in context, the Old Testament). Scripture, therefore, is sanctifying, as it contains all we need for life and godliness. These are important verses for understanding the sufficiency and inspiration of Scripture, as God is behind both. God's Word is enough to transform the Christian.

Later in his letter, Peter gives us references to the nature of Scripture and the origins of the canon. Notice what 2 Peter says in 3:2: ". . . that you should remember the predictions of the holy prophets and the commandment of the Lord and Savior through your apostles." Peter makes it clear that he has two major sources of authority in his world as to how you hear from God: 1) the Old Testament and 2) the Apostles. Peter puts the apostolic words on par with Scripture itself. This suggests that Peter has a robust doctrine of Scripture in terms of its inspiration, but he also has a very clear idea that there is new Scripture, from the Apostles, in his own day that people are using: ". . . just as our beloved brother Paul also wrote to you according to the wisdom given him, as he does in all his letters [plural] when he speaks in them of these matters" (2 Peter 3:15–16). In fact, Peter talks as if it is common knowledge that people know who the Apostle Paul is (notice he does not introduce Paul to his readers) and that his letters are authoritative Scripture.

Because Scripture is *God-breathed* and *men were moved by the Holy Spirit* to write it, it is unique revelation. The events of the supernatural creation of the world and the cataclysmic global Flood are then a reliable, historical account of the creation of the world and humanity since they

---

35. See Schreiner, *1, 2 Peter, Jude*, 294.

were uniquely revealed by God to His prophets and Apostles. Scripture, therefore, is trustworthy and authoritative when it comes to history and thereby is trustworthy in the scientific inferences from that history. Those who deny the full authority of Scripture by arguing it contains human error are classic examples of the disastrous effects of trying to make God's inspired Word fit with that of man's ever-changing, fallible opinions. Christianity essentially is antithetical to evolution. Since the rise of Darwinian evolution in the 19th century, it has become the custom to reinterpret the biblical account of creation in light of this. This has led to the decline of the Church within the Western world as the whole point of Darwinian evolution is to show that there is no need for a supernatural Creator, since nature can do the creating by itself. This ultimately leads to a rejection of God and His Word. The question we must ask ourselves, then, as Christians is: Do we have the same view of Scripture as the Apostles (and our Lord and Savior), or are we being deceived by a lesser view of Scripture, given to us by certain influential theologians and pastors?

CHAPTER FOUR

SCOFFERS IN THE LAST DAYS

This is now the second letter that I am writing to you, beloved. In both of them I am stirring up your sincere mind by way of reminder, that you should remember the predictions of the holy prophets and the commandment of the Lord and Savior through your apostles, knowing this first of all, that scoffers will come in the last days with scoffing, following their own sinful desires (2 Peter 3:1–3).

The Apostle Peter begins his third chapter by telling his readers he wants to remind them of something: namely the words of the holy prophets and the commandment of the Lord and Savior through the Apostles. Why does Peter do this? Because he is reminding believers that the arrival of the scoffers was prophesied for the last days. These opponents that Peter warned about were actually no more than false teachers within the Church (2 Peter 2:1, 13; cf. Jude 4). Reminders are often necessary because the nature of humanity is that we are a forgetful people, and when we forget, there are consequences. Keep in mind, for much of their history, the nation of Israel forgot what God had done for them (e.g., redeeming them out of Egypt, giving them His law and taking them into the Promised Land), and when they did this, it always ended in tragedy, and God justly brought judgment upon them (see Judges 2:6–15; Jeremiah 29:1–23). An even more fitting example is the Apostle Peter himself. He knew the penalty for not remembering since he had the personal experience of forgetting the words of the Lord Jesus. In the lead up to his arrest and trial, Jesus told Peter he would deny knowing him three times, something Peter said he would not do (Matthew 26:34–35). During Jesus' trial, His words came to pass when Peter, having been asked by a servant girl in the courtyard for a third time if he knew Jesus, denied that he ever knew Him. When he remembered Jesus' prediction, he left the courtyard and wept bitterly (Matthew 26:75). If we are not to repeat the mistake of the nation of Israel and the Apostle Peter, then it is important for us to not only remember but also believe what God has said to us in His Word regarding the supernatural creation of the world and the global Flood.

The purpose of Peter's reminder is to stir up the "sincere (pure) minds" of believers, which is in contrast to the scoffers, who only have contempt for personal holiness and are like irrational animals following their sinful desires (2 Peter 2:12). In other words, we find our answers to the scoffers in Scripture, and we come to that with a pure mind (*dianoia*).[1] Peter also exhorts believers to prepare their minds for action, which will require discipline (1 Peter 1:13). Scripture, then, is sufficient — not only to transform the Christian (2 Peter 1:3–4) but also to deal with the arguments of the scoffers. In a similar fashion, the Apostle Paul exhorts Christians, "Do not be conformed to this world, but be transformed by the renewal of your mind" (Romans 12:2). The word "world" (*aiōn*) in this context refers to the thinking of the age. The reason that our minds (*nous*)[2] need to be renewed is because in the Fall of man (Genesis 3), they became futile and darkened (Romans 1:21). As Christians, we need to understand that there are only two kinds of mind in this world: the debased mind (Romans 1:28) and the discerning mind (Romans 12:2).[3] The debased mind, trapped in sin, believes the *lie* (*tō pseudei*, Romans 1:25)[4] and worships and serves the creature rather than the Creator. Whereas the discerning mind has been transformed, having been freed from sin,

---

1. In 2 Peter 3:1, the word *dianoia* refers to the mind as a mode of thinking (disposition, thought). See Walter Bauer, BDAG: *A Greek-English Lexicon of the New Testament* Third Edition (Chicago, IL: The University of Chicago Press, 2000), 234.

2. In Romans 12:2, the word translated mind, *nous*, refers to the way of thinking (attitude). See BDAG: *A Greek-English Lexicon of the New Testament*, 680.

3. Theologian Peter Jones uses this example of the "debased mind" and "discerning mind" to show the difference between the pagan and Christian worldview, see Peter Jones, *The Other Worldview: Exposing Christianity's Greatest Threat* (Bellingham, WA: Kirkdale Press, 2015), 162–178.

4. Since Paul has Genesis 1 in mind throughout Romans 1, he may be referring to *the* original lie in Genesis 3 (see John 8:44) and not just any old falsehood (i.e., "a lie," see ESV).

it is now free to worship and serve the Creator, who is blessed forever, amen! Becoming a Christian does not erase all effects of sin — even as Christians, we still have the capacity to think like the world if we do not allow Scripture to renew our minds and walk in step with the Holy Spirit (see Galatians 5:16–18). In the Christian's spiritual battle, the key element that is being fought over is the mind:

> For the weapons of our warfare are not of the flesh but have divine power to destroy strongholds. We destroy arguments and every lofty opinion raised against the knowledge of God, and take every thought captive to obey Christ. . . (2 Corinthians 10:4–5).

The Apostle Paul uses a military metaphor here in order to explain what he means. The arguments we are to destroy are the "strongholds" by which unbelievers are held captive against the invasion of the knowledge of God. These "strongholds" are the intellectual arguments used by unbelievers against the gospel. As Christians, we are coming against these great ideas (evolution, millions of years) — which have become people's "strongholds" — that, unless unbelievers change their minds, will end up being their tombs. The nature of the spiritual war we are in is to destroy the "arguments," which is the Greek word *logismos* and refers to the reasoning or thought process that people are held captive by, and we are called to bring those thoughts captive to Christ. Christians are the instruments by which God brings the truth of the gospel to destroy error. However, if we do not take every thought captive and make them obedient to Christ, then those thoughts (e.g., evolution, millions of years, etc.) will take us captive.

Paul also warns Christians that just as the serpent (Satan) appealed to Eve's mind to get her to disobey God's Word, so he wants to deceive Christian minds (2 Corinthians 11:3). For this reason, our minds need to be daily renewed by God's Word so that we are not conformed to the world and do not adopt its thinking patterns (see Ephesians 4:17–24). So, rather than seeing the mind as a terrible thing and head knowledge as a disease that needs to be cured, we should love God the way Jesus told us to:

> And he [Jesus] said to him, "You shall love the Lord your God with all your heart and with all your soul and with all your mind" (Matthew 22:37).

This is not to say we become "puffed up with knowledge" (1 Corinthians 8:1) but that we use our minds to think biblically when it comes to the issues such as creation and evolution. Rather than dulling our minds with the thinking of the world, we need to educate our mind by applying it to the knowledge in God's Word (Proverbs 22:17).

As we saw in the last chapter, Peter makes it clear that he has two major sources of authority as to how believers are to hear from God: 1) the Old Testament and 2) the Apostles. The first group mentioned by Peter are the "Holy Prophets," which is the prophetic word of the Old Testament (see Acts 3:21). In the Old Testament, there are many passages where the prophets speak of judgment for those who scoff at the delayed judgment of God (Isaiah 5:18–20; Jeremiah 5:12–24; Malachi 2:17). The second group are "your apostles," who are those particular Apostles who first brought the gospel to the believers he is writing to, who passed on "the commandment of the Lord and Savior." What is noteworthy here are the authoritative titles used of Jesus (Lord and Savior), as they not only express His sovereignty but also counter the scoffer's argument. As theologian Michael Green points out:

> Note that Peter again uses the full title Lord and Saviour, probably because he is about to emphasize the future element in salvation which the scoffers ridicule. Jesus is not only saviour from the past (1:1–4), and in the present (2:20), but for the future as well. To deny the second coming of Jesus is to deny Jesus as Saviour.[5]

The argument of Peter to aid us in not falling victim to the scoffers comes from Scripture. As believers, we have been given a pure mind that can be stirred up, and what stirs it up is Scripture.

Scoffers and the Last Days

Finding people who scoff at the biblical account of creation and the Flood in our secular culture is not hard to do these days. The reality is that in today's world, it is normal for secular society to scoff at, twist, and take out of context the content of the Bible. In fact, it is indeed common for many scoffers to apply a view of criticism to Christianity that says it is not important to be factually correct in reporting what the

5. Michael Green, *2 Peter and Jude, Tyndale New Testament Commentaries* (Leicester: InterVarsity Press, 1987), 136.

Bible says, but it is acceptable to make what they believe is a "morally" correct judgment about the text. At the popular level, for example, in his bestselling book *The God Delusion*, well-known atheist Richard Dawkins says of the account of the Flood:

> The legend of the animals going into the ark two by two is charming, but the moral of the story of Noah is appalling. God took a dim view of humans, so he (with the exception of one family) drowned the lot of them including children and also, for good measure, the rest of the (presumably blameless) animals as well. Of course, irritated theologians will protest that we don't take the book of Genesis literally any more. But that is my whole point! We pick and choose which bits of scripture to believe, which bits to write off as symbols or allegories. Such picking and choosing is a matter of personal decision, just as much, or as little, as the atheists' decision to follow this moral precept or that was a personal decision, without an absolute foundation. If one of these is "morality flying by the seat of its pants", so is the other. In any case, despite the good intentions of the sophisticated theologian, a frighteningly large number of people still do take their scriptures, including the story of Noah, literally.[6]

Dawkins' comments on the Flood account are not about the truth but simply about scoffing and being "morally" correct. Let's think about what he is saying. Why would it be frightening that a large number of people take the text "literally" — or more precisely, "plainly" — according to its literary genre (historical narrative)? Remember, Dawkins is an atheist, so for anyone to take the text "literally" (that God is real and has acted in history) is simply unacceptable to his naturalistic worldview. So, when Dawkins reads the text of Scripture, keep in mind that he does not believe that God exists or that He reveals Himself to people. The biblical narrative is judged by Dawkins (and other atheists) as if God has not revealed Himself. Ultimately, he is not critiquing what the Bible says but rather is critiquing a misrepresentation of the biblical event. If Dawkins had taken the time to properly interact with the Flood account, he would have realized that God judged the people in Noah's day not because He took a dim view of humans but for a number of clear reasons:

---

6. Richard Dawkins, The God Delusion (Great Britain: Bantam Press, 2006), 269.

The wickedness of man.
Every intent of the thoughts of man's heart was only evil continually.
The earth was corrupt.
The earth was filled with violence.
All flesh (including the animals) had corrupted their way upon
    the earth (Genesis 6:5–13).

Despite man's wickedness, God showed Himself to be gracious in that He patiently waited while the Ark was being prepared (1 Peter 3:20). What Dawkins needs to explain is how God's judgment of wicked people can be "morally appalling" in a naturalistic worldview in which he believes there is "no evil and no good."[7] As an atheist, Dawkins has no foundation upon which to define something as "morally appalling," as even leading atheist philosophers admit that atheism implies amorality. Atheist Joel Marks, Professor Emeritus of Philosophy at the University of New Haven, states:

> The long and the short of it is that I became convinced that atheism implies amorality; and since I am an atheist, I must therefore embrace amorality. . . . [T]he religious fundamentalists are correct: without God, there is no morality. But they are incorrect, I still believe, about there being a God. Hence, I believe, there is no morality.[8]

Atheists have no rational justification for questioning the character of God, given that they have no objective moral foundation on which to do so. Morality for an atheist is just a matter of opinion. From an evolutionary point of view, if we are just evolved animals, then there is no such thing as absolute morality. Yet, absolute morality is needed to make ethical judgments, and to make absolute ethical judgments, you need the God of the Bible. This is not to say that you need to profess belief in God to argue morality, but you do need God to have absolute morality. In the Christian worldview, God is good and is the standard of goodness,

---

7. In his book *River Out of Eden*, Dawkins has famously stated: "The universe we observe has precisely the properties we should expect if there is, at bottom, no design, no purpose, no evil and no good, nothing but blind pitiless indifference." Richard Dawkins, *River Out of Eden: A Darwinian View of Life* (New York: Basic Books/Harper Collins, 1995), 133.
8. Joel Marks, "An Amoral Manifesto (Part I)," *Philosophy Now* (August/September 2010). Marks does distinguish between hard atheists (himself), who believe in amorality, and soft atheists (like Richard Dawkins), who reject God but believe in morality.

so apart from God, any standard of our own making would be necessarily arbitrary and ultimately self-refuting. The reason human beings possess an innate sense of morality is because we are made in the image of God and His law has been written on our hearts (Genesis 1:27; Romans 2:15). If your worldview cannot give a justification for things like morality, then it should be rejected. As Christians, we need to consider the account of the Flood (and other judgment passages in Scripture) in light of what the Bible states about God and humanity:

- God is the sovereign Creator and therefore has the right to do what He pleases (Psalm 135:6; Daniel 4:35).

- God is holy, just, righteous, gracious, merciful, compassionate, and loving (Isaiah 6:3; Exodus 34:6–7; John 3:16).

- God created a very good world (Genesis 1:31).

- The world we now live in is a fallen, sin-cursed world (Roman 5:12, 8:19–22).

- There are no truly good people (i.e., good by God's standard) since we have all sinned and fallen short of God's glory (Romans 3:9–19, 23; Colossians 1:21).

- We do not deserve God's mercy; we deserve God's justice (Psalm 103:10, 130:3; Romans 6:23).

The coming "scoffers" of the Apostle Peter's day are the false teachers he had criticized in 2 Peter 2:1–22. Scoffing is not a rational argument against the truth; it is basically an argument by ridicule, as it is meant to bring dishonor to a person. Peter's priority is to warn his readers to be mindful of the coming attacks from the false teachers — the scoffers. We need to remember that there is a difference between error and false teaching. For example, Apollos' understanding of the Christian message departed at least at one point from the teaching of the Apostles in the Book of Acts: The only baptism he knew of was the baptism of repentance taught by John the Baptist; he did not know about baptism in Jesus' name as proclaimed by the Apostles (cf. Acts 2:38). However, when he was taken aside and corrected by Priscilla and Aquila, he began to teach the truth (Acts 18:24–28). A false teacher is not just someone who teaches falsehood but is someone who rejects authority and is uncorrectable (2 Peter 2:10; Jude 8). The difference between error and false teaching is that while error can be corrected, false teaching is something that strikes at the very heart of the gospel and of the truth of God's Word.

The term "knowing this first" is not referring to the first in the list of things; rather, it means the first in priority (cf. 2 Peter 1:20). The priority for Peter is to alert his readers to the presence of the coming scoffers, which is a sign that the last days have arrived. The "last days" are a reference to the era from Christ's first coming until His return (cf. Acts 2:17). It is not about the "quantity" but the "quality" of time.[9] The author of Hebrews tells us that these "last days" (*eschatou tōn hēmerōn*) is a time when God has fully and finally revealed Himself in the person of His Son, the Lord Jesus (see Hebrews 1:1–2). This is a privileged time; it is a time when the gospel has gone out into all the world and we await the return of Jesus. The Christian's life is not meant to be lived on a cruise ship but on a battleship, as it is lived in *the* day of salvation when believers, as Christ's ambassadors, proclaim the message of reconciliation with God the Father (2 Corinthians 5:21–6:2). But it is not surprising that these scoffers or false teachers would come, as according to the Apostles, the last days would be characterized by false teaching and apostasy:

- Now the Spirit expressly says that in *later times* [*hysterois kairois*] some will depart from the faith by devoting themselves to deceitful spirits and teachings of demons. . . (1 Timothy 4:1; emphasis mine).

- But understand this, that in the *last days* [*eschatais hēmerais*] there will come times of difficulty (2 Timothy 3:1; emphasis mine; cf. 2–5, 12–13).

- Come now, you rich, weep and howl for the miseries that are coming upon you. Your riches have rotted and your garments are moth-eaten. Your gold and silver have corroded, and their corrosion will be evidence against you and will eat your flesh like fire. You have laid up treasure in the *last days* [*eschatais hēmerais*] (James 5:1–3; emphasis mine).

---

9. Kistemaker, "2 Peter," 477.

- Children, it is the *last hour* [*eschatē hōra*], and as you have heard that antichrist is coming, so now many antichrists have come. Therefore we know that it is the last hour (1 John 2:18; emphasis mine).

- They said to you, "In the *last time* [*eschatou chronou*] there will be scoffers, following their own ungodly passions" (Jude 18; emphasis mine).

These passages are not just talking about something that will take place at the end of the age, as the Apostles saw this false teaching happening in their own congregations, but would dominate throughout the Church age.

Scoffing at God's Word is not a new phenomenon, as it has taken place throughout biblical history. In the garden in Eden, Eve "scoffed" at the truth of God's Word and instead accepted the lie of the serpent over it (Genesis 3:1–5; cf. 2 Corinthians 11:3). When Moses brought God's Word to Pharaoh and asked him to let the nation of Israel leave Egypt or face the coming judgment of the plagues, Pharaoh "scoffed" at him, saying: "Who is the LORD, that I should obey his voice and let Israel go?" (Exodus 5:2). Because of their continual disobedience of His Word, God ultimately brought judgment, through the Babylonians, upon the nation of Israel because ". . . they kept mocking the messengers of God, despising his words and scoffing at his prophets, until the wrath of the LORD rose against his people, until there was no remedy" (2 Chronicles 36:16). Even after the Babylonian exile, when the people of Israel returned to the land, Tobiah and Sanballat rose up and scoffed at Nehemiah's plan to rebuild the wall around Jerusalem (Nehemiah 2:10, 19; 4:1). In fact, scoffers were common in the Old Testament and were to be avoided by God's people (Psalm 1:1, 35:16; Proverbs 1:22, 9:7–8, 13:1, 14:6).

In the days of Jesus, the leading theologians of the day, the Pharisees, "scoffed" at the idea that Jesus was the fulfilment of the messianic prophecies in the Old Testament (John 7:47–52). And when Jesus was hanging on the Cross, the Jewish rulers ". . . scoffed at him, saying, 'He saved others; let him save himself, if he is the Christ of God, his Chosen One!'" (Luke 23:35). After hearing the gospel message on Mars Hill, many of the Athenians "scoffed" at the idea that there could be a physical resurrection of the body, even though God had already attested to this by raising Jesus from the dead (Acts 17:30–32). Near the close of the first century, the Apostle John had to deal with false teaching of the docetists (from *dokeo*, "to appear"), who "scoffed" at the idea of Jesus, rather than being truly human, only appeared to be human (see 1 John 1:1–3, 4:1–3). False teaching and "scoffing" didn't stop with the end of the Apostles but continued after they had passed away just as the Apostle Paul warned: "I know that after my departure fierce wolves will come in among you, not sparing the flock; and from among your own selves will arise men speaking twisted things, to draw away the disciples after them" (Acts 20:29–30).

In the second century, when Christianity broke into the Greco-Roman world, the Greek philosopher and critic of Christianity Celsus scoffed at Christians by labelling them "ignorant," "unintelligent," "uninstructed," and "foolish" (see *Contra Celsus*, 3.44). In the third century, the false teacher Arius (256–336), an Alexandrian Presbyter, "scoffed" at the idea that Jesus was the Creator of the world and instead argued that He (the Son) was the first created being.[10] The fourth century saw another false teacher arise and scoff at a different aspect of God's Word. The British theologian Pelagius (360–420) "scoffed" at God's Word by rejecting the scriptural teaching that Adam's disobedience rendered mankind inherently sinful (see Romans 5:12–19). For Pelagius, there was no connection between Adam's sin and ours, and therefore, Adam's transgression bore no consequence to the essential nature of the human race.[11] The list of false teachers and scoffers throughout the centuries goes on and on: such as Joseph Smith (1805–1844), the founder of Mormonism; Ellen G. White (1827–1915), the false prophetess of the Seventh Day Adventists; and Charles Taze Russel (1852–1916), whose teachings helped start the Jehovah's Witnesses.

Although there have been many scoffers of God's Word throughout history, there are three men in particular who have helped lay a foundation for people today to scoff at the Bible's account of the supernatural creation of the world and the divine judgment of it through a global Flood through their ideas of the old age of the earth and the evolution of life: James Hutton, Charles Lyell, and Charles Darwin.

10. The Bible clearly teaches that Jesus is the Creator of all things and is not a created being (John 1:1–3; Hebrews 1:2, 8–10; Colossians 1:16).

11. In the year A.D. 418, the Council of Carthage condemned the teachings of Pelagius, as did the Council of Ephesus in A.D. 431. The Council of Carthage even stated: "Whoever says, that Adam was created mortal, and would, even without sin, have died by natural necessity, let him be anathema."

Modern-day Scoffing of Creation and the Flood

Modern-day scoffing at God's Word, especially at the supernatural creation of the world and the global Flood, is not unusual, and we only have to think of men such as Bill Nye, Richard Dawkins, Sam Harris, Daniel Dennett, David Attenborough, Lawrence Krauss, and both the late Stephen Hawking and Christopher Hitchens. These men, all scientists (except Hitchens), through their writings and work in the media, openly scoff at the biblical account of creation and the Flood and openly ridicule those who believe it. These modern-day scoffers did not appear in a vacuum. They have built on the arguments of a previous generation of men who openly scoffed at God's Word.

Until the 1800s, the dominant view of the history of the world, at least in Europe, was the biblical view of creation and a global Flood. But in the late 18th and early 19th centuries, new theories of earth's history began to be proposed.[12] It was at this time that the idea of the great age of the earth began to be developed, which subsequently challenged the historicity of the early chapters of Genesis. In the 18th and 19th centuries, building on the back of the Enlightenment, or the age of reason (1685–1815), which elevated human reason above supernatural revelation (i.e., God's Word), three men in particular began this modern attack on the supernatural events of creation and the Flood.

The first of these men is James Hutton (1726–1797), a Scottish geologist and deist (the belief in a creator who does not intervene in the universe) who viewed earth's history as cyclical and is famous in the history of the debate over the age of the earth. Hutton's geological work at Siccar Point, a rocky headland on the east coast of Scotland, helped hail him as "the founding father of geology." Hutton considered Siccar Point to be proof of his uniformitarian ideas of geological development, and this belief significantly undermined the biblical account of creation and the Flood. Today, there is a sign at Siccar Point commemorating Hutton's work that reads:

> The rocks at Siccar Point were the defining proof for his revolutionary Theory of the Earth. Most people at this time thought the world no older than a few thousand years. Hutton realised

---

12. For a more in-depth discussion of this history, see Terry Mortenson, *The Great Turning Point: The Church's Catastrophic Mistake on Geology — Before Darwin* (Green Forest, AR: Master Books, 2004).

that earth processes are cyclical and that geological time is virtu-ally unlimited . . . Hutton's theory released science and philoso-phy from limitations of the biblical age of the earth (6000 years old). Though bitterly disputed at the time, it is now accepted as a fundamental of science.

Hutton, just like any other scientist, was not a neutral observer of the geological evidence (no one is). For instance, before going out into the field and actually examining the evidence, Hutton argued that we can only interpret the world around us by present-day processes:

> The past history of our globe must be explained by what can be seen to be happening *now*. . . . No powers are to be employed that are not *natural* to the globe, no action to be admitted except those of which we know the principle.[13] (emphasis mine)

What Hutton was actually arguing was that when it comes to earth's history, we cannot appeal to such things as the Bible; more specifically, we cannot appeal to the Flood in Noah's day to interpret the rock layers. According to Hutton, any interpretation of the rock layers had to be nat-ural. Hutton's philosophical bias (naturalism) has become part and parcel of scientific thinking today.

Hutton's views in his book *The Theory of the Earth* (1788) helped give rise to the philosophy of uniformitarianism. It was his philosophical bias of naturalism and explaining the world only by present processes that began to dominate the study of geology from around 1840, and every geologist since then has been trained to think with the assumptions of uniformitarian naturalism (see chapter 6).

Hutton's work would later be built on by influential Scottish law-yer-geologist Charles Lyell (1797–1875) in his three-volume work *Prin-ciples of Geology* (1830–1833). Like Hutton, Lyell was also a deist. Lyell took Hutton's views and popularized them. In his book *Principles of Geology*, Lyell presented the theory that the landforms and rock layers of the earth we observe now are the product of vast ages of slow gradual processes. This idea is commonly known as uniformitarianism, which

---

13. James Hutton, "Theory of the Earth," a paper (with the same title of his 1795 book) communicated to the Royal Society of Edinburgh and published in *Transactions of the Royal Society of Edinburgh*, 1785; cited with approval in A. Holmes, *Principles of Physical Geology* 2nd edition (Great Britain: Thomas Nelson and Sons Ltd., 1965), 43–44.

Simon standing next to the "James Hutton" sign at Siccar Point in 2015 and the rocky headland that convinced Hutton of the old age of the earth.

assumes that the processes we observe in our present world are the way it has always been. What may be unknown to many people, however, is that Lyell had made it clear that he had an anti-Bible agenda. In 1830, he wrote to George Scrope, a Member of Parliament and fellow uniformitarian geologist, outlining the ultimate purpose of his geological writings:

> I am sure you may get into Q.R. [Quarterly Review] what will free the science [of geology] from Moses, for if treated seriously, the [church] party are quite prepared for it. A bishop, Buckland ascertained (we suppose [Bishop] Sumner), gave Ure a dressing in the British Critic and Theological Review. They see at last the mischief and scandal brought on them by Mosaic systems. . . . I conceived the idea five or six years ago, that if ever the Mosaic geology could be set down [put aside] without giving offence, it would be in an historical sketch, and you must abstract mine, in order to have as little to say as possible yourself.[14]

In the 19th century, the majority of people would have recognized that Moses was the author of the Book of Genesis, so freeing science from Moses meant denying the origin and history of the world as described in Genesis. Lyell realized if he could get rid of (set down) the Flood account in Genesis (Moses), then he would re-write history (historical sketch), and he has succeeded in doing that. It was Lyell's first volume

---

14. Charles Lyell: Letter to George Scrope, June 14, 1830, in K. Lyell [Lyell's sister-in-law], *Life, Letters and Journals of Sir Charles Lyell, Bart. I* (London: John Murray, 1881), 268–271.

of *Principles of Geology*, perhaps more than anything else, which greatly influenced the famous English naturalist Charles Darwin (1809–1882) in his thinking. The idea of an old earth was foundational to Darwin's evolutionary ideas. During Darwin's famous five-year voyage around the world on the HMS *Beagle* (1831–1836), he read *Principles of Geology* and would later admit to a friend:

> I always feel as if my books came half out of Lyell's brains & that I never acknowledge this sufficiently, nor do I know how I can, without saying so in so many words — for I have always thought that the great merit of the Principles [*Principles of Geology*] was that it altered the whole tone of one's mind & therefore that when seeing a thing never seen by Lyell, one yet saw it partially through his eyes.[15]

Only a few weeks into his voyage, Darwin was converted to Lyell's gradualism and uniformitarian geology, as it gave him a new framework for his interpretation of what he was seeing in the world. The whole understanding of deep time impacted Darwin's thinking, providing an impetus for developing his theory of evolution. In 1859 in his book *Origin of the Species*, Darwin proposed that life evolved over millions of years from a common ancestor. Darwin basically believed that all the time that is there in geology provided enough time for the little changes in biology. As historian of science Reijer Hooykaas explains:

> Charles Darwin (1809–1882) was strongly influenced by Lyell's uniformitarianism, but he also acknowledged the progression of the animal world as revealed by palaeontology. . . . The doctrine of evolution as enunciated by Darwin borrowed from uniformitarianism the idea of extremely long periods, extremely slow changes, and continuous changes, but not the idea of [intelligent] progress, which . . . was held by the opponents of uniformity.[16]

It was the rise of uniformitarian science in the 1800s that caused a re-evaluation of how the early chapters of Genesis were interpreted. The belief that earth's history was millions of years old changed the way the

15. Charles Darwin, letter to Leonard Horner, August 29, 1844, http://www.darwinproject.ac.uk/entry-771.
16. R. Hooykaas, *The Principle of Uniformity in Geology, Biology and Theology* (Netherlands: E.J. Brill, 1963), 101.

days of creation were interpreted, as it seemed that the geological data for an old earth was too convincing to maintain a belief that God created the world in six 24-hour days and that He destroyed the world with a global Flood as described in the Book of Genesis. The many modern various attempts to harmonize Genesis with old-earth geology and old-universe cosmology (Progressive Creation, Gap Theory, Day Age View, Cosmic Temple View, Theistic Evolution) are novel to this current generation.

Unfortunately, the ideas of Hutton, Lyell, and Darwin have played a vital role in the Church abandoning its belief in the biblical account of creation and the Flood, which had disastrous effects on the Church and the Western world. The Darwinian revolution did not begin in 1859 with the publication of *Origin of the Species*, as Darwin could never have postulated his idea of evolution without the foundation of millions of years of earth's history. The revolution began before that, as one of the 20th century's leading evolutionary biologists Ernst Mayr recognizes:

> The [Darwinian] revolution began when it became obvious that the earth was very ancient rather than having been created only 6000 years ago. This finding was the snowball that started the whole avalanche.[17]

Mayr recognized that once you have the idea of an ancient earth, which is taught as fact that states that there is no God who has acted in history (through creation and the Flood) and that life is just a random accident, then it is going to change how people think about God and the world around them. This is because evolution is not just about molecules turning into people over millions of years, but it is part of an entire worldview that erodes beliefs about God, value, meaning, purpose, and morality. The outcome of decades of indoctrination in evolutionary thinking in secular education is the reason why the majority of the people (71%) living today in Hutton, Lyell, and Darwin's homeland, the UK, accept evolution as fact and tells us why many people now identify as non-religious.[18] They have been given a different worldview; it is the

17. Ernst Mayr, "The Nature of the Darwinian Revolution," *Science*, vol. 176 (June 2, 1972), 988.
18. See "Science and Religion Exploring the Spectrum: New Evolution Survey Shows That Whilst the Majority of People in UK And Canada Accept Evolutionary Science, Non-Religious and Atheist Individuals Show Similar Doubts About the Origins of Humans and Human Consciousness as Religious and Spiritual Individuals," September 5, 2017, https://sciencereligionspectrum.org/in-the-news/press-release-results-of-major-new-survey-on-evolution/#more-1366.

worldview or religion of naturalism (atheism). God is no longer seen as the Creator of all things, but instead, life is simply the process of evolution. The idea of evolution and millions of years gives people today the foundation to scoff at and reject the truthfulness of God's Word.

Following Their Own Sinful Desires

As Christians, we know scoffers exist and that their scoffing is a typical response to the truth of God's Word. But what is the motivation of the scoffers? Is it science, truth, reason, scholarship? No. Peter is quite clear that their motivation is none of these things. It is, in fact, immorality; he uses the Greek word *epithumia* (sinful desires) to encapsulate the scoffers' ungodly sexual desires (see 2 Peter 1:4, 2:10, 18). The scoffers are not only driven by ridicule but also immorality. In chapter 2, Peter describes the false teachers as "sensual," "indulge in the lust of defiling passion and despise authority," "irrational animals," "revel in the daytime," and those who are enticed "by sensual passions of the flesh" (2 Peter 2:2, 10, 12, 13, 18). This is a graphic description of the scoffers and how they live out their own worldview. What we need to realize is that scoffing does not get you to truth, it gets you to your intended goal, and the intended goal of the scoffers is their sinful desires.

The world has witnessed many devastating revolutions, but the sexual revolution may be the most damaging of all. In fact, the Darwinian revolution of the 1800s really paved the way for the sexual revolution that eventually came to fruition in the 1960s. Just before the sexual revolution in the 1960s, the English writer, philosopher, and humanist Aldous Huxley (1894–1963), grandson of T.H. Huxley ("Darwin's Bulldog") and the brother of the atheistic evolutionist Sir Julian Huxley, stated his reason for his anti-Christian stance:

> I had motive for not wanting the world to have a meaning; consequently assumed that it had none, and was able without any difficulty to find satisfying reasons for this assumption. The philosopher who finds no meaning in the world is not concerned exclusively with a problem in pure metaphysics, he is also concerned to prove that there is no valid reason why he personally should not do as he wants to do, or why his friends should not seize political power and govern in the way that they find most advantageous to themselves. . . . For myself, the philosophy of

meaninglessness was essentially an instrument of liberation, sexual and political.[19]

The attractiveness of Darwinian evolution is not because it is scientific but that it is morally appealing to people. Many of the leading atheistic intellectuals of the 20th century lived unethical lives. The English philosopher, mathematician, and political activist Bertrand Russell (1872–1970) was married four times and had numerous affairs, and the French existentialist philosopher Jean Paul Sartre (1905–1980) was an exploiter of women (most notably, his open marriage with feminist Simone de Beauvoir).[20] Once God is removed as the moral lawgiver, people are free to make their own rules. Today, we are seeing the fruit of the sexual revolution reaped in Western culture, as many of the radicals of the 1960s have long occupied influential places in government, universities, and media and have used these platforms to spread their worldview. In our modern Western culture, the twisted and corrupt changes that are taking place display themselves in the following behaviors (among others):

- Homosexuality
- Bisexuality
- Polygamy
- Pansexuality
- Transgenderism
- Transvestitism
- Non-binary
- Abortion on demand

Where did all these beliefs come from? The current sexual agenda that is being promoted in our culture by these graduates of the sixties culture is part and parcel of a neo-pagan view of the world that has shaped the current millennial generation. What is happening now in western culture is not just the influence of secularism but also the return of ancient paganism (i.e., those who worship creation, Romans 1:25). Although many may view paganism as an outdated religion that was practiced by people many thousands of years ago, it is alive and well today.[21]

---

19. Aldous Huxley, *Ends and Means* (New York, NY: Harper & Brothers, 1937), 270.
20. See Paul Johnson, *Intellectuals: From Marx and Tolstoy to Sartre and Chomsky* (New York: Harper Collins Publishers, 1988).
21. Jones, *The Other Worldview*, 50–81.

The neo-pagan worldview is essentially monistic (attributing oneness or singleness to existence) and is founded upon an eastern worldview. The monistic worldview "sees the world as self-creating (or perpetually existing) and self-explanatory. Everything is made up of the same stuff, whether matter, spirit, or a mixture. ... Although there is apparent differentiation and even hierarchy, all distinctions are, in principle, eliminated, and everything has the same worth."[22] It is important to understand that the practices of homosexuality and transgenderism have not appeared in a vacuum, but the celebration of them is the perfect expression of a neo-pagan (monistic) worldview.

It is no surprise that, since the beginning of the sexual revolution in the 1960s, we have witnessed a progressive public sexual tsunami. All the above beliefs are now part and parcel of the western worldview and examples of how morality has become so twisted and corrupted. Cultural approval of issues such as homosexuality and transgenderism is a progressive development of a whole analysis of monistic thinking (the denial of distinctions between God and the world). The goal of neo-paganism is to relativize everything that seems different, to join the opposites and get rid of the distinctions God has made in His creation because of their belief that all is "one" (i.e., non-binary = not two). For example, heterosexuality celebrates otherness (Greek, *héteros* = other), whereas homosexuality (Greek, *homo* = same) celebrates the sameness of everything, which is the definition of the neo-pagan worldview. In the biblical worldview, however, distinctions are the product of the Creator's work in creation: most notably male and female (Genesis 1:27; cf. 1:4, 6, 9–10, 14–18). The one solution to this problem of the neo-pagan worldview is the biblical worldview, as it rightly sees distinctions in the world: the main one being that God is our Creator and mankind is His creation.

Once you lose moral reasoning, you will lose behavioral normality. This is why we are seeing people in Western culture becoming so confused about their identity. These beliefs are now seen as normal and natural for Millennials (born in 1980s or 1990s) and Post-Millennials (born between 1996–2010), and for anyone to question or object to any of these is viewed as hate speech for which people should be punished. Millennials and Post-Millennials have a different worldview to that of their parents' or grandparents' generation. In fact, it has even led to pride in

22. Ibid., 12.

the Millennial and Post-Millennial generations, as they see themselves as autonomous before God in the things they do, say, and write, and they not only celebrate this immorality but also force it upon people. Yet, this autonomous attitude is not new (there is nothing new under the sun), as it echoes King David's lament in Psalm 12, which records the godly man's struggling with the evil prevalent in his nation. The question on the lips of the rebellious man in Psalm 12:4 (NASB) is, "Who is lord over us?" The result of this sort of attitude is that "vileness is exalted" among the people (Psalm 12:8). Even though our current cultural situation may cause us to feel that we should remain silent or even flee, we must instead respond just as David did, by calling out to the Lord in his time of need (Psalm 12:1, 3). David knew that, unlike the wicked who spoke falsely, the words of the Lord are pure (Psalm 12:6), and He will guard the godly (Psalm 12:7).

The reality of the matter is that scoffers come ridiculing the idea of the future coming of Jesus Christ in judgment and salvation not because of their intellect but because it fits their immorality since they do not want a judge who will hold them accountable for their sin. The reason the scoffers deny creation and the Flood is the same reason they deny the coming of Jesus; they don't want to be held accountable, and it frees them up to enjoy their lust without restraint and without guilt. The debate over creation and evolution ultimately is not an intellectual argument, it is a moral argument. When it comes to these issues, we need to keep in mind what Scripture tells us about our fallen human nature:

And this is the judgment: the light has come into the world, and people loved the darkness rather than the light because their works were evil. For everyone who does wicked things hates the light and does not come to the light, lest his works should be exposed (John 3:19–20).

The world's rejection of Jesus' Second Coming is due to humankind's sinful condition, since people would prefer to cling to the darkness rather than come into the light lest the light expose their sinfulness. In order to see through our spiritual blindness, we first need someone to liberate us from our slavery to sin, which is why Jesus said, "So if the Son sets you free, you will be free indeed" (John 8:36; cf. 34–35). There is a correlation between beliefs and actions, but it also works the other way since actions affect beliefs. Moral behavior affects what we believe. That means that our own personal holiness is part of our doctrinal purity. The reason Christians should doubt false teachers is not only because of their teaching but also because their false teaching is rooted in their immorality. Moreover, as Christians, we need to guard our character because it affects our doctrine. Peter had already exhorted the Christians to whom he was writing:

> Beloved, I urge you as sojourners and exiles to abstain from the passions of the flesh, which wage war against your soul. Keep your conduct among the Gentiles honorable, so that when they speak against you as evildoers, they may see your good deeds and glorify God on the day of visitation (1 Peter 2:11–12).

Likewise, the Apostle Paul told Timothy: "Keep a close watch on yourself and on the teaching. Persist in this, for by so doing you will save both yourself and your hearers" (1 Timothy 4:16). Paul is referring to Timothy's conduct and his doctrine, as he knows that a person's teaching cannot be separated from personal holiness (1 Timothy 4:6, 12). Today, atheists, agnostics, and secularists scoff at belief in the return of Christ; however, these have nothing to do with the lack of evidence for God's existence but are simply tools for sinners to indulge in their own lusts. It is the desires of the scoffers that govern how they conduct themselves. Although many scoffers of Christianity present their objections as intellectual, they are, in fact, often based on their sinful impulses.

As Christians, we need to remember that if we stand on God's Word and preach the gospel faithfully, the culture will scoff at us, but if we compromise the Bible with the thinking of the culture, they will still scoff at us. So why compromise to begin with? When we preach the Word of God faithfully, some will scoff, some will want to know more, and some will believe (cf. Acts 17:32–34). When it comes to our cultural situation today, we should also keep in mind that the Book of Acts tells us that Christianity was born into a time of adversity, immorality, and scoffing in a world where the Church was in the minority. At that time, Christians had to find a way to be faithful in an age when they were not (culturally) in control. Even when the Roman emperor claimed to be Lord and the moral code was decidedly in opposition to Scripture, the Holy Spirit gave that early Church the ability to be faithful and to preach the Word of God without fear or compromise. He did it then, and He can do so now.

Apologetics is not about temporally setting Christ aside so that we can engage in a rational discussion, or even about status or fame or being in control of the culture, but about living day by day under the lordship of Christ (1 Peter 3:15). The Apostle Paul reminds us that scoffing at the truth of the gospel is ultimately bound up in the foolishness of unbelief:

> For the word of the cross is folly to those who are perishing, but to us who are being saved it is the power of God. For it is written, "I will destroy the wisdom of the wise, and the discernment of the discerning I will thwart." Where is the one who is wise? Where is the scribe? Where is the debater of this age? Has not God made foolish the wisdom of the world? For since, in the wisdom of God, the world did not know God through wisdom, it pleased God through the folly of what we preach to save those who believe. For Jews demand signs and Greeks seek wisdom, but we preach Christ crucified, a stumbling block to Jews and folly to Gentiles, but to those who are called, both Jews and Greeks, Christ the power of God and the wisdom of God. For the foolishness of God is wiser than men, and the weakness of God is stronger than men (1 Corinthians 1:18–25).

The Christian message is based on what God has communicated to us through His Word (v. 18, *logos*), but in their human wisdom, those who are perishing see it as foolishness. The opposite of foolishness is wisdom, which is found in the power of God's Word (cf. Romans 1:16). This is why a biblical apologetic, taught by the Spirit of God, will reject the priority of the natural man's reasoning and the thinking of the world (1 Corinthians 2:13–14). It is only by God's intervention through the light of knowledge of the glory of God that can change the state of those who are perishing (2 Corinthians 4:6–7). Paul reminded the Corinthian Church that autonomous human wisdom cannot benefit us before God, as He rejects all that rests on human wisdom (1 Corinthians 3:19). Instead, Paul reminded them that Christ, who is the wisdom of God, is far superior to that of any human philosophy. The wisdom of the Greeks could not recognize the most profound wisdom of all when they were challenged with it. The truth of the supernatural creation of the world and its destruction through the global Flood embodies true wisdom — the wisdom of God, not the wisdom of the age. Whereas the culture may scoff at the truth of God's Word and see it as folly, our duty as Christians is to proclaim its truth regardless of the consequences, just as the Apostle Peter did (see Acts 4:19–20).

CHAPTER FIVE

WHERE IS THE PROMISE OF HIS COMING?

2 Peter 3:4

They will say, "Where is the promise of his coming? For ever since the fathers fell asleep, all things are continuing as they were from the beginning of creation" (2 Peter 3:4).

The Apostle Peter was known for his preaching that Jesus was not just the fulfilment of the messianic expectations of the nation of Israel but that He was also the Savior of the world (see Acts 2:14–41, 3:12–26, 10:34–43). But Peter was not only known for his preaching, as there is good literary and historical evidence that inform us that Mark's gospel came from the teaching and preaching of the Apostle Peter (see Mark 1:16, 16:7; cf. Acts 12:12–17, 15:37; 1 Peter 5:13).[1] The gospel of Mark starts with the words: "The beginning of the gospel of Jesus Christ, the Son of God" (Mark 1:1).[2] These opening words are of great interest. The word "beginning" (*archē*) "recalls the opening words of Genesis, and

1. It is was understood that Papias, the early church bishop of Hierapolis in Phrygia, in the early 2nd century (101–108), wrote that Mark relied on the Apostle Peter for his information. For a defense of this view, see David E. Garland, *A Theology of Mark's Gospel: Biblical Theology of the New Testament* (Grand Rapids, MI: Zondervan, 2015), 53–67. Interestingly, Garland notes that "Simon Peter is the first and last mentioned disciple in the gospel (1:16, where his name is mentioned twice in the Greek text; and 16:7). These 'two references form an inclusion around the whole story, suggesting that Peter is the witness whose testimony includes the whole.' " Garland, *A Theology of Mark's Gospel*, 66.
2. This verse contains a textual variant, as the title "Son of God" is absent in a few manuscripts. However, the originality of the reading "Son of God" can be argued on internal grounds (see below): See Garland, *A Theology of Mark's Gospel*, 195–197.

Mark writes about a new beginning in salvation history that God inaugurates."[3] This new beginning comes about through the authoritative message of the apostolic proclamation of the "gospel" concerning Jesus being declared to be *the* Son of God (see Mark 1:11, 9:7, 14:61, 15:39).[4] Jesus' words, actions, death, and Resurrection all affirm that He truly was the Son of God. In His earthly ministry, Jesus also described Himself as the divine yet human figure, the "Son of Man" (Mark 14:62; cf. Daniel 7:13–14), who came "not to be served but to serve, and to give his life as a ransom for many" (Mark 10:45; cf. 1 Peter 1:18–19). In offering Himself freely as a "ransom," Jesus was paying the necessary debt to free people from their captivity to sin so that they could be counted as righteous (cf. Isaiah 53:10–11; 2 Corinthians 5:21). Jesus' ransom for sinners took place when He suffered and died on the Cross of Calvary, which He prophesied to His disciples would take place before it happened:

> And he began to teach them that the Son of Man must suffer many things and be rejected by the elders and the chief priests and the scribes and be killed, and after three days rise again (Mark 8:31).

Not only did Jesus prophesy His death and Resurrection, but He also said that people will be judged at His Second Coming by whether or not they confessed Him without shame:

> For whoever is ashamed of me and of my words in this adulterous and sinful generation, of him will the Son of Man also be ashamed when he comes in the glory of his Father with the holy angels (Mark 8:38).

Jesus also said of His Second Coming: "But concerning that day or that hour, no one knows, not even the angels in heaven, nor the Son, but only the Father" (Mark 13:32; cf. 13:24–27).[5] The fact that no one

---

3. Ibid., 101.

4. These references to Jesus as *the* "Son of God" all appear at crucial points in His ministry: baptism, transfiguration, trial, and crucifixion. The title "Son of God" means that Jesus is on a level with God and divine authority (see Mark 14:61–62; cf. John 5:18).

5. Garland notes, "The ascending order of 'no one,' 'the angels in heaven,' 'the Son,' and 'the Father,' puts Jesus next to the Father in the divine hierarchy." Garland, *A Theology of Mark's Gospel*, 307. Many cults and false religions wrongly use this passage to argue that, since Jesus did not know all things, He cannot be God. Jesus' teaching, however, shows that His not "knowing" the day or the hour was a conscious self-limitation. As the God-man, Jesus possessed divine attributes, or He would have ceased to be God, but He chose not always to employ them.

knows when Jesus will return is the reason why believers need to "stay awake" and be ready for it (Mark 13:35). After Jesus had been crucified, when His words concerning His Resurrection from the dead came to pass, the disciples and Peter were told to go and meet Him in Galilee (Mark 16:6–7). While in Galilee, Jesus met the 11 disciples on a mountain that He had directed them to go to, and there He commissioned them to make disciples of all nations and to teach them to observe everything He commanded (Matthew 28:16–20). Sometime after this, Jesus and His disciples went back down to Judea to Bethany, to the Mount of Olives, and from there He ascended into heaven (Luke 24:50–53; cf. Mark 11:1).

By the time the Apostle Peter had written his second letter to those early Christians, it had been almost 30 years since he stood on the Mount of Olives (Acts 1:12) with the other disciples and saw Jesus ascend into heaven:

> And when he had said these things, as they were looking on, he was lifted up, and a cloud took him out of their sight. And while they were gazing into heaven as he went, behold, two men stood by them in white robes, and said, "Men of Galilee, why do you stand looking into heaven? This Jesus, who was taken up from you into heaven, will come in the same way as you saw him go into heaven" (Acts 1:9–11).

In a period of ministry which lasted 40 days (Acts 1:3), before He had ascended into heaven, Jesus appeared to His disciples and spoke to them about the kingdom of God and told them to wait in Jerusalem until they were clothed in the Spirit and then to begin their mission from there (Acts 1:8; cf. 8:12, 14:22, 19:8, 20:25, 28:23, 31). Although we are not told everything Jesus taught about the kingdom of God, what we do know is that Jesus told His disciples that repentance and forgiveness of sins should be preached to all the world (Luke 24:45–47; cf. Acts 2:38, 3:19, 8:22, 10:43, 11:18, 20:21, 26:20). This promise of redemption takes place in the Book of Acts when Peter and the rest of the disciples go out in the power of the Holy Spirit to take the gospel to all the nations of the world (Acts 1:8, 13:47). Not only did the Apostles preach about repentance and forgiveness of sins on their missionary journeys, but they also proclaimed that God would judge the world. At the end of his address to the people from the nations gathered at Cornelius' house, the Apostle Peter said:

> And he commanded us to preach to the people and to testify that he is the one appointed by God to be judge of the living and the dead. To him all the prophets bear witness that everyone who believes in him receives forgiveness of sins through his name (Acts 10:42–43).

Similarly, when the Apostle Paul spoke to the Athenians at the Areopagus, he concluded his addresses by saying:

> The times of ignorance God overlooked, but now he commands all people everywhere to repent, because he has fixed a day on which he will judge the world in righteousness by a man whom he has appointed; and of this he has given assurance to all by raising him from the dead (Acts 17:30–31; cf. 24:25).

Because of their ignorance, God in His mercy has not judged the idolatry of the nations as severely as He might have (cf. Romans 3:25).[6] This is why, in these "last days" with the full revelation of the arrival and work of Jesus, the Apostles declare the gospel message to be first and foremost a command that people repent of their sins because there is a fixed day of judgment. The proof of Jesus' right to be judge of the living and the dead is, of course, His own Resurrection from the dead (Acts 2:32–36; cf. 10:40–42). The Apostle Paul clearly taught that Jesus' Resurrection from the dead is proof of His lordship and judicial authority (cf. Romans 1:4). The disciples firmly believed that with the return (*parousia*) of Jesus would follow the judgment of the world. This is important to keep in mind, as it does not fit the scoffer's scheme of things that nothing changes, because the *parousia* involves not only the judgment of the world but also, according to the Apostle Peter, the "restoration" (*apokatastasis*) of all things (Acts 3:19–21). After the 40 days, Jesus was lifted up, and a cloud took Him out of their sight. The cloud that took Jesus was a manifestation of His divine glory, just as the cloud that covered (*shekhinah*) the tent of meeting and God's glory filled the tabernacle was a visible sign that God had taken up residence there (Exodus 40:34–35). This was not the first time some of the disciples had seen His divine glory. At Jesus' transfiguration after seeing His glory,

---

6. In Acts, the term *ignorant* is used of Jews and Gentiles since they both need to repent and be reconciled to God through Christ (Acts 3:17, 13:27, 14:16).

"... a cloud overshadowed them [Peter, James, and John], and a voice came out of the cloud, 'This is my beloved Son; listen to him' " (Mark 9:7). This language also recalls Jesus' own words about His return when He comes to bring judgment: "... they will see the Son of Man coming in clouds with great power and glory" (Mark 13:26; cf. Revelation 1:7). The transfiguration, ascension, and *parousia* are all manifestations of Jesus' divine glory.[7]

For Christians today, it's been over 2,000 years since Jesus ascended into heaven, and nothing has changed, as there are still scoffers around who scoff at the return of Jesus in judgment of the world. Jesus Himself warned us that there would be those who "pay no attention" to His return (Matthew 22:5), yet at the same time, He told those who believe in Him to be dressed and ready for action, found awake and engaging in business until He comes (Luke 12:35, 37; 19:13). No doubt Peter had these things in mind when he also reminded believers that while we await the return of our Lord and Savior, we are exhorted to live godly lives as we await Jesus' return and use the time as an opportunity to call people to repentance and salvation (2 Peter 3:14–15; cf. Titus 2:12–13).

This chapter will look at how the influence of uniformitarian thinking (all things are continuing as they were from the beginning) has led to a lack of confidence in and even a denial of the physical return of Christ.

Where Is the Promise of His Coming?

In 2018 and 2020, Ligonier Ministries conducted a survey to find out what American evangelical Christians thought about God, Jesus Christ, sin, and eternity. One of the questions they asked people ages 18–34 was did they believe that "There will be a time when Jesus Christ returns to judge all the people who have lived."[8] The results of the question were:

2018	2020
15% strongly disagreed	15% strongly disagreed
7% somewhat disagreed	8% somewhat disagreed
13% were not sure	15% were not sure
22% somewhat agreed	21% somewhat agreed
43% strongly agreed	41% strongly agreed

7. See F.F. Bruce, *The Book of Acts: NICOT* – Revised Edition (Grand Rapids, MI: W.B. Eerdmans, 1989), 38.
8. See Statement 19: "There will be a time when Jesus Christ returns to judge all the people who have lived." "The State of Theology," https://thestateoftheology.com/.

The fact that only 43% in 2018 and 41% in 2020 of people who identify as evangelical Christians (only an additional 22% [2018] and 21% [2020] somewhat agreed) agreed that Jesus would come again to judge the world is a sad reflection of the current skepticism many Christians have with the Bible. While different influences have played their part in this, there can be no doubt that in the Western world, the Darwinian view of nature has brought about a skepticism to the supernatural claims in the Bible. The question Peter was dealing with from the scoffers as part of their reasoning for rejecting the coming judgment is: "Where is the promise of his coming?" The term "coming" (*parousia*) refers to the arrival and future return of Jesus Christ to this earth (see Matthew 24:3, 27, 37, 39; 1 Thessalonians 2:19, 4:15). While the scoffers denied the divine promise of Jesus' return (2 Peter 3:9), which is guaranteed according to Peter (2 Peter 1:4), they made their own promises of sexual freedom (2 Peter 2:19). The question "Where is . . ." is not new but is common among those who could be seen as skeptics in biblical history (Psalm 42:3, 79:10; Malachi 2:17).

The foundation of the scoffer's question is based on a lack of God's intervention in human history, beginning with the doctrine of creation. The scoffers saw the world as unchanging, and therefore, any divine intervention like the return of Jesus just does not take place. This is similar to the claim from today's naturalistic skeptics who argue that because the world is governed solely by natural laws, divine intervention (miracles) can never happen. This is to forget that the laws that govern the world are God's laws; He created them, so He can choose to intervene in the world if He so wishes. God is not a prisoner to them. The laws of nature do not forbid miracles, they just describe what normally happens; they do not say whether someone can intervene or not. The scoffer's denial that Jesus would return and that judgment would come with Him is not asked in innocence but is, in fact, a demand for evidence.

Today, the demand for evidence of Christianity comes largely because of the idea of evolution and millions of years of history being in direct opposition to the biblical view of history. In fact, it was Charles Darwin who understood that his hypothesis that life naturally evolved from a common ancestor was in direct opposition not only to the fact that God created life supernaturally but also to the rest of biblical history that followed. Before we look at how Darwin's evolutionary hypothesis impacted his own view of the Bible and Jesus' return, it is necessary to see the influences that helped form his thinking. It is quite common for people to assume that Darwin was a Christian until he found "science" and then lost his faith, but this narrative is not at all true. Charles Robert Darwin, an amateur naturalist, geologist, and biologist, was born on February 12, 1809, in Shrewsbury, England, and was the son of Robert and Susannah Darwin. Darwin's father was a wealthy doctor who attended the local Church of England, St Chad's; however, he was "at heart probably an atheist."[9] Darwin's grandfather Erasmus Darwin, who embraced enlightenment thinking, was also a skeptic of Christianity. On the other hand, Darwin's mother, Susannah, part of the Wedgwood pottery family, was a Unitarian (the belief that God is one person) who took Charles to the local Unitarian Church in Shrewsbury, and at age 8, he went for a year (1817) to a local school run by the Unitarian minister George Case. So, Darwin's formative years involved one parent who was an atheist and the other a Unitarian, so he didn't even grow up in a Bible-believing Christian home.

After Darwin had finished his studies at Shrewsbury School as a boarder (1818–25), he went to study medicine at Edinburgh University (1825–27). Darwin, however, did not enjoy the field of medicine, so instead, his father encouraged him to go to Cambridge University (1828–31) to study theology in order to become a clergyman. This was because Darwin's father thought that being a clergyman would at least have been a respectable profession for young Charles (at least at that time in Victorian England). Darwin's life as a clergyman in the 1800s in England would have been a very nice life, brought in a good living, and also given him lots of time to pursue his real interest — the study of the natural world. Darwin pondered the request from his father to study theology and asked for some time to think about it. In his autobiography, in 1828, he reflects on this moment:

> I asked for some time to consider, as from what little I had heard and thought on the subject *I had scruples about declaring my belief in all the dogmas of the Church of England*; though otherwise I liked the thought of being a country clergyman . . . and as *I did not then in the least doubt the strict and literal truth of every word of the Bible*, I soon persuaded myself that our Creed must be

9. Janet Browne, *Charles Darwin: Voyaging* (London: Pimlico, 2003), 9.

fully accepted. It never struck me how illogical it was to say that *I believed in what I could not understand and what is in fact unintelligible*[10] (emphasis mine).

At this moment in Darwin's life, we begin to see the confusion in his mind, as on the one hand, he claims to believe the literal truth of the Bible, and yet at the same time, he says he couldn't understand it as it was unintelligible. Darwin would go on to accept his father's advice, studying theology at Christ's College Cambridge. While at Cambridge, Darwin read William Paley's *Natural Theology*, the leading intelligent design argument of the day, of which Darwin said: "I do not think I hardly ever admired a book more than Paley's 'Natural Theology.' I could almost formerly have said it by heart."[11] In reality, however, Darwin would spend most of his life trying to explain away design in nature without the need of an intelligent being. After graduating from Cambridge University with a degree in theology, he went to be a companion for Captain FitzRoy on the HMS Beagle voyage to survey the South American coast (1831–36). In his autobiography, he goes on to reflect on the time from October 1, 1836, to January 1839:

> During these two years I was led to think much about religion. Whilst on board the Beagle *I was quite orthodox*, and I remember being heartily laughed at by several of the officers (though themselves orthodox) for quoting *the Bible as an unanswerable authority on some point of morality*. I suppose it was the novelty of the argument that amused them. But I had gradually come, by this time, to see that the Old Testament from its *manifestly false history of the world*, with the Tower of Babel, the rainbow as a sign, etc., etc., and from its attributing to God the feelings of a revengeful tyrant, was *no more to be trusted than the sacred books of the Hindoos [sic], or the beliefs of any barbarian*[12] (emphasis mine).

Between 1837–39, Darwin had gradually come to believe that the history in the Bible was false (doubting the account of the Flood and Tower of Babel) and was no more to be trusted than other sacred books of the

10. Nora Barlow, ed., *The Autobiography of Charles Darwin, 1809–1882* (New York: W.W. Norton, 1958), 49.
11. *Life and Letters of Charles Darwin*, Vol. 2, C. Darwin to John Lubbock, November 15, 1859 (New York: D. Appleton and Co., 1911), 15.
12. Ibid., 85.

pagans. How is this orthodox Christianity? Even though the Church of England, at that time, was in the midst of compromising the Bible with the idea of millions of years, they still believed, to some extent, that Genesis was a historical revelation from God. It is clear that Darwin was not orthodox at all but was very confused about what he believed. Regardless of his impact on the scientific world, Darwin's evolutionary ideas had consequences for not only how he viewed the Bible but how he understood the person of Jesus Christ. Influenced by naturalistic philosophers (like David Hume, 1711–1776), Darwin rejected the miracles in the Bible:

> The more we know of the fixed laws of nature the more incredible do miracles become — that the men at that time were ignorant and credulous to a degree almost incomprehensible by us, — that the Gospels cannot be proved to have been written simultaneously with the events, — that they differ in many important details, far too important as it seemed to me to be admitted as the usual inaccuracies of eye-witnesses; — by such reflections as these.[13]

Darwin's rejection of the miraculous, however, was logically fallacious, as he rejected the miraculous because of the fixed laws of nature. But he can only know the laws of nature are fixed if he knows beforehand that all miraculous reports are false. This is a circular argument. He rejects miracles by rejecting the Bible, but he rejects the Bible because it contains miracles. Miracles do not break the laws of nature but are rather additions to them. Darwin's rejection of the miraculous was also snobbish, as he believed that people in the first century believed in miracles out of ignorance. This is not true, as Mary the mother of Jesus knew it took a man and woman to make a baby (Luke 1:34). Contrary to what Darwin believed about the four gospels, they actually give us an agreeable and accurate eyewitness account from the 1st century of the miracles done by Jesus.[14] For most of his life, Darwin had largely kept silent on his religious

---

13. Ibid., 85–96.
14. Today most scholars would agree that all four canonical Gospels should be dated to the 1st century A.D. This would take us closer to the events (such as the miraculous accounts) which are reported to have taken place. So, if you want an accurate report of what Jesus did (such as miracles), then there is no better source for this than the eyewitnesses. For example, the Gospel of John tells us that the author (the Apostle John) was an eyewitness to what took place (John 19:35, 21:24). Moreover, the Early Church father Irenaeus (A.D. 130–202) tells us that the Apostle John wrote the Gospel of John, and he got his information from Polycarp (A.D. 69–156), who was a disciple of the Apostle John.

views; for example, in 1866 he wrote: "My opinion is not worth more than that of any other man who has thought on such subjects."[15] This changed, however, in 1880 when, two years before his death, Darwin was asked a question by a young barrister named F.A. McDermott for his views on the New Testament. Darwin replied to McDermott:

> I am sorry to have to inform you that I do not believe in the Bible as a divine revelation, & therefore not in Jesus Christ as the son of God.[16]

Along with his rejection of the inspiration of the Bible and the divinity of Jesus, Darwin also rejected the belief that God would finally judge people, calling hell a "damnable doctrine."[17] Just like an acid, Darwin's evolutionary ideas slowly eroded doctrines that are essential to the Christian faith. Even though Darwin is the icon of many atheists today, he never was one.[18] Understanding the implications of his evolutionary ideas led Darwin to admit he was an agnostic, and he died as one at the age of 73 in 1882.[19] Despite the reports, Darwin never converted to Christianity on his deathbed, nor did he renounce evolution. It is so important to understand Darwin's evolutionary ideas and the conclusions he came to regarding the Bible because people do ask: "Is it possible to be a theist, i.e., believe there is a 'god' of some kind, and believe in evolution?" Well, even Darwin himself believed one could be "an ardent Theist & an evolutionist" (naming Charles Kingsley and Asa Gray as examples), although he did qualify that by saying: "Whether a man deserves to be called a theist depends on the definition of the term."[20] Creationists do not say that belief in God rules out belief in evolution. However, they do argue that the whole point of Darwinian evolution is to show that there is no need for a supernatural Creator, since nature can do the creating by itself. This ultimately leads to a rejection of God, such as Darwin did.

15. See "To M. E. Boole," December 14, 1866, https://www.darwinproject.ac.uk/letter/DCP-LETT-5307.xml.
16. See C.R. Darwin to F.A. McDermott, November 24, 1880, http://www.darwinproject.ac.uk/entry-12851.
17. *The Autobiography of Charles Darwin*, ed. Nora Barlow (New York: W.W. Norton, 1993), 87.
18. Famous atheist Richard Dawkins stated, "Darwin made it possible to be an intellectually fulfilled atheist." *The Blind Watchmaker* (W. W. Norton, New York), 198.
19. See C.R. Darwin to John Fordyce, May 7, 1879, www.darwinproject.ac.uk/entry-12041.
20. Ibid.

WHERE IS THE PROMISE OF HIS COMING?

In trying to mix Christianity and evolution together, Charles Darwin would have been the first to disagree. In Darwin's understanding of the world, there never was a time that it was very good. Randal Keynes (Darwin's great-great-grandson) wrote in *Annie's Box: Charles Darwin, his Daughter and Human Evolution* (a book focusing on Darwin's family life): "After Annie's death, Charles set the Christian faith firmly behind him."[21] Keynes notes that the death of Darwin's daughter (aged 10) marked a great turning point in Darwin's life because Darwin realized that somewhere along the line, you have to ask the question: "What kind of god would deliberately use a process of death, disease, famine, and struggle to make the world, and then declare it to be very good (Genesis 1:31)?" This is a good question to think about if you believe God used millions of years of evolution to create the world. Because where is the intelligence of a "god" that creates some creatures to survive for millions of years before he creates new and more complex creatures to survive for millions of years before he creates new creatures who are a little more complex? Then add to this millions of years of the death and extinction of many or most of this "god's" creations before he creates man. Therefore, what philosopher David Hull wrote in his review of intelligent design advocate Phillip Johnson's book *Darwin on Trial* applies not only to evolution but to any view of origins that accepts the millions-of-years interpretation of the rock layers:

> The problem that biological evolution poses for natural theologians is the sort of God that a Darwinian version of evolution implies. . . . The evolutionary process is rife with happenstance, contingency, incredible waste, death, pain and horror. . . . Whatever the God implied by evolutionary theory and the data of natural history may be like, He is not the Protestant God of waste not, want not. He is also not a loving God who cares about His productions. He is not even the awful God portrayed in the book of Job. The God of the Galápagos is careless, wasteful, indifferent, almost diabolical. He is certainly not the sort of God to whom anyone would be inclined to pray.[22]

---

21. Randal Keynes, *Annie's Box: Charles Darwin, his Daughter and Human Evolution* (London: Fourth Estate, 2001), 222.
22. David L. Hull, review of Phillip Johnson's *Darwin on Trial*, "The God of the Galápagos," *Nature*, Vol. 352 (August 8, 1991), 485–6.

Biblical creationists have often warned about the consequences of synthesizing evolution and millions of years into the text of Scripture since this not only affects how the early chapters of Genesis are interpreted, but it also affects the coherency and internal consistency of the biblical message of creation, the Fall, redemption, and ultimately the return of Christ, who will bring an end to history. Moreover, a logical, consistent application of theistic evolution can lead to heretical teaching, such as the belief that Jesus erred in His teaching and that Adam did not exist.[23]

Just as Darwin's evolutionary ideas shaped the way he thought about the inspiration of the Bible and the deity of Jesus, so his ideas would also cause many of the leading theologians of the 20th century to scoff at key doctrines of the faith, including Jesus' Second Coming. An example of the consequences of interpreting Scripture in light of evolution and millions of years of history can be seen in theologian Ernest Best's commentary *The First and Second Epistles to the Thessalonians*. In his commentary, Best admits that Paul's concept of Christ's return "is a public and cosmic event taking place at a definite date in history."[24] He describes first-century Christians as those who accepted the cosmological belief that God created the universe during a dated period of a few thousand years before Christ. However, because Best believes that we now know the world is billions of years old and not a few thousand, the end of the world is also moved so far away that there is no need to calculate it. Because of this, he reasons: "We must therefore exclude the conception of the End in a physical sense."[25] For Best,

> All this means that the parousia was an integral part of an existing framework which thought of the world as created a few thousand years earlier and ending in at least a comparable, if not a much shorter, period in the future. If we jettison this, and jettison it we must today, does any place remain for the parousia? As such there is no place.[26]

Best goes on to say of the end of the world:

23. For examples of this, see my book: Simon Turpin, *Adam: The First and the Last: Responding to Modern Attacks on Adam and Christ* (Leominister: DayOne Publications, 2018).
24. Ernest Best, *The First and Second Epistles to the Thessalonians* (New York: Harper, 1972), 360.
25. Ibid., 363.
26. Ibid., 367.

The End then is not to be conceived as the End of history, as a public event which can be seen as an intervention of God into the world process. Christ bears a similar relation to the End as to the Beginning: he is creator and consummator. But in neither case is he to be tied to the universe in any way science would find recognizable or which the historian could record. The End is not an event in history but outside it.[27]

Because Best was just being consistent in his application of evolution and millions of years, he not only rejected Genesis 1–11 as being historical but also rejected the physical return of Jesus to the earth. Instead, Best re-interprets the *parousia* as being an event outside of history (i.e., symbolic). Best realized that Paul and the early Christians accepted that Jesus' return was to be a historical public event but rejected it because he has succumbed to a "greater authority" — evolution and millions of years.

All Things Continue as They Were from the Beginning of Creation

As well as being motivated by an argument from ridicule and their immorality, the scoffers also base their arguments for the rejection of Jesus' return in judgment on the idea that "all things continue as they were from the beginning of creation." The scoffers' statement "the beginning of creation" (*ap' archēs ktiseōs*) is referring to the past history of the heavens and earth that are in view, the beginning of the whole creation in Genesis 1 (see also Mark 10:6; 1 John 1:1, 2:13–14). The scoffers' argument is that, since the fathers (Old Testament patriarchs)[28] fell asleep (a euphemism for death), nothing has changed since the beginning of creation; in other words, there has been no supernatural intervention. The scoffers denied, and Peter affirmed, the promise of eschatological judgment that is found within the Old Testament. Peter's opponents are denying any divine intervention in human affairs while at the same time twisting the Old Testament Scriptures. The scoffers' claim was that there has never been any supernatural intervention in creation is very similar to the Greek philosopher Epicurus (341–270 B.C.), who stated:

But, in truth, the universal whole always was such as it now is, and always will be such. For there is nothing into which it can

---

27. Ibid., 370.
28. The phrase "the fathers" probably refers to the Old Testament patriarchs, as every other reference to "the fathers" in the New Testament means this: see Acts 3:13; Romans 9:5; Hebrews 1:1.

change; for there is nothing beyond this universal whole which can penetrate into it, and produce any change in it.[29]

The idea of uniformitarianism is not a modern idea but was part of the Greek worldview. In the modern era, the argument for uniformitarianism, which was promoted by Charles Lyell, basically states:

> Uniformitarianism proclaims that "The present is the key to the past." As originally conceived, it asserted that nothing had happened in the past that is not happening now. All geological and biological changes take place, and have always taken place, at an imperceptible rate. Only over periods of millions of years can a difference be noticed — evolution from microbe to man, the growth of a mountain range.[30]

According to uniformitarianism, only the present can be used to understand the history of the world. In other words, when we look at the present world today, we can assume only that the rock layers have been laid down slowly over millions of years. This belief in the uniformity of natural processes now underpins all of modern geology. What we need to understand is that there are three key assumptions in the philosophy of uniformitarianism naturalism:

1. Nature or matter is all that exists.[31]
2. Everything can, and indeed must, be explained by time plus chance plus the laws of nature working on matter.
3. Processes of geological change have always been operating in the past at the same rate, frequency, and power as today.[32]

Uniformitarianism is built on the idea of deep time, which is central to the evolutionary argument, as evolutionist George Wald points out:

> Time is in fact the hero of the plot. The time with which we have to deal is of the order of two billion years [the age of the earth in 1954]. What we regard as impossible on the basis of human experience is

---

29. See G.L. Green, *Jude and 2 Peter Baker Exegetical Commentary on the New Testament* (Grand Rapids, MI: Baker Academic, 2008), 318.
30. James E. Strickling, Jr., *Origins — Today's Science, Tomorrow's Myth: An Objective Study of Creationism, Evolution, and Catastrophism* (New York, NY: Vantage Press, 1986), 4.
31. Not all scientists believe this, but many scientists (even those who believe in God) do their science as if it were true.
32. I am grateful to Dr. Terry Mortenson for these three points.

meaningless here. Given so much time, the "impossible" becomes possible, the possible probable, and the probable virtually certain. One has only to wait: time itself performs the miracles.[33]

Notice that in Wald's day (1954), the age of the earth was 2 billion years old. Yet today, secular scientists would date the age of the earth to be around 4.5 billion years old. In 65 years, the earth has aged 2.3 billion years! Really, what this should tell us is that there is something about the assumptions that are being made when it comes to dating methods (see below). What this also tells us about Wald's statement is that he admits deep time is needed to "perform the miracles." Why is Wald (a naturalistic evolutionist) talking about miracles? Is it not religious people who are supposed to believe in miracles? This is the internal inconsistency of the naturalistic worldview. The reality of evolutionary position is that it needs miracles in order for its own worldview to be true. The "gods" of the evolutionists who are needed to perform these miracles are time, chance, and Mother Nature. Of course, these are just like the gods of the nations — idols who cannot create and will perish from the earth (cf. Psalm 96:5; Jeremiah 10:11).

Uniformitarianism assumes that the processes we observe in our present world are the way they have always been (based on naturalism). This is a common assumption even among theistic evolutionists and old-earth creationists. However, if the initial conditions have not always been the same as we observe today or happening at the same rate, then this philosophy fails, as does the idea of an old earth and universe. God's revelation, and not our understanding of the present, is the key to understanding the past. Uniformitarianism has nothing to do with observation or the evidence, but scoffers believe it to avoid interpreting evidence of catastrophic processes through the lens of events such as Noah's Flood. Derek Ager, a British geologist, speaking of Lyell and his followers in his book *The Nature of the Stratigraphical Record*, reviewed the early 19th-century development of catastrophism and uniformitarianism and made this revealing comment:

> My excuse for this lengthy and amateur digression into history is that I have been trying to show how I think geology got into the hands of the theoreticians [the uniformitarians, in Ager's view] who were conditioned by the social and political history of their day more than by observations in the field. . . . In other words,

33. George Wald, "The Origin of Life," *Scientific American*, 191:48, August 1954.

we have allowed ourselves to be brain-washed into avoiding any interpretation of the past that involves extreme and what might be termed "catastrophic" processes.[34]

The idea of the great age of the earth came from the belief that the fossil record was laid down slowly over millions of years, which, as Ager admits, has nothing to do with observation in the field. Once we understand that admission, accepting that the world has not always operated under uniformitarian assumptions also informs our understanding of the age of the earth. When we see something that scientists have dated to be millions of years old, we need to remember that age is based on an assumed evolutionary history which is then used to prove that evolutionary history. Biblical creationists do not deny scientific evidence or methods of measurement that are used to determine the age of things. What we do point out is that all evidence is interpreted through a bias and that all the dating methods that are used to interpret the evidence that give long ages make several assumptions:

1. The initial conditions are known (no initial inheritance).
2. The amount of parent and daughter element is known to have not been altered by other processes in the past (no contamination).
3. The decay rate has stayed constant (no changed rates).

One specific dating method, carbon-14, or C-14, actually confirms a young age for the earth. For example, C-14 breaks down relatively quickly with a half-life of 5,730 years. Material older than about 95,000 years should have no C-14, yet we still find it in coal and diamonds, which are supposed to be billions of years old.[35] The fact that we find C-14 in diamonds confirms the biblical timescale of creation but is a problem for evolutionists.

It is important to recognize that none of the above assumptions are provable because no scientists were there in the past to observe, measure, or test them. The reason why scientists accept certain dating methods (such as uranium to lead or potassium to argon) is because they work to give them the millions of years they already believe in. Moreover, the assump-

34. Derek Ager, *The Nature of the Stratigraphical Record* (London: Macmillan, 1981), 46–47.
35. See Andrew Snelling, "Carbon-14 in Fossils and Diamonds: An Evolution Dilemma," *Answers*, January–March 2011, https://answersingenesis.org/geology/carbon-14/carbon-14-in-fossils-and-diamonds/.

tions are not even reasonable because all three have been repeatedly falsified. There are several lines of evidence that demonstrate conclusively that decay rates were grossly accelerated during a recent past catastrophic event. A concrete example of this is the well-known catastrophe that took place at Mount St. Helens in Washington, USA, on May 18, 1980.[36] After the eruption at Mount St. Helens, a new lava dome began to build inside the blown-out crater. The formation of this dome was directly observed after the initial eruption. Samples were then collected from lavas in the lava dome, whose ages were known through observation, as the lavas had flowed out of the volcano and the molten rock had crystalized and cooled them in 1986. In 1996, the samples were taken to a laboratory, and the results from the potassium to argon (K-Ar) dating were calculated to be at 0.35 million years old. The question is, why was the age of the rock, which was known from observation to be 10 years old, given to be 0.35 million years old? Because it had inherited the daughter element argon (inherited excess Ar-40) when it solidified. When the rock cooled and crystalized, it trapped some of the argon in the rock. When it was analyzed, the calculated age was based on the assumption that all the argon had come from potassium decay. The rock was artificially old because it contained the argon to begin with. See the chart on the following page for more examples like this one from Mount St. Helens where the true age of the rocks is known from observation and the answer to age that was given has been wrong.[37]

If the calculated ages can be wrong on rocks that we know the age of, then how can we trust the potassium to argon age dating method on ancient rocks of which we do not have the historical documentation? Our starting point for any dating method is either a history position that God has revealed to us or a faith position about the unobservable past. The history position that God has revealed to us includes some of the details of what the early earth was like and how it has changed:

1. A very good creation (Genesis 1:31)
2. The Fall (Genesis 3)
3. The global Flood (Genesis 6–8)

36. See Dr. Steve Austin, "Excess Argon Within Mineral Concentrates from the New Dacite Lava Dome at Mount St Helens Volcano," Answers in Genesis, December 1, 1996, https://answersingenesis.org/geology/mount-st-helens/argon-in-mineral-concentrates-from-mount-st-helens-volcano/.
37. See "More and More Wrong Dates," June 1, 2001, https://answersingenesis.org/geology/radiometric-dating/more-and-more-wrong-dates/.

Historic Lava Flow	Potassium-argon Dating
Hualalai, basalt (Hawaii, A.D. 1800–1801)	1.4–1.6 million years "old"
Mt Etna, basalt (Sicily, 122 B.C.)	0.25 million years "old"
Mt Etna, basalt (Sicily, A.D. 1792)	0.35 million years "old"
Mt Lassen, plagioclase (California, A.D. 1915)	0.11 million years "old"
Sunset Crater, basalt (Arizona, A.D. 1064–1065)	0.25–0.27 million years "old"

Or it is the faith position that states that however processes are operating now is how they have always been operating, i.e., the present is the key to the past. The starting position for understanding the age of the earth is a choice between faith in the God who was there or the opinion of men who were not.

There are, however, many Christians who object: "But how can the majority of scientists who do not believe that the earth is young be wrong?" Even though it may be true that the majority of scientists do not believe in biblical creation, it does not follow that we should simply accept what the majority believe (this argument undermines Jesus' own teaching — see Matthew 7:13–14). This sort of claim is also disastrous to a Christian's own belief in the miraculous. For example, the majority of scientists do not believe in the virgin birth, the Resurrection, or the miracles of Jesus. Yet would they abandon their belief in these vital doctrines until scientists were persuaded of the truth by "scientific testing and evidence"? The reason that the majority of scientists do not accept biblical creation is not because of the evidence — everyone has the same evidence to examine — but because it does not fit their naturalistic worldview.

There are three things that are important to keep in mind when it comes to the issue of evolution and the age of the earth: 1) the distinction between observation science and historical science, 2) the distinction between God's revelation in Scripture and creation, and 3) all evidence is viewed through a particular worldview.

Observational Science and Historical Science

In the discussion about creation and the Flood, it is also vitally important to understand a valid distinction between historical science and observational science. Historical science seeks to reconstruct the unrepeatable, unobservable past by looking at the evidence of the past events that produced what we see in the present. And such historical reconstructions are very dependent on a scientist's belief system or worldview. On the other hand, observational science uses repeatable, observable, testable experiments to find out how things in the present world operate so that we can find cures for disease, produce new technology, or make other scientific advancements. Evolutionary scientists even recognize this distinction. The late Harvard zoologist Ernst Mayr pointed out,

> Evolution is a *historical* process that cannot be proven by the same arguments and methods by which purely physical or *functional* phenomena can be documented[38] (emphasis mine).

The age of the earth falls in the category of historical, not observational, science. Scientists who have been influenced by uniformitarianism have basically made up the history of planet earth, a history that is taught throughout the education system and has, sadly, become "proven science" in the minds of the public. The long-age, evolutionary story of planet earth (indeed the whole universe) is not based on observational evidence but is part of a secular faith (i.e., religion) that denies supernatural revelation. The debate over creation and the Flood is not a battle between science and Scripture but between two different worldviews and how science is to be used to interpret the evidence.

God's Revelation in Scripture and Creation

In order to defend the idea of evolution and millions of years, some Christians have even referred to nature as the "sixty-seventh book of the Bible." In saying this, they grant God's revelation in creation (general revelation) equal weight with the Bible, calling it one of "two books" God gave us to understand how He created the world. However, Christians who hold to the "two books" analogy must go outside God's special revelation to find support for their views. God revelation in creation says nothing about our ability to discern how earth functioned in the unobservable past (see Psalm 19:1–6; Romans1:18–21). General revelation is limited, as it has a general content and is revealed to a general audience. This does not mean that we cannot learn anything from studying nature.

---

38. Ernst Mayr, *What Evolution Is* (New York: Basic Books, 2001), 13.

It just means that our interpretation of what we observe must be consistent with the revelation of Scripture. The Bible is God's eyewitness testimony that enables us to rightly interpret the present physical evidence so we can reconstruct earth's history since creation. Therefore, it is not biblically sound to label the claims and interpretations a scientist makes about the evidence a general revelation.

God's special revelation also informs us that the creation itself has been corrupted by the Curse and that sin has affected how people view general revelation. The New Testament uses various words to describe the ruin of humanity's intellect: futile (Romans 1:21), debased (Romans (1:28), deceived (Colossians 2:4), and darkened (Ephesians 4:18). Only by having our mind renewed in Christ and our thinking guided by the Holy Spirit can we rightly understand the special revelation of Scripture and then apply that to interpreting general revelation. Theologian Louis Berkhof states, "Since the entrance of sin into the world, man can gather true knowledge about God from His general revelation only if he studies it in the light of Scripture."[39] God has given us special revelation as the glasses to rightly understand His general revelation.

The most important distinction between the two is that, biblically speaking, special revelation precedes and grounds our understanding of general revelation. For example, in Genesis 1 we read, "And God said, 'Let there be light,' and there was light" (Genesis 1:3). Special revelation brings general revelation into existence. Once creation came into existence and was completed, God told Adam what to do in the garden He had created (Genesis 2:16–17). Both special and general revelation are complementary concepts: one cannot exist without the other. If we isolate one from the other, we will end up with problems, such as when observations of nature are used to support evolution or millions of years. However, our scientific observations and interpretations of the creation are not equivalent to Scripture and cannot be used to modify our understanding of special revelation.

It's important to remember that God's Word offers us direct statements of truth while nature does not speak. Since general and special revelation both proceed from God, they cannot ultimately conflict with each other, and they do not conflict when we use special revelation to correctly interpret general revelation.

39. Louis Berkhof, *Introductory Volume to Systematic Theology* (Grand Rapids, MI: Eerdmans, 1932), 60.

Worldview Matters

As Christians, we also need to understand there is no neutral ground when it comes to worldview issues such as creation and evolution. The Bible makes this clear in several ways:

> For the mind that is set on the flesh is hostile to God, for it does not submit to God's law; indeed, it cannot (Romans 8:7).

> The natural person does not accept the things of the Spirit of God, for they are folly to him, and he is not able to understand them because they are spiritually discerned (1 Corinthians 2:14).

Since the Bible indicates that there is no such thing as "neutrality," when it comes to our thinking about worldview issues, the claim of neutrality is itself unbiblical. Ultimately, the reason why creationists and evolutionists disagree is because of the presuppositions they bring to the evidence.[40]

Biblical Timescale	Evolutionary Timescale
Presuppositions • Supernaturalism • Catastrophism (global Flood)	Presuppositions • Naturalism • Uniformitarianism (rates and conditions are constant)
Conclusions	Conclusions
• Creation in 6 days a few thousand years ago	• Billions of years of cosmic, biological, and geological evolution

It is important to grasp these presuppositions, as there are a number of people who would try to argue that human reasoning suggests the earth looks old because today's natural processes alone would have required billions of years to build the earth's rocks and landscapes. But this interpretation of the world is again built upon the unprovable assumption of uniformitarianism. We cannot assume that something looks old if we do not know when it came into being. When God created things originally in Genesis 1, they were fully functional from the beginning. Think about it. How old would Adam have looked when God created him? Adam and Eve were created as mature adults ready to be fruitful and multiply

---

40. This chart comes from a presentation by Dr. Jason Lisle.

(Genesis 1:28). God did not create a "baby" Adam, but just as with the rest of creation, He created him mature. So, if you had met Adam just after he was created, you would mistakenly assume he was older than he was. Adam also witnessed the sudden appearance of a fully "mature" Eve (Genesis 2:20–23). On Day Three of creation week, God created fruit trees already bearing fruit (Genesis 1:11–13). Why? Because three days later He created Adam and Eve, who would need to eat fruit. If God had planted seeds and waited for them to grow, Adam and Eve would have gone hungry. God created a fully formed and fully functioning creation to begin with. This is consistent with the miracles of our Creator. Think about when Jesus turned water into wine at a wedding in Cana in Galilee (see John 2:1–11). Jesus, the Creator (John 1:1–3), was told by His mother that the wine had run out, so He called for the servants to fill up six stone water jars (each holding 20 or 30 gallons). When the servants drew out the water to give some to the master of the feast, it had become wine. After tasting it, the master did not know where it had come from. Jesus did not deceive the master of the marriage feast in Cana when He instantly turned water into wine. The master deceived himself for thinking that wine was old, having come from grapes produced by natural processes, instead of listening to the testimony of the eyewitnesses (the servants). In the same way, we deceive ourselves if we ignore God's eyewitness account of creation and the Flood found in the Bible.

Those today who scoff at the return of Jesus at the end of history, based on the argument that there has been no divine intervention that has materially changed the nature of the world, find themselves blinded by the same philosophy as the scoffers in Peter's day (uniformitarianism). As we will see in the next two chapters, the examples Peter gives of God's intervention in human history through creation and the Flood speak against the argument that nothing has changed since the beginning of creation. This is why we can be certain that the same God who brought creation into existence and entered into His creation to redeem a fallen world is the One who will come back in judgment of it.

CHAPTER SIX

DELIBERATELY OVERLOOKING CREATION

2 Peter 3:6

For they deliberately overlook this fact, that the heavens existed long ago, and the earth was formed out of water and through water by the word of God. . . (2 Peter 3:5).

In the past, the leading astronomers of the age, men like Nicolaus Copernicus (1473–1543), Galileo Galilei (1564–1642), and Johannes Kepler (1571–1630), gave God the glory and honor for His work in creation. Today, however, astronomy is one of those scientific fields that the scoffers often use to challenge the Bible. We live in a time when many scientists scoff at God as the Creator of the cosmos because of the prevailing naturalistic model of the origin of the universe, the big bang. A book of Professor Stephen Hawking's writings, published posthumously, begins by asking the question: "Is there a God?" In the book, Hawking argues that our universe consists of just two elements, energy and space, which he says ". . . were spontaneously invented in an event we now call the Big Bang."[1] Hawking then goes on to say: "The laws of physics demand the existence of something called 'negative energy.' "[2] He explains this through an illustration:

Imagine a man wants to build a hill on a flat piece of land. The hill will represent the universe. To make this hill he digs a hole

---

1. Stephen Hawking, *Brief Answers to the Big Questions* (London: John Murray Publishers, 2018), 31.
2. Ibid., 32.

in the ground and uses that soil to dig [*sic*] his hill. But of course he's not just making a hill — he's also making a hole, in effect a negative version of the hill. The stuff that was in the hole has now become the hill, so it all perfectly balances out. This is the principle behind what happened at the beginning of the universe. ... When the Big bang produced a massive amount of positive energy, it simultaneously produced the same amount of negative energy. In this way the positive and the negative add up to zero, always. It's a law of nature. ... So what does this mean in our quest to find out if there is a God? It means that if the universe adds up to nothing, then you don't need a God to create it. The universe is the ultimate free lunch.[3]

Although Hawking's illustration is designed to disprove God's existence, when you think about the scenario he has set up, it fails drastically. The shovel and the material all existed in time and space before the man started to build the hill, and each needed a cause to begin with (not to mention the man was necessary to dig and build the hill, just as God was necessary to create the universe). The fact of the matter is that there is no good physical or naturalistic explanation for the origin of the universe.

The atheist objection to the supernatural creation of the universe seems to fall back on: ". . . the postulate of a designer or creator only raises the unanswerable question of who designed the designer or created the creator."[4] But this is not an unanswerable question — the atheist just does not like the answer. Since we know time began to exist (Genesis 1:1), it obviously had a cause.[5] Therefore, whatever caused time must be timeless (i.e., eternal). The Bible tells us that the God who created the universe does not have a beginning or end, as He inhabits eternity, and that He does not have a cause, as He is self-existent: the I AM, or more literally, "He who causes to be" (Exodus 3:14; cf. Isaiah 57:15; Psalm 90:2). Not only does the objection assume that God is a created being, but it is also irrelevant as to what it is trying to prove. Think about it. Atheists do not believe God exists, so they do not believe anyone created God. Christians believe God is eternal, so they do not believe God is created. Neither atheists nor Christians believe God was created, so why do atheists bring up this question?

3. Ibid., 32–33.
4. Christopher Hitchens, *God Is Not Great: The Case Against Religion* (London: Atlanta Books, 2007), 71.
5. The universe cannot be eternal because it is suffering the effects of entropy.

Hawking's scoffing at the existence of God ended with him denying God's coming judgment:

> There is probably no heaven and no afterlife either. I think belief in an afterlife is just wishful thinking. There is no reliable evidence for it, and it flies in the face of everything we know in science.[6]

Given that Hawking has already accepted a naturalistic understanding of the universe, what evidence would he have accepted for heaven or an afterlife since he had already ruled out a supernatural explanation? Many atheists, like Hawking, seem to think that science is the answer to all of life's questions. However, there are many questions that science cannot account for, even if they are rational to accept. One example of this is logical truth. Science cannot account for logical truth, as it presupposes logic, so to try and prove it by science would be arguing in a circle. Hawking's lack of belief in meta-physical truth (such as heaven) also cannot be proven by science, as science deals with the observable present material world. Trying to find heaven by using science would be like trying to find plastic by using a metal detector. It is a category error. It is necessary and rational to believe that the world is real before going out to investigate it, but it cannot be proven scientifically. It must be accepted by faith.

The reality of the matter is that for many atheists, no evidence will ever be enough to convince them of God's existence or the reality of heaven, as they will always explain evidence away because they have a prior commitment to the philosophy of naturalism.[7] What many atheists don't seem to realize or want to acknowledge is that naturalism itself is a self-defeating worldview, as it undermines the very faculties it takes in order to affirm reasoning and therefore by extension be able to do science. If humans are simply just the result of random, chance evolutionary processes and our brains are also the product of random chemical reactions, then there is no basis to trust our reasoning faculties (as the brain would be controlled by physics and chemistry). For example, is what evolutionists say about evolution just their neurons firing, or is there an objectivity to it that transcends everyone else's objectivity? If we are just "dancing to

---

6. Hawking, *Brief Answers to the Big Questions*, 38.
7. In a conversation with fellow atheist Peter Boghossian, Richard Dawkins admitted that no evidence would convince him of God's existence, as he could always explain it away (relevant section 12:30–15:27). See "Richard Dawkins in conversation with Peter Boghossian," https://www.youtube.com/watch?v=RoQurwEZmmQ.

our DNA,"[8] then reason disappears. In order to do science, it is necessary to use objective reason. But atheism undermines objective reason because it reduces everything to physics and chemistry. From a naturalistic evolutionary perspective, "our brains were shaped for fitness, not for truth,"[9] which means that a person's beliefs do not have to be true, they just have to grant survival value. If atheistic naturalism were true, then there is no objective reasoning nor freedom to our thoughts and therefore no reason to trust the thoughts that our brains produce because they were not designed to obtain truth. In fact, if the brain is not designed, then for the atheist, all their thoughts and beliefs become rationally unjustified when it comes to asserting or evaluating truth claims.[10] Therefore, if naturalism were true, how can atheists, like Stephen Hawking, call on Christians (or anybody) to be reasonable or rational?

Atheists are emotionally committed to an underlying worldview that undermines the very reasoning processes that they need to account for intelligibility. Under atheist presuppositions, you cannot intelligibly account for reason. In other words, atheists may believe in reason, but they have no foundation to support that belief. Atheism is an arbitrary, irrational, and blind faith (i.e., without evidence), all the while dressed up as being reasonable. Ultimately, the atheist who wants to be rational has departed from their philosophy of naturalism. In the Christian worldview, reason and rationality are understandable because they reflect the nature and character of God, but if the history of the world is just "... full of sound and fury, but signifies nothing,"[11] as some atheists claim, then there is really no reason to be rational. The Christian worldview is the only one that can give an account for reason and rationality, as all reasoning itself depends upon the God who is reasonable (cf. Isaiah 1:18).

8. Richard Dawkins has said: "The universe we observe has . . . no design, no purpose, no evil and no good, nothing but blind, pitiless indifference. . . . DNA neither knows nor cares. DNA just is. And we dance to its music." Dawkins, *River out of Eden*, 133.
9. This is the view of atheist professor of psychology at Harvard University Steven Pinker. Steven Pinker, *How the Mind Works* (New York, NY: W.W. Norton and Company, 1997), 305.
10. This is not a Christian argument but was Charles Darwin's: ". . . with me the horrid doubt always arises whether the convictions of man's mind, which has been developed from the mind of the lower animals, are of any value or at all trustworthy. Would any one trust in the convictions of a monkey's mind, if there are any convictions in such a mind?" Charles Darwin to William Graham, Darwin Correspondence Project, Letter No. 13230, dated July 3, 1881.
11. See atheist philosopher at Duke University Alex Rosenberg, *The Atheist's Guide to Reality: Enjoying Life Without Illusions* (W.W. Norton & Company, 2011), 3.

Hawking's argument that God does not exist fits with the Apostle Peter's argument that the scoffers "deliberately overlook" the evidence of God's acts in history. The fact that the scoffers "deliberately overlook" the events of biblical history also fits with what the Apostle Paul tells us about humanity and its rejection of God in Romans 1:18–20:

> For the wrath of God is revealed from heaven against all ungodliness and unrighteousness of men, who by their unrighteousness suppress the truth. For what can be known about God is plain to them, because God has shown it to them. For his invisible attributes, namely, his eternal power and divine nature, have been clearly perceived, ever since the creation of the world, in the things that have been made. So they are without excuse.

Paul states that God's wrath is revealed against the ungodly and unrighteous, "who by their unrighteousness suppress the truth." This suppression of the truth is that which can be known about God in creation. The reason men can suppress the truth is that they are creatures of God, made in His image, and because of His clear witness in creation. When people suppress the truth, they become "futile in their thinking" (Romans 1:21; cf. Ephesians 4:17). Paul's argument is that human beings already know God exists through His revelation in creation, so no one has an excuse. This includes all people living in all places and all times.[12] People have been able to understand God's revelation of Himself since the very beginning of His creation (see Acts 14:15–17, 17:18–31). The words "the creation of the world" (*apo ktiseōs kosmou*) refer to the beginning of the creation week in Genesis 1. Paul is saying that God's revelation of Himself through creation has been clear since the creation week in Genesis 1, which refutes an evolutionary or long-age view of creation since man

---

12. John Frame shows why these verses are not just about certain people living in the past: "The aorist translated 'knew,' 'honor,' 'give thanks,' and 'became futile' in verse 21 and beyond have led some readers to think Paul is talking about people living in a past time, not his own contemporaries. But that would imply that Paul is giving his contemporaries a pass from his solemn indictment. Note: 1) This passage, again, is part of an argument convicting all people of sin, all past, present, and future [Romans 3:9ff]. So it presupposes that people in all times and places 'know God.' The aorists therefore do not designate a particular time of occurrence for the events they mention. 2) More generally, this passage is part of Paul's description to the Roman church of the gospel he proclaims (vv.16–17). Clearly, the pagans he mentions in verses 18–32 are pagans to whom he preaches his gospel in his present labors. 3) Paul establishes his time reference at the beginning of the passage by a present active participle, *katechonton*, in verse 18." John Frame, *Systematic Theology: An Introduction to Christian Belief* (Phillipsburg, NJ: P&R Publishing Group, 2013), 711.

(Adam and Eve) is as old as the rest of creation. The truth that Paul says is being suppressed is Genesis 1:1: "In the beginning, God created the heavens and the earth." As Christians, we need to keep in mind the theological reality that God is our Creator and that man in his inherent sin nature is in active rebellion against Him. Therefore, we cannot base our apologetic methodology on the assumption that fallen man will make unbiased decisions on the existence of God because they will not do that (Romans 8:7–8; 1 Corinthians 2:14). Unbelievers are not in a neutral position when it comes to the existence of God. God's creatures have no right to judge their Creator or His existence. Those who do not hold to the view that God created the world and that we are creatures of God are not thinking rationally but irrationally, even foolishly (see Psalm 14:1), and are doing that in unrighteousness; it is an ethical problem.[13]

In Christian apologetics today, it is common for Christians to defend the existence of God by arguing something like the following: "The majority of the evidence points to the greater probability for the existence of God." This is because many Christians think that if we give people enough evidence for God, they will be convinced. The problem with this idea is that the unbeliever, by virtue of their unbelief, will take the evidence and interpret it according to their unbelief; the idolatry Paul saw in Athens was the result of suppressing the truth of God's revelation in creation (see Acts 17:23).[14] The reason the Greek philosophers in Athens (Mars Hill) rejected Paul's message (which included the resurrection of the dead) was not because of the evidence but because it did not fit their worldview. The Stoics had a pantheistic concept of God and believed reason "as the principle which was inherent in the structuring of the universe and by which men ought to live."[15] The Epicureans, however, had a similar worldview to today's atheists in that they were materialists, believing in the atomic theory, and so "for them either the gods did not exist, or they were so far removed from the world as to exercise no influence on its affairs."[16] The idea of "rising" (*anistēmi*) from the dead was literally "to raise up by bringing back to life."[17] This view was incompatible with the Athenian view of life, as they believed that "once a man dies and the

13. Irrationality is a state in respect to reason; it does not mean that unbelievers are unintelligent.
14. Paul's apologetic in Acts 17:22–34 is based on his theology in Romans 1:18–32.
15. I. Howard Marshall, *Acts: Tyndale New Testament Commentaries* (Leicester, England: InterVarsity Press, 1986), 284.
16. Ibid., 284.
17. BDAG: *A Greek-English Lexicon of the New Testament*, 83.

earth drinks up his blood, there is no resurrection."[18] This is why many of them scoffed at the resurrection; by the cultural standard of wisdom, it was foolishness to them (Acts 17:32; 1 Corinthians 1:23).

Despite the naturalistic and materialistic worldview that rejects the Resurrection of Jesus, the evidence for it is verifiable. Jesus' death by crucifixion is one of the best-established facts of ancient history, something even atheist scholars admit.[19] We know Jesus was alive after His death because His many post-Resurrection appearances proved He had risen from the dead (Matthew 28:16; Luke 24:13–15, 36–39; John 20:11–23, 21:1–14). It did not happen in secret. There were numerous eyewitnesses to it and trustworthy pieces of evidence to support it, such as the conversion of skeptical witnesses, the empty tomb, etc. In 1 Corinthians 15:3–7, Paul even makes use of an early credal statement from the eyewitnesses of the risen Jesus that pre-dates the writing of the letter (A.D. 55) by a number of years, with some scholars placing its formulation to within almost months (some scholars say 2–3 years) of the actual event of the crucifixion.[20] What is more, even atheist scholars recognize that Jesus' disciples were convinced that they had seen Jesus alive after His death.[21] Given the historical evidence for the Resurrection of Jesus, it would seem the reasons to reject it would either be a prior commitment to naturalism or the implication that we need to listen to what He says when it comes to sin, judgment, and salvation (see Mark 8:34–38).

---

18. F.F. Bruce, *The Book of ACTS: New International Commentary on the Old Testament* (Grand Rapids, MI: W.B. Eerdmans Publishing Company, 1988), 343.
19. Atheist professor of the history and literature of early Christianity Gerd Lüdemann admits: "Jesus' death as a consequence of crucifixion is indisputable." Gerd Lüdemann, *The Resurrection of Christ: A Historical Inquiry* (Amherst, NY: Prometheus Books, 2004), 41.
20. New Testament scholar James D.G. Dunn says of the credal statement in 1 Corinthians 15:3–7: "This tradition, we can be entirely confident, was formulated as tradition within months of Jesus' death." See James D.G. Dunn, *Jesus Remembered* (Grand Rapids, MI: W.B. Eerdmans Publishing Company, 2003), 825.
21. Gerd Lüdemann admits: "It may be taken as historically cetain that Peter and the disciples had experiences after Jesus' death in which Jesus appeared to them as the risen Christ." Gerd Lüdemann, *What Really Happened to Jesus: A Historical Approach to the Resurrection* (Louisville, KY: John Knox Press, 1995), 80. Lüdemann believes these events were the product of hallucinatory experiences probably brought about by guilt-complexes. However, after His Resurrection Jesus not only appeared to numerous individuals but He also appeared at least three times to groups of people (Matthew 28:16; Luke 24:13–15; 36–39; John 20:11–23; 21:1–14). Generally, groups of people do not hallucinate at the same time as it is not contagious but is a personal experience. Moreover, hallucination does not account for the empty tomb or the conversion of Paul (Saul) as he was not grieving but trying to destroy the church (Acts 9:1–5; Galatians 1:13).

The problem is not the evidence for the Resurrection but what people will do with the evidence. Evidence only has value when God uses it to clear the ground of unbelief. Paul did not present the Resurrection of Jesus as a neutral fact, open to the interpretation of the Athenian philosophers, but as the focal point of the history of redemption. As part of the history of redemption, Paul proclaimed the fact of creation (Acts 17:24), the fact of the human race being in Adam (Acts 17:26), and the fact of the Resurrection, which leads to the fact of the final judgment (Acts 17:31). Any apologetic perspective that leaves you appealing to the person as an autonomous authority to judge the evidence as to what is acceptable is not biblical. This does not fit with the authoritative proclamation that we see in Acts 17, where Paul speaks of the future judgment of the world; there is no opting out of it if you do not agree with the evidence.

Deliberately Overlooking

Peter begins his argument against the scoffers' worldview that "all things continue as they were since creation" by arguing that God's supernatural act of creation represents a divine intervention in the world. The universe has not always existed but was brought into existence at a moment in time by the very word of God. The scoffers of Peter's day are very much like modern-day skeptics in that they "deliberately overlook" the facts of biblical history: creation and the Flood. The first words of verse five, "they deliberately overlook" (*lanthanei gar autos touto thelontas*), express the self will of the scoffers in their unbelief. It is important to consider how these words should be understood since Bible versions render these words differently:

- "deliberately overlook" (ESV)
- "they willingly are ignorant" (KJV)
- "they deliberately forget" (NIV)
- "when they maintain this, it escapes their notice" (NASB)

Although the difference in meaning is minor, the translation "when they maintain this, it escapes their notice" (NASB) makes better sense of the Greek words.[22] The scoffers, Peter suggests, are not ignorant or naïve, but "when they maintain this, it escapes their notice" that the continuity of human history runs counter to the fact of biblical history in Genesis 1 (and 6–8); Peter's reference to heavens and earth is a clear reference back to the creation account in Genesis 1. The scoffers are people who deliberately ignore the fundamental truths of Scripture.

22. See Schreiner, *1,2 Peter, Jude*, 375; Moo, *2 Peter*, 168–169.

In our modern era of history, it is the naturalistic interpretation of the origin and evolution of the universe and the subsequent evolution of life that scoffers look to today to explain the universe without the need for a Creator. Darwinian evolution is the belief that change over enough time can lead to the common ancestry of all species on earth that we see today. The driving forces behind this process are natural selection and mutations. However, there are two major problems with this model of evolution: 1) mutations do not add the novel traits necessary for molecules-to-man evolution, and 2) natural selection does not lead to the changes that, given time, change one kind of animal into another.[23] A popular argument that is used to try to prove evolution is to say that "humans evolve new characteristics to help us survive in the world." This argument, however, equivocates on the term *evolution*, which is a common practice in evolutionary arguments. The word *evolution* is often used by evolutionists to refer to descent from a common ancestor. But evolution also refers to change in a generic sense. Even though both definitions are accurate, they should not be confused in an argument. The evolutionist is basically arguing: "I know evolution is true (we evolved from a common ancestor) because we see evolution (change within human characteristics) happening all the time." The fact that human characteristics are changing does not mean we share a common ancestor with ape-like creatures. The evidence from Scripture and the sequencing of the human genome are consistent with all humans sharing ancestry with one pair of human parents, Adam and Eve (Genesis 3:20; 1 Corinthians 15:45).[24] The question, though, of how the first cell even came into existence is also a puzzling one for evolutionists, as George Whitesides, professor of chemistry at Harvard, acknowledges:

> **The Origin of Life.** This problem is one of the big ones in science. It begins to place life, and us, in the universe. Most chemists believe, as do I, that life emerged spontaneously from mixtures of

---

23. Antibiotic resistance of bacteria is often used by evolutionists as an argument for evolution in action. Yet, this is the opposite of evolution and is just another example of natural selection working in conjunction with mutations. The bacteria becoming resistant to antibiotics through mutation involves a loss of genetic information, which is the opposite of what evolution needs to generate more complex organisms.

24. See Dr. Nathaniel Jeanson and Dr. Jeffrey Tomkins, "Genetics Confirms the Recent, Supernatural Creation of Adam and Eve," in *Searching for Adam: Genesis & the Truth About Man's Origin*, ed. Terry Mortenson (Green Forest, AR: Master Books, 2016), 287–330.

molecules in the prebiotic Earth. How? I have no idea. ... On the basis of all the chemistry that I know, it seems to me astonishingly improbable.[25]

It is statements like this that show that it is not the evidence that drives scientists to make such claims but a particular ideology (evolution). It is also one of the reasons evolutionists will try to limit the discussion of evolution to merely biological evolution — the development of the first lifeform into the enormous and diverse assortment of living things we see today. But they want to set aside chemical evolution — how the first life-form evolved from lifeless chemicals. They do this because they cannot explain the origin of life through any known natural processes.

Evolution is not just about the development of the first lifeform into the diversity we see today, but is really a three-part hypothesis to explain all of reality: 1) biological evolution (life), 2) geological evolution (earth), and 3) cosmological evolution (planets, stars, and galaxies). An online course from Harvard University explains what is meant by cosmic evolution:

Cosmic evolution is the study of the many varied changes in the assembly and composition of energy, matter and life in the thinning and cooling Universe.[26]

In cosmic evolution, the big bang is the prevailing model used by many secular cosmologists to argue that the universe came out of nothing (the absence of anything); there was no space, matter, time, or energy, and then suddenly, there was something around 13.8 billion years ago.[27] People often ask, "What was here before the big bang?" But that really is an improper question, as the word "here" implies the concept of "space," and "before" implies the concept of "time," but neither of these existed. So, before the big bang, there was absolutely nothing. To many people, this may even sound theistic (that there was nothing then something), but in the big bang model, there is no reason or purpose for it — it just happened. Additionally, this story about the origin of the universe is based upon a naturalistic worldview. The two major premises of naturalism are:

25. See Dr. Nathaniel Jeanson and Dr. Jeffrey Tomkins, "Genetics Confirms the Recent, Supernatural Creation of Adam and Eve," in *Searching for Adam: Genesis & the Truth About Man's Origin*, ed. Terry Mortenson (Green Forest, AR: Master Books, 2016), 287–330.
26. See https://www.cfa.harvard.edu/~ejchaisson/cosmic_evolution/docs/splash.html.
27. Because the age of the universe is based upon naturalistic assumptions, the dates for its age will continue to change.

1. The belief that nature is all there is.
2. Everything, including origins, must be explained by time, chance, and the laws of nature. This philosophy is used today by scientists to interpret observational data.

The big bang is not only the dominant secular interpretation of the origin of the world, but many Christians who believe in an old earth have also adopted it into their thinking, arguing that God used the big bang to create the world. In his book *Seven Days that Divide the World*, Christian apologist Professor John Lennox's understanding of the age of the universe is controlled more by the big bang theory than the biblical text:

> The standard (Big Bang) Model developed by physicists and cosmologists can be seen as a scientific unpacking of the implications of the statement, "In the beginning God created the heavens and the earth." There is a certain irony here, in that the very same big bang cosmological model of the universe that confirms the biblical claim that there was a beginning also implies that the universe is very old.[28]

To claim that God used the big bang, however, not only misunderstands the big bang but, more importantly, the biblical text (see below). But if you believe God used the big bang to create, then what happens when secular scientists change their minds on the big bang? In 2004, in an article called "Bucking the Big Bang" in *New Scientist*, a number of prominent secular scientists questioned the big bang, arguing that it "relies on a growing number of hypothetical entities, things that we have *never observed* — inflation, dark matter and dark energy are the most prominent examples"[29] (emphasis mine). More recently, in 2019, another article, "What if there was no Big Bang and we live in an ever-cycling universe?" appeared in New Scientist attacking the big bang and instead

---

28. John Lennox, *Seven Days That Divide the World: The Beginning According to Genesis and Science* (Grand Rapids, MI: Zondervan, 2011), 154. For a critique of Lennox's view of Genesis, see my review of his book: Simon Turpin, "Review of John Lennox's Book *Seven Days That Divide the World: The Beginning According to Genesis and Science*," June 27, 2012, https://answersingenesis.org/reviews/books/review-of-seven-days-that-divide-the-world-john-lennox/.
29. See "An Open Letter to the Scientific Community" (Published in *New Scientist*, May 22, 2004), https://web.archive.org/web/20140401081546/http:/cosmologystatement.org/.

proposed the hypotheses of an oscillating universe (an infinite cycle).[30] The problem is that it is not even a testable scientific model. All this just shows the desperate attempt by secular scientists to come up with an explanation of the universe that does not involve a personal Creator.

There are, however, many other scientists who reject cosmic evolution. These scientists base their worldview on the Bible. The two major premises of a biblical worldview are:

1. The triune, eternal, good, all-knowing, all-powerful, holy God exists, and He created everything else.
2. The Bible, God's completely truthful eyewitness testimony, explains the key events in history so that we can correctly interpret the evidence for the origin and history of creation.[31]

This is a very different worldview to the naturalistic one. In the biblical worldview, the reason everything exists is for God's glory and His purposes (Isaiah 43:7, 46:10).[32] The God of the Bible is not silent; He is a speaking God who has communicated to us through His revelation in the Bible. Because the Bible is trustworthy and authoritative when it comes to history, it is trustworthy in the scientific inferences from that history. In fact, there are many ways in which the heavens and the earth affirm the biblical account of creation and declare the glory of God (Psalm 19:1). For example, there are many lines of observational scientific evidence that confirm the universe is only thousands of years old rather than billions. One of these is the excess internal heat of three of the four giant planets. Jupiter emits twice as much energy as it receives from the sun, but such a process could not last billions of years. For example, when you take a baked potato out of the microwave, that heat is radiated out into the atmosphere. However, the heat will not radiate out forever since it only has so much heat to give out. Eventually it will cool off. Jupiter (the size of about ten earths across) is not going to cool off very much in a few thousand years, but if it were billions of years old, then why is it not an icicle by now? This is a problem for the secular view of the cosmos.

30. See Anna Ijjas, "What if there was no big bang and we live in an ever-cycling universe?" August 14, 2019, https://www.newscientist.com/article/mg24332430-800-what-if-there-was-no-big-bang-and-we-live-in-an-ever-cycling-universe/.
31. I am thankful to Dr. Terry Mortenson for these points.
32. ". . . thus, says the LORD . . . I created for my glory" (Isaiah 43:1, 7). "I am God, and there is none like me . . . and I will accomplish all my purpose" (Isaiah 46:9–10).

Another line of evidence would be the existence of comets. Comets are made of icy material that is being continually depleted as solar wind and radiation blast the material into space. So, a typical comet can last no more than 100,000 years (the upper limit). Evolutionary astronomers realize this and must believe that new comets replace the vanishing ones. They imagine that a hypothetical "Oort Cloud" provides a vast reservoir of new comets — the only problem with this is that no one has ever observed an Oort Cloud. Interestingly, in 2015, the Rosetta spacecraft discovered molecular oxygen in the cloud of gas surrounding the comet P67 it was tracking, to which the study's author said:

> If we have O2 [oxygen] at the beginning of the formation of the comet, how did it survive so long? All the models say it shouldn't survive for so long, which tells us something about the building of our solar system.[33]

It was rightly observed that the molecular oxygen should not have lasted so long on comet P67, but rather than telling us something about the building of the solar system, what it really confirms is that the comet and universe are not as old as secular scientists think. Other things such as the decay of the earth's magnetic field and the recession of the moon from the earth also point to a young universe.[34]

The Apostle Peter's appeals to God's revelation in Genesis 1 to counter the scoffers is important to understand, as it undercuts their argument that God has not intervened in the world. The world in which we live has not always been here; God brought it about at a moment in time.

The Heavens Existed Long Ago

Peter tells us that "the heavens existed long ago" (2 Peter 3:5), but when was this? Was it 13.8 billion years ago, according to secular cosmology? Or around 6,000 years ago, according to biblical chronology? The fact that Peter notes that "the heavens existed long ago" does not point to the earth being millions of years old. The words "long ago" in Greek use the adverb *ekpalai*, and it only occurs one other time in the New Testament, in 2 Peter 2:3: "And in their greed they will exploit you with false words. Their condemnation from *long ago* is not idle, and their destruction is

33. See "Surprise discovery suggests 'gentle' start for Solar System," October 28, 2015, https://www.bbc.co.uk/news/science-environment-34660576.
34. See Jason Lisle, *Taking Back Astronomy: The Heavens Declare Creation and Science Confirms It* (Green Forest, AR: Master Books, 2006).

not asleep." The word itself is a relative term and comes from the prefix *ek* (out of), which is added to the root *palai* (old). Elsewhere in the New Testament, *palai* is used to refer to events that took place in human history (Matthew 11:21; Mark 15:44; Hebrews 1:1).

For many Christians, the Bible is silent on this issue of the age of the earth, but does Genesis tell us about how long ago the heavens existed? One reason that many Christians believe that Genesis says nothing about the age of the earth is that they believe it can easily be harmonized with modern secular scientific cosmology (big bang). This harmonization often involves eisegesis (reading into the text) and fails to look closely at the details of the text of Genesis 1.

The very first verse of Genesis is one of the most famous verses in the Bible: "In the beginning, God created the heavens and the earth." These words have long been seen by many creationists as God's first creative act. However, that is not the only understanding of Genesis 1:1 among Old Testament scholars and biblical creationists. There is very good reason to view Genesis 1:1 as an introduction or title to the entire creation narrative. Understanding Genesis 1:1 as a title (rather than the first creative act of Day One) means that Day Two is the creation of atmosphere and space (Genesis 1:6–8).[35] There are at least three reasons to understand Genesis 1:1 as an introductory title: 1) the phrase "heaven and earth" is a merism, 2) Genesis 1:1 together with Genesis 2:1–3 functions as an *inclusio*, and 3) the grammatical relationship between Genesis 1:1 and 1:2 suggest Genesis 1:1 is an introductory title.[36] Another way of saying this is that Genesis 1:1 tells us, "In the beginning God made everything," and verses 2–31 tell us how He did it.

If Genesis 1:1 is a title to the narrative and the heavens are made on Day Two, then the question is, when did God create the earth? The Hebrew word for earth, *'eres*, occurs in Genesis 1:1 and then in 1:2.[37] In Genesis 1:1, however, the "the earth" (*hāāres*) is used with "the heavens" (*haššāmayim*) to form a combination that designates the world or universe

35. One of the reasons for not understanding Genesis 1:1 as referring to creation of heaven (i.e., the atmosphere) is that what God does on Day Two with the expanse means that heaven would have been created twice.
36. For a more detailed discussion of Genesis 1:1 as a title (rather than of the creation of space and time), see Dr. Danny Faulkner with Lee Anderson Jr, *The Created Cosmos: What the Bible Reveals About Astronomy* (Green Forest, AR: Master Books, 2016), 43–47.
37. In Hebrew, *'eres* has more than one meaning and can refer to: 1) the whole earth; 2) land; 3) ground, surface of the ground; or 4) people of the land.

(a merism).[38] In Genesis 1:2, the earth is not the same as 1:1, as it begins a new subject: "The earth was without form and void, and darkness was over the face of the deep. And the Spirit of God was hovering over the face of the waters." These words do not follow sequentially from Genesis 1:1 but rather describe the state of the world and the beginning of the creation process, which is summarized in 1:1.[39] In verse 2, the earth is pictured as being "without form and void" (tōhû wābōhû) or rather "unfilled and unformed." In other words, it is in an unfinished state and is uninhabitable. At this stage in creation, the earth was in such a state that man could not live in it, but God did not create the earth for this purpose. The prophet Isaiah tells us: "For thus says the LORD, who created the heavens (he is God!), who formed the earth and made it (he established it; he did not create it empty, he formed it to be inhabited!)" (Isaiah 45:18). Since God's purpose in forming the earth was for it to be inhabited, it makes sense that creation took place over a short period of time, in six days. Why would God wait billions of years if His whole purpose is to have human life on the earth? It is estimated today, by naturalistic scientists, that the universe is around 13.8 billion years old, which means that man was created after 99.99997 percent of those billions of years had passed. This evolutionary timeline makes no sense considering what the Bible teaches about God's purpose in forming the earth to be inhabited or that God created man at the beginning of creation (cf. Mark 10:6).

What would later become the earth started off covered with water. In Genesis 1:2, the earth is not the earth we live on today, as that did not appear until Day Three (Genesis 1:9); rather, it is the raw material God will use to shape into our planet earth. It "is sort of like a lump of clay or a piece of stone that an artist acquires but has not yet begun to work on."[40] Verse 2 is a description about the original unfinished condition of the earth when God first created it. In Genesis 1:2 the earth is unformed and unfilled, but 1:3–31 will tell how God formed and filled up His creation described in verse 2. There is no need to place a gap anywhere in 1:1–2 as some do, unless you are trying to fit millions of years into the text.

In verse 3 God shatters the darkness mentioned in verse 2 by saying: " 'Let there be light,' and there was light." The divine speech "let there

38. A merism is a figure of speech by which a single thing is referred to by a conventional phrase, e.g., head to toe. In Genesis 1:1 heaven and earth are two opposite parts that refer to the whole created order.
39. See E.J. Young, Studies in Genesis One (Phillipsburg, NJ: P&R Publishing, 1964), 30.
40. Faulkner, The Created Cosmos, 55.

be . . ." describes creation and history coming into existence together. Then in verse 4 God separates the light from the darkness, and in verse 5 He calls the darkness "night" — both have the definite article. The only darkness that has been mentioned so far is in verse 2, which means that verse 2 is describing the state of the earth at the beginning of the first night. Verse 5 has the first night between evening and morning, as it defines the day. The initial period in Genesis 1:5 is "day one" (*yôm'ehād*),[41] as it is defined by the terms "evening" and "morning," as they make up "one day." The key point in understanding the length of the days in Genesis 1 is that they are, in fact, numbered and are used with the qualifiers "morning" and "evening" (Exodus 18:13; Numbers 7:10–84; 1 Samuel 17:16).[42] Those contextual clues help us comprehend their meaning. Even those who disagree with the young-earth creation position, such as John Walton, acknowledge this:

> I am unpersuaded by the argument that the interpretation of *yôm* in Gen 1 can refer to long periods of time. It is true that *yôm* has a variety of diverse uses, but diversity in the semantic range does not give the interpreter the freedom to choose whichever use suits his or her purposes. Our attempt must always be to identify the meaning that can be supported as the one the author intended. I consider it likely, given the kind of use manifested in Gen 1, that the author had a twenty-four-hour period in mind.[43]

Exodus 20:8–11 teaches that God made everything in six days and has a number of connections with the creation week: a six-plus-one pattern, the "heavens and the earth," "rested the seventh day," "blessed," and

---

41. Genesis 1:5 does not say "the first day" as in most English translations, but "one day," *yôm 'ehād*, which is qualified by evening and morning, which make up one day. See Andrew Steinmann, "אחד As an Ordinal Number and the Meaning of Genesis 1:5," *Journal of the Evangelical Theological Society*, 45, no. 4 (2002): 577–584, http://www.etsjets.org/files/JETS-PDFs/45/45-4/45-4-PP577-584_JETS.pdf.

42. Some argue that Day Seven is not a 24-hour day because "evening and morning" are not used on it. However, Day Seven is not a day of creation but a day of rest; it is not necessary to use the "evening and morning" formula used in Day One through Day Six since it has a rhetorical function that marks the transition from a concluding day to the following day. See Simon Turpin, "Is the Seventh Day 24-Hours Long?" October 27, 2018, https://answersingenesis.org/days-of-creation/seventh-day-24-hours-long/.

43. John Walton, "Reading Genesis 1 as Ancient Cosmology," in *Reading Genesis 1–2: An Evangelical Conversation*, ed. J. Daryl Charles (Peabody, MA: Hendrickson Publishers, 2013), 163.

"made it holy." All of this suggests that one of God's purposes in creating the heavens and the earth within six 24-hour days followed by a literal day of rest was to set up a pattern for His people to follow. The pattern of the creation week is also mentioned in Exodus 31:16–18, as Israel's observance of the Sabbath was a sign of the Mosaic covenant:

> " 'Therefore the people of Israel shall keep the Sabbath, observing the Sabbath throughout their generations, as a covenant forever. It is a sign forever between me and the people of Israel that in six days the Lord made heaven and earth, and on the seventh day he rested and was refreshed.' " And he gave to Moses, when he had finished speaking with him on Mount Sinai, the two tablets of the testimony, tablets of stone, written with the finger of God.

Not only did God speak the words of the commandments to Israel, but He also wrote them upon tablets of stone (Exodus 32:16). This is significant since it is the only part of Scripture that is said to be written directly by the hand of God (Deuteronomy 9:10). Even though the words "finger of God" are figurative language, this should not take away from the fact that something extremely unique took place when God gave these commandments to Moses. Both Exodus 20:8–11 and 31:16–18 make it clear that the events of Genesis 1:1–2:3 occurred in six 24-hour days and affirm that the creation week was a literal, historical week.

It is important to recognize that throughout Genesis 1, God calls His creation "good," *tôb* (vv. 4, 10, 12, 18, 21, 25). But what does it mean that creation was good?[44] At the end of the six days of creation, God's appreciation formula is modified in order to show that His creation is not just "good" but "very good" (*tôb mĕʾōd*, Genesis 1:31). Verse 31 states "all that he had made" instead of just individual items such as light (1:4). God's completed creation is morally very good. When good, *tôb*, is accompanied by *mĕʾōd*, it is a moral evaluation implying much more than a beautiful creation. The phrase "very good" indicates that "God created the

---

44. The Hebrew word "good," *tôb*, has a wide range of meanings: 1) merry (Esther 5:9; Proverbs 15:15); 2) pleasant, desirable (Genesis 2:9, 3:6, 49:15); 3) in order, usable (Genesis 41:35; 2 Kings 3:19, 25); 4) qualitatively good, efficient (2 Samuel 17:7; Job 10:3); 5) pleasing, beautiful (Genesis 26:7; Exodus 2:2); 6) friendly, kind (Genesis 31:24, 29; 2 Chronicles 10:7); 7) good as to character and value (Genesis 2:12; Exodus 3:8; Ecclesiastes 7:1); and 8) morally good (Hosea 8:3; Micah 6:8). See Lee Anderson, "Thoughts on the Goodness of Creation: In What Sense was Creation "Perfect"? November 13, 2013, https://answersingenesis.org/physics/thoughts-on-the-goodness-of-creation-in-what-sense-was-creation-perfect/.

world perfect"[45] with no evil in it. The goodness of God's creation reflects His moral character, as goodness belongs to Him alone (1 Chronicles 16:34; Psalm 34:8, 106:1; cf. Luke 18:19). The main contextual pointer surrounding "very good" is in Genesis 1:29–30, where it indicates that man and animals had a vegetarian diet before the Fall, which, of course, rules out carnivorous activity. Old Testament scholar Victor Hamilton, who is not a young-earth creationist, acknowledges this interpretation:

> At no point is anything (human beings, animals, birds) allowed to take the life of another living being and consume it for food. The dominion assigned to the human couple over the animal world does not include the prerogative to butcher. Instead, humankind survives on a vegetarian diet.[46]

Even after the Fall, Adam and Eve were to eat the herb of the field (Genesis 3:17–19), and it is not until after the Flood that God states, "Every moving thing that lives shall be food for you. And as I gave you the green plants, I give you everything" (Genesis 9:3). Genesis 9:3 clearly describes that a change in diet is permitted at this time. In the beginning, God gave mankind "the green plants," an obvious reference to the vegetarian diet prescribed for Adam, Eve, and the animals in Genesis 1:29–30. But now, after the Flood, God states that everything that moves shall be food for them. In other words, prior to that time, man was not permitted to eat animals, but following the Flood, God instituted a change, and man could then eat meat. In the context of Genesis 1, there is no danger implied because God's creation is morally "very good."

Although some try to argue that the eating of plants would have meant there was death before the Fall, this overlooks the fact that plants are never the subject of the Hebrew word for "life" (*hayyâ*),[47] which is a description of humans, land animals, and sea creatures (Genesis 1:20–21, 24, 30, 2:7, 6:19–20, 9:10–17). The Bible uses terms such as "wither"

45. Critical Old Testament scholar Gerhard von Rad says of the phrase "very good" that it, "expressed and written in a world full of innumerable troubles, preserves an inalienable concern of faith: no evil was laid upon the world by God's hand; neither was his omnipotence limited by any kind of opposing power whatever. When faith speaks of creation, and in doing so directs its eye toward God, then it can only say that God created the world perfect." Gerhard von Rad, *Genesis: Old Testament Library* (London: SCM Press LTD, 1961), 61.
46. Victor Hamilton, *Genesis 1–17: The New International Commentary on the Old Testament* (Grand Rapids, MI: W.B. Eerdmans, 1990), 140.
47. G. Gerleman, "Life," in *The Theological Lexicon of the Old Testament*, vol. 1, ed. E. Jenni and C. Westermann, trans. M.E. Biddle (Peabody, MA: Hendrickson Publishers, 1997), 414.

or "fade" to describe the cessation of plants (Psalm 37:2, 102:11; Isaiah 64:6). In this context, then, the fact that God declares His creation to be "very good" rules out the possibility of any kind of death and suffering before the Fall of man in Genesis 3. The Bible links the reality of death and suffering to the sin of the first man, Adam, which thereby brought corruption into God's "very good" creation (Genesis 2:17, 3:17–19; Romans 5:12, 8:19–22; 1 Corinthians 15:21–22, 26). Before Adam sinned, there was only the blessing of life in creation (Genesis 1:22, 28), but after he disobeyed God's command, man became subject to death and creation was cursed and now lives under the bondage of corruption until the day of its redemption (see Genesis 3:14–19; Romans 8:21).

God's work of creation occurred in six consecutive days, and understanding the chronological information in Genesis 5 and 11 helps determine roughly when this took place. Although some Christians want to assert gaps in the genealogies in Genesis 5 and 11, there are very good arguments against this, as the age of the patriarch is given when the next man is born. See the chart on the following page.[48]

These genealogies intend to communicate an unbroken chronology of Adam to Abraham. The formula expressed throughout these genealogies, "When A had lived x years, he fathered (*yālad*) B," indicates the year in which A "fathered" B, the year in which B became the son of A.[49] At the beginning of the genealogy in Genesis 5:3, Adam names his son Seth and toward the end in Genesis 5:28–29, Lamech names his son Noah, so there cannot be any gaps between father and son in those places. Furthermore, Noah takes his sons Shem, Ham, and Japheth onto the Ark with him (Genesis 5:32, 6:10, 7:13). A no-gap chronology is even implied by the New Testament authors, as Jude, the half-brother of Jesus, tells us, "Enoch, the seventh from Adam" (Jude 14). The genealogies in Genesis 5 and 11 give sufficient details (e.g., numerical data) in order to establish an accurate chronology (see 1 and 2 Kings; 1 and 2 Chronicles). If we combine the time covered in Genesis 5 and 11 (from the Masoretic Hebrew text) with other chronological information in the Bible, then the six days of creation would have occurred around 6,000 years ago. For example, there is roughly 2,000 years from Adam to Abraham; Abraham

---

48. For a persuasive analysis and defense of a no-gap chronology in Genesis 5–11, see Terry Mortenson, "When Was Adam Created?" chap. 5, *Searching for Adam*, (Green Forest, AR: Master Books, 2016).

49. See Jeremy Sexton, "Evangelicalism's Search for Chronological Gaps In Genesis 5 and 11: A Historical, Hermeneutical, and Lingusitic Critique," JETS 61.1 (2018): 5–25.

Adam's *toledoth* Gen. 5:1–32	Age at Begetting. Masoretic Text	Shem's *toledoth* Gen. 11:10–26	Age at Begetting. Masoretic Text
1. Adam	130	1. Shem	100
2. Seth	105	2. Arphaxad	35
3. Enosh	90	3. Salah	30
4. Kenan	70	4. Eber	34
5. Mahalalel	65	5. Paleg	30
6. Jared	162	6. Reu	32
7. Enoch	65	7. Serug	30
8. Methuselah	187	8. Nahor	29
9. Lamech	182	9. Terah (3 sons)	70
10. Noah (3 sons)	500		

lived around 2000 B.C. Then from Abraham to Jesus is roughly another 2,000 years, and from Jesus to today is just over 2,000 years. Even today, both critical and evangelical scholars who disagree with a young-earth creation position recognize that when the genealogies are taken plainly according to the text, the date for creation is around 4174 B.C. Concerning the chronological information in Genesis 5–11, the former regius professor of Hebrew at Oxford University James Barr states,

> But, putting it in broad terms, the Old Testament is clear in placing the date of creation somewhere within the period 5000–4000 B.C. The Jewish calendar still works on this basis, though with somewhat lower figures. . . . According to the biblical world view, the created world, in this year 1983, is roughly six thousand years old.[50]

Likewise, John Walton admits that at face value:

> If we add up numbers, the result is something like the scheme devised in the seventeenth century by Bishop James Ussher, who assigned creation to 4004 B.C.[51]

50. James Barr, *Beyond Fundamentalism* (Philadelphia, PA: Westminster, 1984), 131; cf. 137.
51. Walton, *Genesis*, 48–49.

The chronological history in Genesis 5 and 11 rules out any interpretation that tries to accommodate the current evolutionary framework of cosmology, geology, and anthropology with the Scripture.

Interestingly, using the chronological information in Genesis to combat false teaching is not original to this generation. The conflict over the age of the earth is not new but has always been a debate between pagans and Christians (until, that is, Christians in the early 19th century started to believe what non-Christian geologists said about the age of the creation rather than believing God's Word). Toward the end of the second century, Theophilus, Bishop of Antioch (died A.D. 185), wrote to Autolycus, "an idolater and scorner of Christians,"[52] contrasting the gods of the Greco-Roman world with the God of Christianity. Theophilus accepted the fact that God created in six 24-hour days and that Adam was created from the dust of the ground on Day Six, but he specifically focuses in on the genealogies. In particular, he argued: "All the years from the creation of the world [to Theophilus's day] amount to a total of 5,698 years."[53] Interestingly, Theophilus goes on to write about the chronology of the world set forth by the philosophers Apollonius (Egyptian) and Plato (Greek):

> For some, maintaining that the world was uncreated, went into infinity; and others, asserting that it was created, said that already 153,075 years had passed. . . . For if even a chronological error has been committed by us, of, e.g., 50 or 100, or even 200 years, yet not of thousands and tens of thousands, as Plato and Apollonius and other mendacious authors have hitherto written.[54]

Theophilus rejected the long ages for the world that the Egyptians and the Greeks proposed, clearly regarding the genealogies in Genesis as accurate and authoritative when it came to the age of the world. Unlike other church fathers who allegorized the creation account (e.g., Origen, A.D. 184–253) because they were influenced by the Greek neo-Platonic philosophy of the day, Theophilus stood firm on the authority of Scripture

---

52. Theophilus, 1:1 - Theophilus of Antioch. A.D. 180–185. *Theophilus To Autolycus Book I*. Retrieved from http://www.earlychristianwritings.com/text/theophilus-book1.html.
53. Theophilus was using the chronology of the Greek translation of the Old Testament; the Septuagint (LXX).
54. Theophilus, 3:16, 28, 29 — Theophilus of Antioch. A.D. 180–185. *Theophilus to Autolycus Book III*. Retrieved from http://www.earlychristianwritings.com/text/theophilus-book3.html.

and defended Genesis as an accurate account of history. Theophilus was not the only theologian to take a stand on the biblical account of creation against the attacks of the day. The French theologian, pastor, and Reformer John Calvin (1509–1564) rejected the idea that the six days of creation were a metaphor — a view held in his own day.[55] In his *Institutes of the Christian Religion*, Calvin affirmed that it took six days to create the world over and against the prevailing view of his day, held by many in the Roman Catholic Church, that the world was made in one moment:

> With the same view Moses relates that the work of creation was accomplished not in one moment, but in six days. By this statement we are drawn away from fiction to the one God who thus divided his works into six days, that we may have no reluctance to devote our whole lives to the contemplation of it.[56]

Calvin also believed that the world had not yet ". . . completed its six thousandth year."[57] What is interesting is that Calvin knew his stance on the days of creation and the age of the earth would bring scoffing; in his own day, he also had to deal with a form of atheism associated with the teaching of Epicurus (341–270 B.C.) that believed the world came about by chance:[58]

> Nor will they abstain from their jeers when told that little more than five thousand years have elapsed since the creation of the world. . . . In short, nothing can be stated that they will not assail with derision. . . . Must the creation of the world be passed over in silence? No! The truth of God is too powerful, both here and everywhere to dread the slanders of the ungodly. . . .[59]

Calvin recognized that the same people who scoff at the biblical age of the earth would also scoff at other biblical teaching, but he knew the power of God's Word was too powerful to fear the scoffing of ungodly men. Theophilus and Calvin are examples for us today, as they stood

55. John Calvin, *Genesis*. Repr. (Edinburgh, UK: Banner of Truth, 1984), 78.
56. John Calvin, *Institutes of the Christian Religion* 2nd ed (Peabody, MA: Hendrickson Publications, 2009), 91.
57. Ibid., 90.
58. See "What Did the Reformers Believe about the Age of the Earth?" by Dr. Joel R. Beeke on October 2, 2017, https://answersingenesis.org/age-of-the-earth/what-did-reformers-believe-about-age-earth/.
59. Calvin, *Institutes of the Christian Religion*, 609.

firmly on the authority of Scripture and combatted the false worldviews of their own day with the biblical view of the creation of the world.

The Earth Formed By and Through Water

In the second part of verse 5 in 2 Peter 3, Peter then writes that "the earth was formed out of water and through water." The Greek philosopher Thales of Miletus (640–546 B.C.), who embraced evolutionary ideas, argued that "of the four elements water is the basic one and everything is therefore made out of water. . . ."[60] Peter, of course, is following the biblical account of creation, which is confirmed elsewhere in Scripture: "The earth is the LORD's and the fullness thereof, the world and those who dwell therein, for he has founded it upon the seas and established it upon the rivers" (Psalm 24:1–2). As with many Christian pastors and teachers today, it escaped the scoffers' notice that God created the world out of water and through water. The reference that the earth was formed out of water and by water is an indication that Peter clearly understood Genesis as straightforward, historical narrative according to the plain sense of the text.

The first mention of water in the Genesis account is on Day One when "darkness was over the face of the deep" (1:2). The presence of darkness should not lead us to think there was anything imperfect or evil with creation, as it is God who creates the darkness (Isaiah 45:7). It just reflects the fact that no light existed yet upon the earth. The deep (*tehôm*)[61] here is simply a reference to the deep waters of the world's ocean (Genesis 7:11, 8:2; Psalm 106:9). The Greek translation of the Old Testament (LXX) translates the word "deep" as ἄβυσσος (*abyssos*), from where we get the word *abyss*. The next mention of water is also in 1:2 when the "Spirit of God was hovering over the face of the waters." The Spirit of God is co-participating in creation as He hovers over the waters (*māyim*), preparing the way for the creative word of God and the transformation of the earth, readying it for habitation (Psalm 104:30).[62]

On Day Two of creation God said: "Let there be an expanse in the midst of the waters, and let it separate the waters from the waters" (Genesis 1:6). The word for "expanse" or, as some translations say, "firmament"

---

60. Davids, 2 Peter and Jude, 268.
61. Any notion of trying to identify the Hebrew word for "deep," *tehôm*, with the Babylonian god Tiamat is very doubtful. See Currid, *Genesis 1:1–25:18*, 60–61.
62. The Hebrew word *rûah* can mean either "wind" or "spirit." In the context of Genesis 1, however, *rûah* is modified by *'ĕlōhîm*, which, in the rest of the chapter, always means God.

is *rāqîaʿ*. It does not refer to a "hard dome" or "vault" that goes across the sky, as many theistic evolutionists would believe. Genesis 1 does not depict the sky as a vault resting on foundations. This view is based on taking an ANE worldview and imposing it on the Bible and interpreting phrases like "pillars of the earth" (Psalm 75:3) in woodenly literal manner. Rather, it is probably best to see the "expanse" (*rāqîaʿ*) as referring to outer space or sky, as not only does God equate the expanse with heaven (Genesis 1:8), but on Day Four the sun, moon, and stars are placed in the expanse (see Genesis 1:14–22; cf. Psalm 19:1, 4).[63] On Day Five the "expanse of the heavens" is where the birds fly and the clouds float (Genesis 1:20). Because the earth starts off covered with water, God then separates "the waters that were under the expanse from the waters that were above the expanse" (Genesis 1:7). The expanse separates the waters above, vertically, from the waters below. The waters that are under the expanse are clearly a reference to oceans, seas, and rivers on the earth, but what does the water above the expanse refer to? If the expanse refers to space, then there are some interesting conclusions, as astronomer Dr. Danny Faulkner has pointed out:

> The Bible implies that the boundary of the universe is accompanied by water. Unlike what the canopy model proposes, the waters above the *rāqîaʿ* did not condense at the time of the Flood, and so still ought to be beyond the *rāqîaʿ*. This is borne out by Psalm 148:4, which speaks of waters above the heavens still being there. We do not know who wrote Psalm 148 or when he wrote it, but it almost certainly was long after the Flood. That is to say, in the post-Flood world, the universe is still surrounded by water.[64]

Since the word for water (*māyim*) is used only for liquid water in the Old Testament, then the water above the expanse must have been liquid water. Although some may struggle with the concept of liquid water remaining in that state in space, Faulkner notes that "we know nothing of the physical conditions at the edge of the universe. Indeed, the edge of the universe is a difficult concept to grasp physically."[65]

---

63. See Faulkner, *The Created Cosmos*, 40–49.
64. Ibid., 52.
65. Ibid., 53.

At the beginning of Day Three, the earth is still unformed and unfilled until God says, "Let the waters under the heavens be gathered together into one place, and let the dry land appear" (v. 9). When the waters were gathered together from the rest of the waters, it resulted in the formation of dry land, echoing Peter's words "the earth was formed out of water and through water." Is there any evidence for earth's formation out of water? Well, the earth's earliest rocks in the crystalline basement of every continent that date back to the time of creation all contain minerals that have water molecules in their crystal lattices. This required the presence of water when those minerals and the rocks containing them formed.[66] The focus of verse 9 is on the waters below, which "were gathered together into one place." This seems to suggest that there was a single ocean to begin with. If this is so, then similarly, the dry land which God called earth may also have been in one place, suggesting that there was one land mass or supercontinent to begin with. Then God calls "the dry land Earth, and the waters that were gathered together he called Seas. And God saw that it was good" (1:10). The phrase "God saw that it was good" is absent on Day Two. The reason for this may be that the creation of the expanse was an initial stage to the appearance of the dry land and so the phrase was kept until its completion on Day Three. As we will see, one of the reasons the Apostle Peter refers to the world being created by water is to prepare for the parallel he makes in verse 6 where the world was judged by water (see chapter 8).

Peter's understanding of Genesis is also important to for us today, as he is clearly following the order of creation, which makes it clear that the world was covered with water on Days One and Two, which God then forms into dry land on Day Three. However, the order of the big bang cosmology and subsequent evolutionary development of our solar system completely contradicts the biblical account. In big bang cosmology and the nebular hypothesis of the formation of our planetary system, the earth starts out as a molten blob. The big bang cosmology also has the stars and sun before the earth, but in the biblical cosmology, the physical earth appears on Day Three and the sun, moon, and stars are made on Day Four. Some Christians object to interpreting the days of Genesis 1 as 24-hour days since the sun is not created until Day Four.

This is not a problem with the text but is based on the presupposition that the sun is necessary to have a day marked by evening and morning.

66. This was confirmed in personal correspondence with geologist Dr. Andrew Snelling.

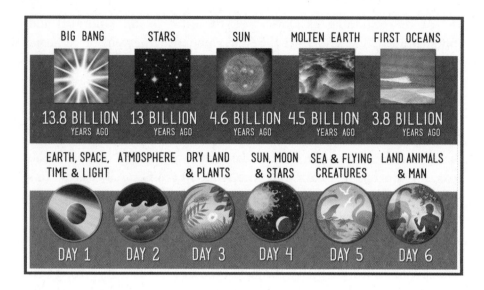

To have an evening and morning on the first three days, all that is needed is a light source, which God created on Day One (Genesis 1:3), and a rotating earth. The light God created was natural and physical. Although the source of light is not specifically mentioned, some suggest that it is the Creator Himself, as He is described as covering Himself in light as a garment, and as part of Israel's future redemption, they were told that God would be their "everlasting light" (Psalm 104:2; Isaiah 60:19; cf. John 1:1–5; 2 Corinthians 4:4–6). The temporary light (*ȏr*) source on Day One was replaced on Day Four by the lights (*mā'ȏr*) that God placed in the expanse of the heavens: the sun, moon, and stars (Genesis 1:14–19). Nevertheless, Days One–Three should not be called "solar days," as the word "solar" means "related to the sun." But as has already been shown, they were 24-hour days. Genesis is clear that the sun was created (not appeared)[67] on Day Four. God is not dependent upon the sun to produce the phenomenon of light (cf. Acts 9:3).

Earth Was Formed by God's Word

Peter not only tells us that the world was "formed" by and through water but that it was "formed" by God's Word (*logos*). The Greek word for "formed" here is the perfect participle *synestōsa* that comes from

---

67. A word for "appear" (*rā'â*) is used in Genesis 1:9 of the dry land, but it is not used on Day Four. Rather, the word "made" (*'āśâ*) is used, which, throughout Genesis 1, is used interchangeably with "create" (*bārā'* in Genesis 1:26–27).

synistēmi, which means "to come to be in a condition of coherence, continue, endure, exist, hold together."[68] Peter is telling us that the earth took its form or shape by God's Word. This is parallel to Paul's comments in Colossians 1:17 that all things "hold together" (*synestēken*) in Christ. The reason Jesus can "hold together" all things is because "in Him dwells all the fullness of the Godhead bodily" (Colossians 2:9; NKJV). The Greek word for "Godhead," *theotēs*, refers to "the state of being God."[69] The writer of Hebrews also echoes Paul's words referring to Christ: ". . . he upholds the universe by the word of his power" (Hebrews 1:3). These words anticipate Peter's own claim: "But by the same word the heavens and earth that now exist are stored up for fire. . ." (2 Peter 3:7). The reason things in our present world stay the same (laws of gravity, nature, logic, etc.) is because God upholds all things together by the power of His Word. God's Word is the most powerful thing in all creation, and without its sustaining power, things would fall apart. While the heavens declare the glory of God and speak of His existence (Psalm 19:1), it is the Word of God that converts the soul (Psalm 19:7). The Word of God is powerful not only to convert but to convict, to conform, to console, and to correct (2 Timothy 3:16; Titus 1:9). It is even more powerful than any other object we could hold in our hands (Hebrews 4:12). It is so powerful that it brings forth people physically from the dead and produces faith in the life of a spiritually dead sinner (John 11:43; Romans 10:17).

It is the power of God's Word that brings creation into existence. Genesis 1:3–30 clearly tells us that the divine command brought creation into existence, as it repeatedly states, "and God said" and then notes the event that happened immediately within the confines of the context of a 24-hour day:

Narration	"God said..." (1:3, 6, 9, 11, 14, 20, 24, 26)
Commandment	"let there be..." (1:3, 6, 9, 11, 14, 20, 24, 26)
Fulfillment	"there was" (1:3, 7, 9, 11, 15, 24, 30)
Evaluation	"God saw that it was good" (1:4, 10, 12, 18, 21, 25, 31)
Conclusion	"there was evening and morning" (1:5, 8, 13, 19, 23, 31)

68. BDAG: *A Greek-English Lexicon of the New Testament*, 973.
69. Thayer, *Thayer's Greek-English Lexicon of the New Testament*, 288.

God's creative act also shows the length He took to create. In the context of Genesis 1, the divine command "Let there be" is a jussive form of the verb, which is followed by "and it was so," which reveals rapid fulfilment of that command with no process. The theme of God creating through His Word is picked up by the Psalmist:

> By the word of the LORD the heavens were made, and by the breath of his mouth all their host. . . . For he spoke, and it came to be; he commanded, and it stood firm (Psalm 33:6, 9).

The New Testament further attests to this by God the Father, who spoke through His Son, the Word, to create the world (e.g., John 1:1–3; Colossians 1:16; Hebrews 1:2). When the eternal Son of God took on flesh (John 1:14) as Jesus, His first recorded miracle revealed His glory as the Creator, turning water into wine (John 2:1–11). We see the instant nature of His miracles very clearly in His encounter with the Roman centurion in Matthew 8:5–13 where the centurion's servant was healed the very moment Jesus commanded it. In fact, His miracles were ordinarily instantaneous (e.g., Mark 10:52; Luke 18:42–43). Hebrews 11:3 also affirms that the world was made by "the word of God." The author of Hebrews has in mind the divine command, "Let there be light" (Genesis 1:3), interpreting it in the fashion of Psalm 33:6, 9. So when Jesus, the Word, spoke the divine command, "Let there be light" (Genesis 1:3), we have very good reasons to conclude that it did not take millions of years for it to come into existence. Since God is the Creator of time, He does not need time to create. In fact, God has expressly told us why He took so long to create (see Exodus 20:11, 31:17). When God created the world there was no struggle — it was effortless. He simply spoke things into existence by the power of His Word (Psalm 148:1–6). Not only was creation an expression of His speech, but it originated by His will. He did it freely without being compelled (Revelation 4:11). Creation shows God's sovereignty over all things. As Creator, all things are under His rule because He is the one who made all things (Psalm 24:1–2).

Peter's claim that "the earth was formed out of water and through water by the word of God" was necessary to counter the arguments of the scoffers. Those details, Peter argued, were not forgotten by the scoffers, but rather they had "escaped their notice" of how God had acted in history.

CHAPTER SEVEN

DELIBERATELY OVERLOOKING THE FLOOD

2 Peter 3:6

. . . and that by means of these the world that then existed was deluged with water and perished (2 Peter 3:6).

The words "millions of years ago" have become the mantra of the evolutionary worldview, and as a consequence of their promotion through various mediums (media, museums, science textbooks, etc.), they are now deeply imbedded in the minds of people in modern culture. Because of this, many people take as an established scientific fact the idea that the earth is millions of years old rather than realising this to be part of a worldview that is based upon naturalistic assumptions. This assumption of uniformitarian naturalism that "all things are continuing as they were from the beginning of creation" (2 Peter 3:4) is the reason that the evidence for the global Flood "escapes the notice" of the scoffers (2 Peter 3:5).

The second event of biblical history that "escapes the notice" of the scoffers is the global Flood with which God judged the entire world in the days of Noah. In recent history, as we have already seen (chapter 5), it was the rise of uniformitarian science in the 1800s that caused a re-evaluation of how the early chapters of Genesis were interpreted. The geological data that supposedly demonstrated the history of the earth to be millions of years old was simply too convincing to maintain a belief in the global Flood mentioned in Genesis 6–9. But this does not just escape the notice of the scoffers, as, sadly, many Christians have embraced (maybe unwittingly) the scoffer's assumptions (all things are continuing as they were from the beginning of creation) and reject the biblical testimony of a global Flood. Christian apologist Dr. William Lane Craig made some interesting comments on this issue in an episode of his *Defenders Podcast* that aired in September 2019. He stated:

> Take for example the attempt to explain away the Earth's sedimentation on the basis of so-called flood geology — Noah's Flood. The idea that there was ever a worldwide flood that destroyed all terrestrial life on Earth and laid down the Earth's sediments is a fantasy. . . . Truly Young Earth Creationists live in a different universe than most of us do. This is crank science and Christians should not be attracted to it.[1]

Truly creationists do live in a different universe; it is the universe where the revelation of God reigns supreme when it comes to the issue of origins. In this universe, the revelation of God will always be folly to those with an unbelieving worldview (1 Corinthians 2:14, 3:19). For Dr. Craig, it seems the reason we should abandon young earth creation (or biblical creation!) is that, as Christians, we do not want to be seen as anti-intellectual.[2] Yet who is it that assumes Christianity to be anti-intellectual? The answer is the secular academy! What Christians face today is a choice between earning the respect of the secular, unbelieving world by accepting evolution, or being faithful to Scripture. The belief in a global Flood that laid down the vast majority of earth's sedimentary rock layers does not mean we have to abandon modern science; rather, what it means is that we reject an interpretation of the scientific data based upon the ideological presuppositions of uniformitarian naturalism. Because Dr. Craig has accepted the ideological presuppositions of the evolutionary worldview, it is no wonder that he dismisses Flood geology as "fantasy"

---

1. See Dr. William Lane Craig, "Excursus on Creation of Life and Biological Diversity (Part 27): Scientific Evidence Pertinent to the Origin and Evolution of Biological Complexity," September 4, 2019, https://www.reasonablefaith.org/podcasts/defenders-podcast-series-3/excursus-on-creation-of-life-and-biological-diversity/excursus-on-creation-of-life-and-biological-diversity-part-27.
2. This does not mean Christians should be anti-intellectual, as we should love God with all our minds, but we should not embrace the wisdom of the world.

and scoffs at young earth creationists. How then would Dr. Craig have people view the Flood? In the same podcast, he went on to say:

> I'm not assuming that the Bible is wrong. On the contrary, I said that the two most plausible interpretations of these passages is either the literal Young Earth view or the mytho-historical view. What I would say is that in light of modern science, history, and linguistics, the literalistic interpretation is falsified. So one isn't assuming that it's false. Rather, it's saying that in light of the evidence that we have it has been falsified. There was no worldwide flood a few thousand years ago that destroyed all terrestrial life. And you can't squeeze plate tectonics and mountain building into a few hundred years between the Flood and the call of Abraham.[3]

Again, when Dr. Craig argues that "modern science" falsifies the "Young Earth view," it is important to understand what he means. It is his belief in the big bang and uniformitarian geology (historical science, not observational science) that rules out believing in Genesis as historical truth. Dr. Craig rightly realizes that ". . . the language of Genesis 6–9 just doesn't seem to be consistent with a local flood,"[4] but at the same time, he also believes ". . . it's very plausible that there is some kind of local flood that lies at the historical root of the story."[5] Dr. Craig believes the Flood account is ". . . not simply a straightforward literalistic historical account, but it's a mytho-historical account."[6] The mytho-historical interpretation (see chapter 3) means that the events in Genesis 1–11, like the Flood, happened but that they have been portrayed in the language of myth and symbol (so they are not intended to be read "literally"). By stereotyping the biblical creation (young earth) position as "literalistic," Dr. Craig tries to show how it is wrong while advancing his own interpretation as the correct one. Biblical creationists do not interpret Genesis 1 in a "literalistic" fashion; rather, using the historical-grammatical approach, they take the text plainly according to its literary genre (historical narrative). Dr. Craig's understanding that Genesis is mytho-historical also overlooks how Jesus (and Peter) understood and treated the Flood account:

3. Craig, "Excursus on Creation of Life and Biological Diversity (Part 27)."
4. Ibid.
5. Ibid.
6. Ibid.

Just as it was in the days of Noah, so will it be in the days of the Son of Man. They were eating and drinking and marrying and being given in marriage, until the day when Noah entered the ark, and the flood came and destroyed them all (Luke 17:26–27).

Jesus does not just refer to the individuals as historical but cites parts of the narrative (such as eating, drinking, marrying, and entering the Ark) as real historical events. The Flood is not just a story with a theological point, as Jesus uses it as analogy with the judgment at the end of the age, which will also be a global historical event. Christians like Dr. Craig who embrace an evolutionary view of the history of the world are only helping to "scoff" at the biblical testimony of God's worldwide judgment through a global Flood. The belief that the Flood of Noah's day is couched in "mytho-historical" language has nothing to do with what the biblical text teaches, but is a consequence of accepting the idea that the earth is millions of years old. Those who believe in an old earth are naturally forced to believe in a local flood since the idea of the great age of the earth came from the belief that the fossil record was laid down over millions of years. Either the fossil record is the evidence of millions of years, or it is largely the evidence of Noah's Flood. It cannot be both; it is not logical to believe both in millions of years and a global Flood.

As the Apostle Peter continues his argument against the scoffers, he tells us that it was by the means of the waters and the Word (2 Peter 3:5) that the world at that time perished. The same way God created the world, through water and the Word, is the same way it perished in the days of Noah, and it is by "the same word" (2 Peter 3:7) that He will judge it in the future. How should we understand Peter's reference to the word "world"? Some think the reference to "the world that then existed" is simply referring to the world of men; it was the ungodly humans in Noah's day (living in a limited geographical region) that perished and not the entire planet.[7] In the previous chapter, Peter also spoke of the Flood:

. . . if he did not spare the ancient world, but preserved Noah, a herald of righteousness, with seven others, when he brought a flood upon the world of the ungodly. . . (2 Peter 2:5).

---

7. See Hugh Ross, *The Genesis Question* (Colorado Springs, CO: NavPress, 1998), 143; Green, *2 Peter and Jude*, 14.

Peter speaks here of the Flood as an example of God's not sparing "the ancient world" (*archaiou kosmou*) but bringing judgment upon the "world of the ungodly" (*kosmō asebōn*). His focus is not only upon the ungodly people but upon the entire world, as the Flood functions as the preview of the final judgment of the world that is still to come (2 Peter 2:4, 9). Peter also speaks of the Ark as a vessel of salvation, and only eight people survived the Flood, which means that the Flood could not have been local (1 Peter 3:20; 2 Peter 2:5).

In the present verse (2 Peter 3:6), Peter calls it "the world that then existed" (*ho tote kosmos*). It was the world that existed in Noah's day that was deluged with water that perished. The word Peter uses here for "world" is the Greek word κόσμος (*kosmos*), and although it can refer to the inhabited world, a better choice of word for a limited geographical region would have been γῆς (*ges* — land, earth, and ground). In context, the word *kosmos* refers to a judgment that affects more than just people in a limited region. It is a reference to the world as the sum total of the planet. The world that then existed "perished" by the Flood waters, and they returned the world back to its watery beginning as they undid the work in Genesis 1:6–10 by which the world was formed. Peter previously warned of the destruction of the scoffers (2 Peter 2:3) and will warn of the coming destruction of the ungodly (2 Peter 3:7). The judgment at the time of the Flood, while directed at human sin, would have certainly affected the entire physical world.[8] This is clear from the water mentioned in Genesis 7:11 that is used in the destruction of the world: the fountains of the great deep and the windows of heaven. The Flood not only destroyed human life that inhabited the world at that time, but it also destroyed and reshaped the entire physical world (Genesis 6:13). The word Peter uses for "flood" also sheds light on the nature of the Flood. It comes from the Greek word *kataklyzō*, from which we derive our English word *cataclysm* — a clear reference to a global catastrophe (cf. Luke 17:26). If Peter had believed that the Flood in Genesis 6–9 was local, covering only the region of Mesopotamia, then why did he not use the Greek word for an ordinary local flood, *plemmura* (Luke 6:48)? Because, like Jesus, he believed the Flood was a global catastrophe and not a local one.

Peter argues that the scoffers are wrong in what they say because God did judge the world in the past through a global Flood, but if God never

---

8. See Moo, *2 Peter, Jude*, 178.

did destroy the world through a global Flood (i.e., if it never happened or was just local), then Peter's argument that God will once again judge the whole world falls apart. Apart from Scripture, the greatest evidence that God will judge the whole world in the future is the past judgment of the whole world by the Flood that can be seen in the fossil record. But if we deny that the fossil record is the result of the global Flood, then really it is a denial that God has judged the wickedness of the whole world, which only leads to people doubting that He will do it again. Since our authority as Christians is Scripture, then it is necessary to look to it to see what it says about the extent and nature of the Flood.

The Flood: A Local or Global Event?

The rise of uniformitarian geology rather than careful exegesis of Scripture has clearly affected how scholars interpret the Flood account in Genesis. This can be seen from the many commentaries on Genesis that are available to pastors, theological students, and lay people that reject the Flood described in Genesis as a global catastrophe by appealing to conclusions of modern geology.[9] Because of this, many scholars argue that the Flood was only a local event taking place in Mesopotamia. These scholars also object that the plain reading of text of Genesis 6–9 leads to the description of a global catastrophic Flood and offer several objections to it:

1. The Hebrew word for "world" (*'eres*) can also refer to a particular piece of land, not just the whole world.
2. The word "all" (*kōl*) can be used in a non-universal sense.
3. The Hebrew word for "covered" (*kāsâ*) does not mean that the mountains were literally submerged in water.
4. The language used in the Flood narrative is that of appearance or only hyperbolic.

Does the grammar and context of Genesis 6–9 allow for a local flood as certain scholars have suggested? No, not at all. The only way to view the Flood as local is by isolating words from their context and assuming that uniformitarian geology is a proven fact. All the above words need

<hr/>

9. Several of these scholars are: Derek Kinder, *Genesis: An Introduction and Commentary* (Tyndale Old Testament Commentaries, 1967), 93–94; Gordon Wenham, *Exploring the Old Testament: The Pentateuch,* Volume 1 (Great Britain: SPCK, 2003), 30; John Walton, *Genesis The NIV Application Commentary* (Grand Rapids, MI: Zondervan, 2001), 321–329.

to be understood in the overall context of the Flood narrative and the surrounding context of creation and the Tower of Babel event. The introduction to the Flood begins in Genesis 6:5–7, which gives an account of the increasing wickedness of man in the earth that leads up to the reason for the Flood:

> The LORD saw that the wickedness of man was great in the *earth*, and that every intention of the thoughts of his heart was only evil continually. And the LORD regretted that he had made man on the *earth*, and it grieved him to his heart. So the LORD said, "I will blot out man whom I have created from the face of the *land*, man and animals and creeping things and birds of the heavens, for I am sorry that I have made them" (emphasis mine).

Notice the text explains that the wickedness of man had become great on the earth (*'eres*) and that the LORD regretted that He had made man on the earth (*'eres*). It is important to recognize that when we interpret any word, we do not commit the hermeneutical fallacy of the unwarranted adoption of an expanded semantic field. This occurs when one takes a word that can have more than one meaning in a particular context and places it into another context where it cannot have the same meaning. As was pointed out in the last chapter, the Hebrew word *'eres* has more than one meaning and can refer to: 1) the whole earth, 2) land, 3) ground, or 4) people of the land.[10] The context must determine the meaning on each occasion where *'eres* is used. In the account of the Flood in Genesis 6:5–9:17, the word *'eres* (earth, land) is used 47 times[11] while the word *'ădāmâ* is only used 9 times[12] and is usually translated as "land" or "ground" (not "the inhabited world"). Because of the wickedness of man, the LORD said He would blot out man from the face of the land (*'ădāmâ*, the visible surface of the whole earth). The wickedness of man on the earth was the reason for the Flood. The purpose of the Flood was not simply to "blot out" (wipe away; cf. Psalm 51:1) sinful man but to

---

10. F. Brown, S. Driver, and C. Briggs (BDB), *The Brown-Driver-Briggs Hebrew and English Lexicon* (Peabody, MA: Hendrickson Publishers, 2006), 75–76.

11. Genesis 6:5, 6:6, 6:11 x2, 6:12 x2, 6:13 x2, 6:17 x2, 7:3, 7:4, 7:6, 7:10, 7:12, 7:14, 7:17 x2, 7:18, 7:19, 7:21 x2, 7:23, 7:24, 8:1, 8:3, 8:7, 8:9, 8:11, 8:13, 8:14, 8:17x3, 8:19, 8:22, 9:1, 9:2, 9:7, 9:10 x2, 9:11, 9:13, 9:14, 9:16, 9:17.

12. Genesis 6:7, 6:20, 7:4, 7:8, 7:23, 8:8, 8:13, 8:21, 9:2.

destroy the earth and the animals (Genesis 6:13, 17), and only a global catastrophic Flood could do that.[13]

Genesis 6:11–13, 17 then brings us into the context of the Flood where God reveals to Noah His purpose for destroying the earth:

> Now the *earth* was corrupt in *God's sight*, and the earth was *filled* with *violence*. And *God saw* the earth, and behold, it was corrupt, for all flesh had corrupted their way on the earth. And God said to Noah, "I have determined to make an end of all flesh, for the earth is filled with violence through them. Behold, I will destroy them with the earth. . . . For behold, I will bring *a flood* of waters upon the earth to destroy all flesh in which is the breath of life under heaven. Everything that is on the earth shall die (emphasis mine).

These verses also help clarify the meaning of the word *'eres*, as they refer to the earth God created in Genesis 1. Genesis 6:11 tells us that the "earth" (*'eres*) was corrupt in God's sight and filled with violence. The earth that was "filled" with violence is the same earth that God commanded humanity (Adam and Eve) to "fill" up in Genesis 1:28 (Be fruitful and multiply and fill the earth); this can only be a reference to the whole earth and not just to the region of Mesopotamia. When we think of the geography at the time of the Flood, we should not make the mistake of looking at today's world and reading its geography back into the text of Genesis 6. Genesis 1 indicates that the world which God originally created was a single continent (Genesis 1:9–13). Today's continents are the result of the catastrophic plate tectonics that occurred at the beginning of the Flood when the earth's crust split apart along lines traversing the globe.[14] After the Flood, just as God commanded Adam and Eve to be fruitful and multiply and to fill the earth, He also gives

---

13. The destruction of the entire world at the time of the Flood often raises the question of how many people perished at the time of the Flood. There are at least two different suggestions as to how many people died during the Flood. Some, based on modern population growth, suggest numbers from as low as 235 million to as high as 3 billion people. See Henry Morris, *Biblical Cosmology and Modern Science* (Grand Rapids, MI: Baker Book House, 1970), 77–78. Others, based on an argument of the wicked nature of mankind, believe the pre-Flood population was probably just a few hundred thousand people. See Ken Ham and Bodie Hodge, "How Many People Died in the Flood?" in *A Flood of Evidence: 40 Reasons Noah and the Ark Still Matter* (Green Forest, AR: Master Books, 2016), 283–291.
14. See Dr. John Baumgardner's website, https://www.globalflood.org/.

Noah this same command (Genesis 9:1). Again, the command given to Noah "to fill the earth" is quite clearly a reference to the whole earth and not just a specific place in Mesopotamia. This can be seen from the disobedience of the people who migrated east to the land of Shinar in resisting God's command to "increase" and "fill the earth" by staying in one place at the Tower of Babel, which is why the Lord had to disperse them over the face of all the earth (Genesis 11:8). In a similar fashion, Genesis 6:12 also helps us understand the extent of the Flood as it recalls Genesis 6:5: "The LORD saw that the wickedness of man was great in the earth [*'eres*]." This echoes Genesis 1:31, which states, "God saw all that He had made and behold it was very good." The "very good" earth (*'eres*) that God created has now become "wicked," and this wickedness is all-inclusive (all people) except for Noah. Genesis 6:11–12 therefore sets up the context of the Flood, which was in God's sight (literally before God), "that is, before the eyes of God, which rove over the whole earth (compare Genesis 10:9)."[15] This is not Noah's perspective, but God's, as it is He who sees that the whole earth is corrupt. This refutes the idea that the Flood only appeared to cover the then-known land mass (the limited perspective of the biblical author). While the purpose of the Ark was to keep offspring alive on the face of the earth, it also reveals God's grace in preserving humanity. If the Flood was only local, limited only to the area of Mesopotamia, then it seems a strange thing for God to ask Noah to build such a large vessel when He could have simply asked Noah to move out of the area of Mesopotamia.

As the Flood narrative moves on to Genesis 7:19–23, it is here again that the text clearly spells out the extent of the Flood:

> And the waters prevailed so mightily on the earth that *all* the high mountains under the *whole* heaven were covered. The waters prevailed above the mountains, covering them fifteen cubits deep. And *all* flesh died that moved on the earth, birds, livestock, beasts, *all* swarming creatures that swarm on the earth, and *all* mankind. *Everything* on the dry land in whose nostrils was the breath of life died. He blotted out *every* living thing that was on the face of the ground, man and animals and creeping things and birds of the heavens. They were blotted out from the

---

15. Umberto Cassuto, *Commentary on Genesis II From Noah to Abraham Genesis VI 9 – XI32* (Jerusalem: The Magness Press, The Hebrew University, 1964), 51.

earth. Only Noah was left, and those who were with him in the ark (emphasis mine).

In Genesis 6–9, the Hebrew word *kōl* ("all") is used 72 times. It is correct to say that the word "all" is limited in some biblical passages (cf. Matthew 3:5), but its use in Genesis 6–9 is clearly all-encompassing. The fact that "all flesh" (*kol-bāśār*) died includes all animals and people that lived on the earth (Genesis 6:12, 13, 17, 19, 7:15, 16, 21, 8:17, 9:11, 15, 16, 17). The specific use of the word *kōl* (all/every) in Genesis 7:19–23 clearly indicates that the Flood was global. The ". . . inclusive language 'all/every' occurs eight times (in Hebrew) in vv. 19-23, leaving no doubt about the all-encompassing nature of the destructive flood and the death left behind."[16] The aspect of totality is seen in the use of "all/every" in the narrative of the Flood throughout Genesis 6–9:

- *Every* imagination of the human race was evil (Genesis 6:5).
- *All* flesh had corrupted their way (Genesis 6:13, 17).
- *Everything* on the earth shall die (Genesis 6:17).
- Noah had to save two of *every* kind of animal (Genesis 6:19).
- *Everything* perishes (Genesis 7:21–23 — 6 occurrences).
- After the Flood, *every* kind of creature comes out of the Ark (Genesis 8:17, 19).
- God promises never again to destroy *every* living creature (Genesis 8:21).
- *Every* living animal is given to the human race for food (Genesis 9:3).
- The concluding account of the covenant (Genesis 9:8–17) contains 12 occurrences of *kōl*.[17]

The use of the word *all/every* in Genesis 6–9 is conclusive in showing that the Flood was global in its extent. No area of the globe was left untouched by the Flood waters.

Genesis 7:19–20 offers further evidence to confirm the global extent of the Flood: ". . . all the high mountains under the whole heaven were covered. The waters prevailed above the mountains, covering them fifteen cubits deep." The literal use of the word "covered" (*kāsâ*) means "render

---

16. Mathews, Genesis 1:1–11:26, 380.
17. See Helmer Ringgren, *Theological Dictionary of the Old Testament* Vol. VII (Grand Rapids, MI: W.B Eerdmans, 1995), 138.

invisible," especially when used in the context of water (Exodus 14:28, 15:5, 10; Psalm 78:53, 106:11).[18] The verb *gābar*, which is translated "prevailed" or "rose," is qualified in verse 18 with the adverb "greatly," which is followed in verse 19 by two occurrences of "very greatly" (more and more, *mĕōd' mĕōd*, see NASB). The numerical use of the words waters (x5), increased (x2), rose (x3), and greatly (x3) in 7:17–20 underscores the sense of the escalating waters.[19] If the Flood were local, then how could the waters rise to 15 cubits (8 meters) above the mountains while leaving the rest of the world untouched? Water seeks its own level; therefore, it is impossible that the water of the Flood would only cover local mountains. It was literally all the high mountains everywhere under heaven that were covered 15 cubits deep with water. This was recognized by scholars before the influence of uniformitarian geology. In his day, the medieval Jewish Scholar Ibn Ezra (A.D. 1089–1167) clearly recognized that the extent of the Flood was referring to a global event, as can be seen from his comments on Genesis 7:20:

> There are those who maintain that there is a very tall mountain in Greece that the waters did not cover. However, we believe the words of our God and we put aside the foolish nonsense of man.[20]

The fact that the waters of the Flood covered all the high mountains raises the question as to whether this means that the present-day mountains were covered by the waters of the Flood. Geologist Dr. Andrew Snelling answers this question:

> . . . the sticking point for them [local flood adherents] is whether Genesis is here really suggesting that present-day Mt. Ararat, with an altitude of about 17,000 feet, and beyond that Mt. Everest in the Himalayas, with an altitude of over 29,000 feet, were covered by the Flood waters . . . it is important to note that Mt. Ararat is a volcanic mountain whose lavas cover fossil-bearing sedimentary rocks. Obviously, if these fossil bearing sedimentary rocks beneath Mt. Ararat are a product of the Genesis-Flood, then Mt. Ararat was not prior to the Flood. Similarly, marine-fossil-bear-

---

18. Ibid., 260.
19. See Mathew, *Genesis 1:1–11:26*, 379.
20. Ibn Ezra, *Commentary on the Pentateuch Genesis* (Bereshit). Translated by H. Norman Strickman and Arthur M. Silver (New York: Menorah Publishing Company, Inc, 1988), 109.

ing layers near the summit of Mt. Everest would likewise have been a product of the Flood, so that Mt. Everest, and thus all the Himalayas which are also geologically "recent" mountains, would not have been there prior to the Flood.[21]

This is even suggested in Scripture. Psalm 104:8 identifies a tectonic event that takes place either during, at the end, or after the Flood: "The mountains rose, the valleys sank down to the place that you appointed for them." This implies that the crust of the earth moved in the recessional stage of the Flood so that the mountains arose and the valleys sank down.[22] This would give rise to our present-day mountain ranges, such as the Himalayas.

A further reason why the Flood must have been global is that after the Flood, when Noah and his family come out of the Ark in Genesis 9, God made a covenant (*běrît*) with the rainbow as a sign of the promise, not only with Noah but with his descendants, every living creature, and the earth:

> Then God said to Noah and to his sons with him, "Behold, I establish my covenant with you and your offspring after you, and with every living creature that is with you, the birds, the livestock, and every beast of the earth with you, as many as came out of the ark; it is for every beast of the earth. I establish my covenant with you, that never again shall all flesh be cut off by the waters of the flood, and never again shall there be a flood to destroy the earth." And God said, "This is the sign of the covenant that I make between me and you and every living creature that is with you, for all future generations: I have set my bow in the cloud, and it shall be a sign of the covenant between me and the earth. When I bring clouds over the earth and the bow is seen in the clouds, I will remember my covenant that is between me and you and every living creature of all flesh. And the waters shall never again become a flood to destroy all flesh. When the bow is

---

21. Andrew Snelling, *Earth's Catastrophic Past: Geology, Creation & the Flood Volume 1* (Dallas, TX: Institute for Creation Research, 2009), 28, 30.
22. For an exegetical defense of Psalm 104:8 referring to the Flood, see William D Barrick, "Exegetical Analysis of Psalm 104:8 and Its Possible Implications for Interpreting The Geological Record," 2018, http://www.creationicc.org/2018_papers/12%20Barrick%20Ps%20104%20final.pdf.

in the clouds, I will see it and remember the everlasting covenant between God and every living creature of all flesh that is on the earth." God said to Noah, "This is the sign of the covenant that I have established between me and all flesh that is on the earth" (Genesis 9:8–17).

It is important to understand that the covenant God made with Noah involves the "earth." If Noah's Flood were only local, then the covenant must have been broken many times, as there have been hundreds, if not thousands, of local floods since the time of Noah. The promise God made was unilateral and is everlasting, reinforcing the unconditional and certain commitment of God (Genesis 8:22). The Bible tells us that God is someone who keeps His covenants and is not like mankind, who can lie and change their minds (Deuteronomy 7:9; Numbers 23:19). Before we look at some of the physical evidence for the global Flood, it is important to notice that the language used in the Flood account suggests significant geological implications with violence taking place at the beginning and end of the Flood:

> In the six hundredth year of Noah's life, in the second month, on the seventeenth day of the month, on that day all the fountains of the great deep burst forth, and the windows of the heavens were opened (Genesis 7:11).

In Genesis 6:17, the technical term for "flood" is the Hebrew word *mabbûl*, and it is used only in Genesis 6–9 (except for Psalm 29:10). The Flood waters are the means by which God determined to destroy the earth. The two main sources of water for the Flood are mentioned here. First, the foundations of the great deep (the deep recalls Genesis 1:2) were opened; this refers to subterranean water. The violence at the beginning of the Flood is through the primary source of water in the account: the fountains of the great deep. The Hebrew word *bāqa'*, "burst forth," is loaded with geological significance. For example, when Korah led a rebellion against Moses' leadership, God judged those that followed him so that "the ground under them split apart (*bāqa'*). And the earth opened its mouth and swallowed them up. . ." (Numbers 16:31–32; cf. Judges 15:19; Zechariah 14:4). The word *bāqa'* also occurs with the deep (*těhôm*) in Psalm 78:15, which alludes to God's "splitting" the rock in the wilderness (Exodus 17:6). God also used the great deep as a tool to destroy the armies of Egypt (Isaiah 51:10). Therefore, when that water at the time of the Flood "burst forth," the crust of the earth would have broken apart with water coming up out of it all over the earth.

The second source of water is the windows of the heavens (i.e., the rains above were opened). Genesis 7:12 tells us that the "rain fell upon the earth forty days and forty nights." This time reference for the rain is the time period until the Ark started to float as the rain continued non-stop until the 150th day (Genesis 7:24–8:2). This was not rain (*mātar*) to water plants (Genesis 2:5; cf. 7:4) that came falling down on the earth but a monsoon season type rain. The Hebrew word used for "rain" (*gešem*) in Genesis 7:12 (8:2) can suggest abnormal rainwater, as it is used elsewhere as a metaphor for the LORD's judgment (Ezekiel 13:11, 13). The rain was an expression of God's wrath on the wickedness of man. Genesis 8:3 also records the geological violence at the end of the Flood. This is suggested by the adverb "continually," which is made up of two verbs in the Hebrew (the verb "to go" and the verb "to return"). Old Testament scholar William Barrick explains the significance of the verbs in Genesis 8:3:

> The roots and forms of the last two Hebrew words in 8:3a (*hālôk wāšôb*) present a forceful picture. The two words together focus on the concept of a continual recession of water. However, it is not a focus on mere recession or abatement. That concept is specified with a related construction and a different second verb in 8:5. . . . Applying this concept to 8:3 reveals that the waters were in a constant back and forth motion.[23]

The combination of the two verbs suggests moving water, and moving water carries sediment with it, which surely would have had profound geological implications in shaping the surface of the earth. The language of the global Flood in Genesis 7:11–12 and 8:2 is used by the prophet Isaiah when he compares it to the eschatological judgment of the nations at the coming of God's kingdom (Isaiah 24:18–20; cf. 54:9).

It is important to remember that the Flood is not just about destruction, but the central point of the narrative is about salvation. This can be seen from the focus of a proposed chiastic structure that comes after the *tôlĕdōt* of Noah in Genesis 6:9:

---

23. William Barrick, "Noah's Flood & Its Geological Implications," in *Coming to Grips with Genesis: Biblical Authority and the Age of the Earth*, ed. T. Mortenson and T.H. Ury (Green Forest, AR: Master Books, 2008), 272.

A Noah and his sons (6:10)
  B All life on earth (6:13a)
    C Curse on earth (6:13b)
      D Ark (6:14–16)
        E All living creatures (6:17–20)
          F Food (6:21)
            G Animals in man's hands (7:2–3)
            H Entry into the Ark (7:13–16)
            I Waters increase (7:17–19)
            J Mountains covered (7:20)
            X God remembers Noah (8:1)
            J Mountains are visible (8:5)
            I Waters decrease (8:13–14)
            H Exit from Ark (8:15–19)
            G Animals in man's hands (9:2)
          F Food (9:3–4)
        E All living creatures (9:10a)
      D Ark (9:10b)
    C Blessings on earth (9:13–16)
  B All life on earth (9:17)
A Noah and his sons (9:19)

The central point of the Flood narrative comes in Genesis 8:1: "But God remembered Noah." This does not mean that God forgot about Noah, but rather it is about His covenantal faithfulness, as the word "remember" (*zākar*) is focused on those who have trusted in Him (Genesis 19:29; Exodus 2:24). God is acting according to His earlier promise that He had made showing that He was faithful to His promise in preserving Noah from the destructive waters of the Flood (Genesis 6:18).

Evidence of a Global Flood

Before considering the evidence for the Flood, it is important for Christians to understand some other details of the Flood account. The author of Genesis precisely describes the length of the event of the Flood, as he gives the date when it began (Genesis 7:11), the date when it ended, and when Noah and his family came out of the Ark (Genesis 8:14). This would mean that the Flood lasted exactly one year and 11 days, probably based on a 30-day month and a 360-day year or more, as some creationists believe the month was lunar and the year was exactly 365 days.[24] The duration of the Flood included an initial 40 days of rain (Genesis 7:11–12),[25] 150 days of prevailing waters (Genesis 7:18, 19, 24), and finally 221 days of the waters subsiding and abating (Genesis 8:1–5).[26] No local flood could last this long. From the genealogical information in Genesis 5 and 11 (Masoretic text), the Flood would have occurred roughly around 2518 B.C.; from the creation of Adam to the Flood is around 1,656 years. Not only was the Flood lengthy but so was the Ark. Unlike pictures of the tiny Ark depicted in many children's books, the biblical description of the Ark is of a huge vessel — length: 300 cubits (510 feet); width: 50 cubits (85 feet); height: 30 cubits (51 feet) (Genesis 6:15).[27] The need of such a huge Ark was to save Noah and his family and two (and seven of some) of every "kind" (mîn) of air-breathing, land-dwelling creatures from perishing in the global catastrophe (Genesis 6:18–20, 7:2–3).[28] The dimensions of the Ark are exactly what is required for a cargo ship and is a perfect balance of comfort, stability, and strength. If the Ark was taller or longer or wider, it would have broken apart or even tipped over. Although the Bible mentions the dimensions of the Ark, it does not tell us its shape (it does not say it was a box). The Hebrew word for Ark is tēbâ, and the only other place it appears is in Exodus 2:3, 5, when Moses is rescued from the water by a servant of the daughter of Pharaoh (an Israelite audience would recall the Ark Noah was saved in). It is most likely an Egyptian loan word, as it is related to the Egyptian word for "coffin" (Egyptians believed they were preserving the body for the after-life).[29] The purpose of both arks was to preserve life. It is important to convey the historical nature of the Flood account, as it the foundation on which to understand the evidence for it. This historical event would have radically reshaped the earth.

24. Dr. Danny Faulkner believes that the lunar calendar should be applied to the Flood account. See Danny Faulkner, "How Long Did the Flood Last?" *Answers Research Journal*, 8 (2015): 253–259, May 13, 2015, https://answersingenesis.org/the-flood/how-long-did-the-flood-last/.
25. The 40 days of rain refers to the continuous, torrential rains, but the fountains of the deep did not close and the rains did not stop until the 150th day.
26. For more details on the length of the Flood, see Snelling, *Earth's Catastrophic Past*, 19–25.
27. Ancient vessels generally used the long cubit, which was 20.4 inches.
28. It has been estimated that the number of kinds — living and extinct — that Noah was commanded to take on the Ark was less than 2,000. See Michael Belknap and Tim Chaffey, "How Could All the Animals Fit on the Ark?" April 2, 2019, https://answersingenesis.org/noahs-ark/how-could-all-animals-fit-ark/.
29. See BDB: *Hebrew and English Lexicon*, 1061.

When it comes to the evidence for a global Flood (the rock layers), it is important to remember that when biblical creationists or evolutionists examine the evidence, they both have ideological presuppositions. The presupposition or worldview for the biblical creationist is the revelation of the living God contained within the Bible, whereas for the evolutionist, it is naturalistic uniformitarianism. No one is neutral and free from bias when it comes to interpreting evidence. Because secular scientists start with the wrong assumptions, they therefore come to wrong conclusions. For example, planetary scientists believe that the canyons on Mars were formed in a few weeks by a near-global flood. Yet, there is no confirmation that there is liquid water on Mars today, but Earth's surface is covered in 70% water.[30] Why do these scientists believe there was once something near to a global flood on Mars but not on Earth? Well, if there was once a global Flood on Earth, it means that there is a God who holds people accountable for their sinful actions and judges them appropriately. It is not the evidence that is the problem but the human heart (see Jeremiah 17:9). The reason scoffers do not accept a global Flood is not because of the evidence, but as the Apostle Peter reminds us, it is because it does not fit their worldview (2 Peter 3:3–4).

In a similar fashion, rather than allowing Scripture to inform their understanding of the evidence for the Flood, many theologians, pastors, and lay people have uncritically accepted the testimony of scientists who work within a naturalistic and uniformitarian paradigm, which has controlled geology for the past 150 years. In rejecting the global Flood of Noah's day, the scoffers are really denying that the geological record and the fossils contained in it are the result of God's judgment of a global Flood.

The history of the earth that can be seen in the geological record provides a consistent testimony to the biblical account of the global Flood and not to the idea of sedimentary layers having been laid down over millions of years. There are several evidences that confirm this:

1. Marine creatures buried in rock layers high upon the continents (indicating that the ocean waters had risen to totally inundate the continents).
2. The sedimentary rock layers containing these marine fossils stretch right across the continents where the ocean waters deposited them.

---

30. See Dr. Danny Faulkner, "Global Catastrophe — Anywhere but Earth," July 1, 2018, https://answersingenesis.org/the-flood/global-catastrophe-anywhere-earth/.

3. The sedimentary rock layers and their fossils show evidence of having been rapidly deposited and buried, respectively.
4. The sequence of the sedimentary rock layers show evidence of having been deposited in rapid succession.[31]

Interestingly, there are fossils of sea creatures in rock layers found on every continent in the world that today are high above sea level. The question, then, is how did marine fossils get to be buried in sedimentary rock layers now high (29,000 feet) in a place like the Himalayas? Dr. Andrew Snelling explains:

> There is only one possible explanation — the ocean waters at some time in the past flooded over the continents. Could the continents have then sunk below today's sea level, so that the ocean waters flooded over them? No! Because the continents are made up of rocks that are less dense (lighter) than both the ocean floor rocks and the mantle rocks beneath the continents. The continents, in fact, have an automatic tendency to rise, and thus "float" on the mantle rocks beneath, well above the level of the ocean floor rocks. This is why the continents today have such high elevations compared to the deep ocean floor, and why the ocean basins can accommodate so much water. Rather, the sea level had to rise, so that the ocean waters then flooded up onto, and over, the continents.[32]

The Bible gives us the mechanism that would have caused this. Since the Flood started in the oceans when the fountains of the deep were broken up, the earth's crust would have opened up all around the globe so that the waters flooded the continents (Genesis 7:11, 7:24–8:2). As the ocean waters rose up onto the continents, it brought with it all the creatures that were on the ocean floors that surround the continent. It is not surprising then that the first creatures found in the fossil record are shell and marine invertebrates. In fact, what many people do not realize is that 95% of fossils are marine invertebrates (mostly shellfish); 5% are plants, which include trees and algae; and only 1% are vertebrates of all kinds.

31. Dr. Andrew Snelling provides more detailed evidence of this in his DVD presentation: "Grand Canyon: Testimony to the Biblical Account of Earth History," https://answersingenesis.org/store/product/grand-canyon-testimony-biblical-account-history/.
32. Dr. Andrew Snelling, "What Are Some of the Best Flood Evidences?" in *The New Answers Book 3* (Green Forest, AR: Master Books, 2009), 284–285.

Perhaps some of the clearest evidence of the global Flood can be seen at the Grand Canyon in the USA. The canyon itself stretches 277 miles through northern Arizona with the main portion of the canyon attaining a depth of more than a mile and ranging in width from 4 to 18 miles. Secular geologists would claim that the rock layers in the Grand Canyon represent millions of years of earth's geological history that were formed by the Colorado River. The Colorado River cascades along at about 2,400 feet above sea level within the canyon that cuts across a plateau 7,000–8,500 feet above sea level. But how could the Colorado River cut its way through that plateau thousands of feet above it? The evolutionary scientific community cannot solve this problem. From a biblical viewpoint, the Grand Canyon would have been formed at the end, or sometime soon after, the global Flood. However, some of the basement rocks (schists and granites) are from Day Three of creation week.

Although people are taught that it takes millions of years to form sedimentary rock layers, modern geologic catastrophes such as the one that took place at Mount St. Helens (1980), a volcano in Washington state in the USA, have shown that rock layers can be laid down very quickly. Since the volcanic eruption at Mount St. Helens, thousands of individual layers of rock up to 600 feet thick have accumulated.[33] In fact, 25 feet of stratified deposit accumulated in three hours in just one day (see figure 1).

It did not take a lot of time (millions of years) to form those rock layers; it took the right catastrophic conditions (a Flood). Mud flows from a later eruption at Mount St. Helens (1982) carved out a canyon (known as Little Grand Canyon) up to 140 feet deep in a few hours by

Figure 1: Deposits exposed by mudflow erosion on the North Fork of the Toutle River. The laminated and bedded pyroclastic flow deposit of June 12, 1980, is 25 feet thick in the middle of the cliff. That three-hour deposit is underlain by the pyroclastic flow deposit of May 18, 1980, and overlain by the mudflow deposit of March 19, 1982. (Photo by Dr. Steve Austin, used with permission)

33. See Dr. Steve Austin, "Why Is Mount St. Helens Important to the Origins Controversy?" in *The New Answers Book 3* (Green Forest, AR: Master Books, 2009), 253–261.

Figure 2: Another explosive eruption created destructive mudflows that cut canyons up to 140 feet (43 m) deep in a single day. "Little Grand Canyon of the Toutle River," seen here, is a one-fortieth-scale model of the Grand Canyon. (Photo by Dr. Steve Austin, used with permission)

rapid water flow where there was no canyon before (see figure 2).[34] If this "small" volcanic catastrophe at Mount St. Helens caused those rock layers and canyon to form very quickly, imagine what a global catastrophe could do. There are also areas of the Grand Canyon (e.g., the east Kaibab monocline at Carbon Canyon) that evidence that it did not take millions of years to form the rock layers. These sedimentary layers of Tapeats Sandstone have been folded smoothly almost 90 degrees without breaking or fracturing (deposition of layers laid down in rapid succession). What is interesting is that there is no evidence of metamorphosis over the claimed millions of years since the sedimentary layers were deposited. This strongly indicates that the sedimentary layers were still soft when the earth movements that bent them occurred. This is because for rock to be bent, it must still be soft and wet (unconsolidated), which means that the rock layers were still soft during the period following the Flood and were bent at an angle during folding and later solidified into solid rock (see figure 3). Rather than a lot of time and a little bit of water causing the Grand Canyon to form, an interpretation that better fits with evidence from observable catastrophes is that a lot of water in a little bit of time formed the Grand Canyon.

Figure 3: These folded sedimentary layers had to be soft and pliable at the same time in order for these layers to be folded without fracturing. The folded Tapeats Sandstone can be seen in Carbon Canyon. (Photos courtesy of Dr. Snelling)

34. See John Morris and Steve A. Austin, *Footprints in the Ash* (Green Forest, AR: Master Books, 2003), 75.

Another piece of evidence that points to the global Flood comes from the billions of fossils found throughout the world's rock layers (like in the Grand Canyon). Just as with the rocky layers, many people are taught that fossils are preserved remains of creatures that lived millions of years ago. Fossils do not need long ages to form. Rather, they must form very quickly; otherwise, their tissue and bones will decay, as is recognized by evolutionists:

> Fossilization is a process that can take anything from a few hours to millions of years. . . . The amount of time that it takes for a bone to become completely permineralized is highly variable. If the groundwater is heavily laden with minerals in solution, the process can happen rapidly. Modern bones that fall into mineral springs can become permineralized within a matter of weeks.[35]

While a fossil forming over a few hours can be observed, scientists do not know how fossilization takes millions of years; no scientists have been around long enough to observe this. It doesn't take millions of years to form fossils, it just takes the right conditions. But what does the fossil record reveal? Well, it reveals several evidences that further support a global Flood:

- Evidence of sudden appearance in the fossil record, fully formed and complex, without any ancestors in the layers beneath
- Evidence of many varieties of basic kinds reproducing after their kinds
- Evidence of the basic kinds staying the same (stasis)
- Evidence of death, disease, and suffering
- Evidence of rapid burial in a catastrophe
- Evidence of rapid mass destruction and burial on a global scale in a catastrophe (the Flood)
- Evidence of no evolutionary transitions[36]

The belief in evolutionary transitions (missing links) is part of the argument of the evolution of life. What is significant, however, is that there is no fossil evidence for this. If evolution were true, where are all the

---

35. Philip J. Currie and Eva B. Koppelhus, *101 Questions About Dinosaurs* (New York: Dover Publications, 1996), 11.
36. For more on these evidences, see Dr. Andrew Snelling's presentation: "Rock Strata, Fossils and the Flood."

missing links of one kind of creature turning into another? Over the years, evolutionists have proposed several suggestions for missing links. For example, the proposed missing link *Archaeopteryx* was once said to be the ancestor of the birds, but we now know it was a true bird with true feathers. Then there was *Tiktaalik*, which was considered the best fossil evidence of the supposed transition of creatures from water to land (fish and amphibian) as fins changed into limbs. The anatomical evidence, however, shows that *Tiktaalik* was just a fish.[37] The problem of transitional fossils was, in fact, recognized by Charles Darwin in his book *The Origin of Species* in 1859:

> Why then is not every geological formation and every stratum full of such intermediate links? Geology assuredly does not reveal any such finely graduated organic chain; and this, perhaps, is the most obvious and serious objection which can be urged against the theory. The explanation lies, as I believe, in the extreme imperfection of the geological record.[38]

Darwin realized that there were, in fact, no missing links, but his explanation for this was the "imperfection of the geological record." In 1859, most of the world was unexplored, so Darwin can be excused for this. However, is there any evidence today of transitional fossils when scientists have explored most of the world? David Raup, possibly the greatest palaeontologist of the 20th century, also agreed with Darwin:

> Well, we are now about 120 years after Darwin and the knowledge of the fossil record has been greatly expanded....The record of evolution is still surprisingly jerky and, ironically, we have even fewer examples of evolutionary transition than we had in Darwin's time....Some of the classic cases of Darwinian change in the fossil record...have had to be discarded or modified as a result of more detailed information.[39]

Interestingly, Raup admits that we have fewer examples of transitional fossils than Darwin did in his day, but how can this be, as Darwin said

---

37. See Dr. David Menton, "Is Tiktaalik Evolution's Greatest Missing Link?" in *The New Answers Book 3* (Green Forest, AR: Master Books, 2009), 241–251.
38. Charles Darwin, *The Origin the Species* (London: Penguin Group, Penguin Books Ltd, 1968), 292.
39. D. Raup, "Conflicts Between Darwin and Palaeontology," *Field Museum of Natural History Bulletin* 50, no 1 (1979), 25.

he didn't have any! More recently, in 2001, Ernst Mayr, one of the 20th century's leading evolutionary biologists, also recognized that no transitional fossils have been found:

> Given the fact of evolution, one would expect the fossils to document a gradual steady change from ancestral forms to the descendants. But this is not what the palaeontologist finds. Instead, *he or she finds gaps in just about every phyletic series....* The discovery of unbroken series of species changing gradually into descending species is very rare[40] (emphasis mine).

People think that museums around the world are full of transitional fossils that support evolution, but the experts from Darwin until today have not found a single fossil that unequivocally shows any evolutionary transition. What is seen in the fossil record, however, is evidence of many varieties of basic kinds reproducing after their own kind (Genesis 1 tells us 10 times that God created things after their kind). A biblical "kind" (*mîn*) essentially "represents the basic reproductive boundary of an organism. That is, the offspring of an organism is always the same *kind* as its parents, even though it may display considerable variation."[41] The fossil record confirms the evidence of this stasis (creatures staying the same) within a kind, as snails are always snails, fish are always fish, trilobites are always trilobites, brachiopods are always brachiopods, etc. The evidence for this can be seen from "living fossils." For example, the coelacanth fish, which we find in the fossil record, was thought to

Figure 4: The presence of "living fossils" like this coelacanth casts doubt on the value of evolution as a predictive model — organisms can change rapidly or stay the same for hundreds of millions of years. Other examples of living fossils include wasps, dragonflies, stromatolites, ginkgoes, clams, and the Wollemi pine. Photo by Dean Falk Schnabel, Wikimedia (CC BY-SA 4.0)

---

40. Ernst Mayr, *What Evolution Is* (New York: Basic Books, 2001), 14.
41. Dr. Georgia Purdom, "Variety Within Created Kinds," April 1, 2010, https://answersingenesis.org/creation-science/baraminology/variety-within-created-kinds/.

have died out 65 million years ago until, in 1938, it was found living off the coast of Madagascar (see figure 4). When the fossil record is viewed through a biblical worldview, it is testimony to the global Flood of Noah's day and not to evolution and millions of years.

When it comes to the rock layers and fossils that we see and find all around the world, the most important thing is that it should remind us of the consequences of human sin and God's judgment upon it.

The influence of uniformitarian geology has caused theistic evolutionists and old earth creationists to question whether the Fall in Genesis 3 brought about the physical death of humans and animals as well as natural disasters in creation. So, what were the effects of the Fall for them? Was the Curse that God pronounced on the earth ontological (affecting the very nature of the planet) or functional (affecting the human relationship with the earth)? On the basis of an uniformitarian understanding of the geological and palaeontological evidence, many Christians argue that natural phenomena such as earthquakes have "been part of 'the way things were' on the planet, long before humans existed, let alone sinned."[42] Sadly, many of those Christians who have succumbed to the teaching of long ages of earth's history do not seem bothered by the fact that the fossil record contains death, mutations, disease, suffering, bloodshed, and violence. In fact, for those Christians, it seems that all that the Fall did was to make bad things worse.

Belief in long ages of earth's history contradicts the biblical teaching that Adam's sin brought both moral and natural evil into God's "very good" creation (Genesis 1:31). When the first man Adam disobeyed God's command, his sin physically affected the entire creation. It was not just humanity that was plunged into the "reign of death" (Romans 5:17; cf. Genesis 5:5, 8, 11, 14, 17, 20, 26, 31), as the entire creation experienced the groaning effects of his sin (Romans 8:22). The Hebrew words 'ādām (man) and 'ădāmâ (ground) are closely related and show the related consequences of Adam's disobedience on the ground from which he was taken (Genesis 2:7, 3:17). The curses God pronounces in Genesis 3:14–17 speak of physical judgments against the serpent, animals, the woman, and the ground, speaking against the idea that the text here is just speaking of spiritual death.[43] God's judgment here was not spiritual but physical. One

42. See Christopher J.H. Wright, *Old Testament Ethics for the People of God* (Nottingham, England: InterVarsity Press, 2004), 130.
43. This is not to say there was no spiritual consequences (see Genesis 3:8).

evidence of the change in the way in which the natural world works is the cursed ground, as fallen "thorns and thistles it shall bring forth for you…" (Genesis 3:18).[44] The ground that was cursed was not just the ground in the garden in Eden but the whole earth outside of the garden from which Adam was taken (before he was placed in the garden — Genesis 2:15, 3:23; cf. 5:29). It is the same ground (*ădāmâ*) that was destroyed in the days of Noah that God said He would not curse again (Genesis 8:21). A text that is very relevant to our understanding of Genesis 3, and the result of God's cursing the entire creation, is Romans 8:18–22:

> For I consider that the sufferings of this present time are not worth comparing with the glory that is to be revealed to us. For the creation waits with eager longing for the revealing of the sons of God. For the creation was subjected to futility, not willingly, but because of him who subjected it, in hope that the creation itself will be set free from its bondage to corruption and obtain the freedom of the glory of the children of God. For we know that the whole creation has been groaning together in the pains of childbirth until now.

The Greek word for creation (*ktisis*) in verse 19 in context clearly refers to the non-human creation; the creation is distinguished from humanity in verse 21. In verse 20, Paul explains that creation is anticipating the revealing of the sons of God because it is not the way God intended it to be. It is this way because Adam's sin spoiled God's very good creation, and as a consequence, it is now in frustration. Paul is drawing on the text in Genesis 3:17–19, in which creation is cursed by God due to Adam's sin, and so "futility" means that creation has not filled the purpose for which it was made.[45] However, if Paul did not have Genesis 3 in mind, then the question is when did God subject the creation to futility? There is nothing in Genesis 1 that indicates that there was any kind of corruption in the original creation (Genesis 1:29–31). If the creation were already in a state of futility at its creation, then how could it be subjected to corruption, since it would already be in that state? God's subjecting the creation is clearly a reference to the Curse in Genesis 3:17.

---

44. Secular scientists have found thorns in the fossil record that they have dated to be millions of years that appear way before they claim man existed.
45. See Thomas Schreiner, *Romans: Baker Exegetical Commentary on the New Testament* (Grand Rapids, MI: Baker Academics, 1998), 436.

Paul's comments in verse 20 clearly reflect his belief that the Fall brought about a change in the workings of creation. It is important to keep in mind that Paul has already discussed how the Fall brought about changes in creation (Romans 1:18–25, 5:12).[46] In Romans 8:18–22, Paul continues to trace the consequences of Adam's disobedience to the futility to which creation has been unwillingly subjected and is now corrupted because of his disobedience. Paul makes a direct connection between the liberation of creation and the liberation of the "sons of God." This, however, would be lost if the creation has always been in a state of corruption and futility because it would be unconnected to the fallen state of man. Paul describes the glory that awaits the sons of God in terms of freedom, and this freedom is associated with the state of glory to which the sons of God are destined. The creation itself will be set free from the bondage to corruption and into the glory of the sons of God. Not only that, but Paul also makes it clear that there is going to be a work done in creation itself and not just human beings. Paul's point in verse 22 is that the creation is groaning and suffering, not from natural disasters and suffering before the Fall but from the Fall of Adam in Genesis 3.

There are consequences of synthesizing evolution and millions of years into the text of Scripture since this not only affects how the early chapters of Genesis are interpreted, but it also affects the coherency and internal consistency of the biblical message of creation, the Fall, and redemption. To accept millions of years of human and animal death before the creation and Fall of man undermines the teaching on the full redemptive work of Christ (cf. Colossians 1:20). Jesus did not die on the Cross to defeat an enemy he made at the beginning of creation (cf. 1 Corinthians 15:26). This issue of death and suffering before the Fall is one of the reasons why the age of earth is vital for Christians today to consider, as it impacts how we understand events like the global Flood in Genesis 6–9.

---

46. In Romans 1, he demonstrates how the Fall changed mankind's view of God, as now in the "futility" (1:21, 8:20) of their mind they worship the creature rather than the Creator (Romans 1:18–25). A more specific change in creation is the entrance of sin and death that came into the world through Adam's disobedience (Romans 5:12–19), a clear reference to Genesis 3.

CHAPTER EIGHT

THE JUDGMENT OF
THE UNGODLY

2 Peter 3:7

But by the same word the heavens and earth that now exist are stored up for fire, being kept until the day of judgment and destruction of the ungodly. (2 Peter 3:7)

The first denial of God's words in Scripture was to deny God's judgment, when Satan came to Eve in the guise of a serpent and said: "You will not surely die" (Genesis 3:4; cf. Revelation 12:9; 2 Corinthians 11:3). Satan's words directly contradicted God's command (Genesis 2:17). While God had told Adam death would come the day he ate from one tree, Satan told Eve that death would not take place. Adam and Eve rejected that revelation and instead chose to believe a falsehood about God. Their sin was that they wanted to be gods themselves (Genesis 3:4–5). In this act of disobedience, Adam believed Satan and adopted his own worldview over God's worldview. Adam's disobedience brought God's judgment upon him and Eve (Genesis 3:14–19).

Often when Satan begins a fresh attack on biblical revelation, we first begin to doubt whether God exercises judgment. In a similar way, for many people today, the idea that God would judge people is often rejected as being an archaic understanding of God: a view of God as an angry old man in the sky who judges people for no reason. This caricature of God, however, ignores the biblical notion of God as personal, active, and rightly offended that His creation and holy law are being defiled. God has every right to respond to sin with His righteous judgment (see Exodus 4:14, 15:7, 32:10–12; Romans 1:18–32; Revelation 14:14–20). Behind the idea that God wouldn't judge people is the belief of inherent human goodness, at least in Western secular society. The belief that humans are basically good people is a product of humanistic thinking. Humanism teaches that humanity is born unaffected by sin (instead we are born with a clean slate) and that human nature can be changed by the environment in which we live. This is a similar worldview to that of the scoffer and heretic Pelagius (A.D. 360–420); he taught that human nature left to itself is basically good. It is those who hold this view of human nature who, when they hear the concept of God's judgment, often object by stating: "God surely wouldn't judge and send innocent people to hell, would He?"

The humanist position, that people are basically good, is an inconsistent position. Humanism is founded upon Darwinian evolution, which sees humanity as the product of blind chance, and therefore has no absolute basis to account for such things as goodness (i.e., ethics). The *Humanist Manifesto II* (1973) teaches that "Ethics is autonomous and situational…" and therefore not absolute and universal. So, for humanists to say it is wrong for God to judge any person (not just them) assumes an absolute standard of morality by which they judge God. The problem for those who embrace humanist thinking is that if they want to make moral judgments on anyone (including God), then they need to have absolute moral laws, but in order to have absolute moral laws, you need an absolute moral law giver, something humanists don't have. The optimism of today's humanistic ethics (including secular humanists) is borrowed from Christian ethical and moral assumptions (hope, kindness, mercy, justice, goodness, etc.). This is recognized by atheist historian Tom Holland, who stated: "…modern atheism in the West is Christian atheism. And secularism and liberalism are shot through with Christian ethical and moral presumptions and understandings."[1] In other words, modern atheists (and humanists) borrow their moral standards from the Christian worldview because you cannot consistently live as if there is no transcendent meaning to life. People often talk about living in a post-truth world, but we are moving beyond that into a post-rights world. This is because

---

1. Tom Holland said this at the "Hay Festival" in 2015 in the Q&A time after a lecture he gave entitled 'De-Radicalising Muhammad' (relevant section 49:27), https://www.youtube.com/watch?v=I5slk97ss2Q.

people cannot give a basis for their ethics, why people have value and dignity. But this is no surprise given the cheap view of human nature that humanism (and secular humanism) provides.

The fact that humanists are made in the image of God and therefore have inherent value and worth (which is not the case if you are just the product of evolution) and that the law of God is written on their hearts is why they can have a sense of good and evil and is the reason they can make ethical appeals (Genesis 1:27; Romans 2:15). The belief that humans are basically good people is not a biblical concept, nor does it fit with the reality of the world in which we live (i.e., our sinfulness, Ephesians 2:1–3, 4:18). The Bible tells us that all people are born in sin and are enemies and hostile toward God (Psalm 51:5; Romans 5:10, 8:7; Colossians 1:21). It is important to remember that sin is not first and foremost a deed that is committed but is a condition we have inherited (see Romans 5:19; 1 Corinthians 15:22). Because of this nature we have inherited, our sin causes us to be ignorant of who we really are, i.e., sinners.

God's justice demands that sin be dealt with, which is why there is a real place of final judgment where those who have broken God's law and remain unrepentant about it will go (see Matthew 10:26–28, 25:46; Acts 17:30–31). The problem with the humanistic worldview is that it does not present any good news (gospel) that someone has liberated us from the reign of sin and death. In Christianity, salvation from our sinfulness comes through Jesus' life, death, and resurrection and not through human effort (1 Corinthians 15:1–4; Romans 4:4–8). We need to realize that once you get rid of the idea of judgment as a consequence of our disobedience toward God's Word, then you can entertain anything (covetousness, theft, racism, abortion, euthanasia, same-sex "marriage," gender fluidity, etc.) because people believe there are no consequences to their actions (see Genesis 34; Judges 17:6, 21:25). The reality of this life is that everyone wants some sort of justice when they have been wronged by someone else, but they just don't want justice when they have wronged the God who gives them life. This is what the scoffers were trying to do, convince people of the promise of freedom from moral accountability and final future judgment (2 Peter 2:19).

In verse 7, Peter reaches his conclusion against the scoffers' argument that there was no coming judgment. Just as God judged the world at the time of the Flood, so He will one day judge the present world. The Word that destroyed the world is the same Word that now reserves the present heavens and earth, as opposed to the world that then existed, for judgment by fire. As with the Flood, the extent of the destruction by fire will be a worldwide judgment on the ungodly. This final judgment, however, will not engulf everybody. Just as God preserved Noah and seven others in the judgment of the Flood, He will also spare the godly (2 Peter 2:5) while judging and destroying the ungodly. The word "destruction" (*apōleia*)[2] has been taken by some to refer to the future annihilation of people; however, New Testament scholar Douglas Moo rightly notes that when it is:

> ...applied in the New Testament to the judgement of human beings, must not be taken literally in the sense of annihilation. Indeed, some theologians have taken the language in this sense, but this does not fit the general New Testament teaching about "eternal" punishment. However uncomfortable we may be with the idea, it seems clearly taught in Scripture (e.g., Matt. 25:41, 46; Mark 9:43, 48; Rev. 14:9-11). "Destruction" refers to the cessation of existence in this world and to the final and terrible separation from God involved in condemnation.[3]

The global Flood is the example that Peter, and Jesus (Matthew 24:37–39), use as a guarantee of the future judgment of God. The fact that God already judged the world once with a global judgment is why we know He will do it again, though the coming judgment that awaits the present heavens and earth will be by fire (*pyri*).[4] The belief in a future judgment by fire is not something new to Peter but is a common theme in the Old Testament (Isaiah 29:6; 30:27, 30, 33; Joel 2:30; Zephaniah 1:18; Malachi 4:1). But just as Jesus and Peter pointed to the Flood as a guarantee of future judgment, so they both also pointed to God's judgment of Sodom and Gomorrah by fire as a guarantee of future judgment:

> Likewise, just as it was in the days of Lot — they were eating and drinking, buying and selling, planting and building, but on the day when Lot went out from Sodom, fire and sulfur rained from heaven and destroyed them all — so will it be on the day when the Son of Man is revealed (Luke 17:28–30).

2. Peter uses the verbal and noun form of *apōleia* to designate God's judgment on the wicked (2 Peter 2:1, 3; 3:9, 16).
3. Moo, *2 Peter and Jude*, 172.
4. It is important to recognize that Christians disagree as to whether the future eschatological judgment by fire is literal or a symbolic of the Day of Judgment.

...if by turning the cities of Sodom and Gomorrah to ashes he condemned them to extinction, making them an example of what is going to happen to the ungodly; and if he rescued righteous Lot, greatly distressed by the sensual conduct of the wicked (for as that righteous man lived among them day after day, he was tormenting his righteous soul over their lawless deeds that he saw and heard); then the Lord knows how to rescue the godly from trials, and to keep the unrighteous under punishment until the day of judgment... (2 Peter 2:6–9).

The author of Genesis (Moses) also brings the judgment of the Flood and Sodom and Gomorrah together, as can be seen by the similarities between the accounts:[5]

The Flood	Sodom and Gomorrah
Noah lives among a wicked generation and is described as having "found favor in the eyes of the LORD" (Genesis 6:8).	Lot also finds himself living among a wicked people and "found favor in the sight" of the messengers sent by the LORD (Genesis 19:19).
The LORD warned Noah of the judgment to come (Genesis 6:13).	The LORD warned Abraham of the impending judgment of Sodom and Gomorrah (Genesis 18:17–21).
Sexual indecencies are a reason for the judgment, and drunkenness by a survivor of the disaster, Noah, results in bringing shame on the family (Genesis 6:1–4, 9:22–23).	Sexual indecencies are a reason for the judgment, and drunkenness by a survivor of the disaster, Lot, results in bringing shame on the family (Genesis 19:1–11, 30–38).
In the Flood, it "rained" down with flood waters (Genesis 7:4).	At Sodom and Gomorrah, it "rained" brimstone (Genesis 19:24).
At the end of the Flood, God remembered the covenantal promise He made to Noah (Genesis 8:1).	After God judged Sodom and Gomorrah, He remembered the covenantal promise he made to Abraham (Genesis 19:29).
In the judgment of the Flood, only one family is rescued (Genesis 7:21–23).	In the judgment of Sodom and Gomorrah, only one family is rescued (Genesis 19:15, 25–29).

5. See Mathews, *Genesis 1-11:26*, 362–363.

Just as with the days before the Flood, Jesus spoke of the days before the destruction of Sodom as a time when people were indifferent and solely concerned with the things of this life: eating and drinking, buying and selling, planting and building. In other words, humanity was caught up with material things of life, which caused them to have a lack of concern for the things of God. Then the destruction by fire and sulfur came quickly and unexpectedly and destroyed them all. Likewise, when Peter spoke of the judgment that took place at Sodom and Gomorrah, turning it to ashes, it was to foreshadow the coming future eschatological judgment by fire. The destruction of Sodom and Gomorrah is important, as it serves as a sign of judgment of those who remain unrepentant in their sin against God (Deuteronomy 29:23; Isaiah 1:9–10; Zephaniah 2:9; Romans 9:29; Revelation 11:8). Sodom is seen as the epitome of wickedness and an expression of God's wrath (Jeremiah 23:14). Given the significance that both the Old and New Testaments place on Sodom and Gomorrah as a warning of future judgment by fire, it is important to understand this event. The world today, especially in the West, is very similar to Sodom and Gomorrah, as it affirms and embraces many of the things that God condemns (see below). Significantly, Jesus uses the account of Sodom and Gomorrah in addressing His disciples about being prepared for His second coming to give one of the soberest warnings in the New Testament: "Remember Lot's wife. Whoever seeks to preserve his life will lose it, but whoever loses his life will keep it" (Luke17:32–33).

Moving Toward Sodom

The person mentioned both by Jesus and Peter who stands out in the account of Sodom and Gomorrah is Lot. But who is Lot? Was he a bad man, a wicked man, or even an ungodly man? No. Lot was none of these. Peter, three times, describes Lot as a righteous man who was distressed by the sensual conduct of the wicked and tormented by the lawless deeds that he saw and heard in Sodom (2 Peter 2:7–8). What needs to be considered is how did Lot end up in Sodom, and why did he behave the way he did once he was living there and linger over leaving there on the day of its destruction?

In Genesis 11:10–26, we read of the descendants of Shem (son of Noah), and the last name in that list is Terah, the father of Abram's descendants (Genesis 11:27–25:11). Abram was born around 2166

Basic Old Testament Chronological Scheme	
4174 B.C.	Creation
2518 B.C.	The Flood
2166 B.C.	Birth of Abram
2091 B.C.	Abram leaves Ur
2067 B.C.	Destruction of Sodom
1876 B.C.	Jacob moved to Egypt
1446 B.C.	Exodus from Egypt
1406 B.C.	Israelites crossed into Canaan
967 B.C.	Construction of Solomon's Temple
587 B.C.	Jerusalem fell to the Babylonians*

* Alternatively, based on a short Israelite sojourn in Egypt, others believe creation took place in 4004 B.C., the Flood 2348 B.C., and Abraham was born in 1996 B.C.

B.C.[6] God will later change Abram's name to Abraham (Genesis 17:5). Terah also had two other children, Haran and Nahor, and it was Haran who fathered Lot (Genesis 11:27). Lot was the nephew of Abraham. After Haran dies in Ur of the Chaldeans (Genesis 11:28), Terah takes Abraham (Abram), his wife Sarah (Sarai), and Lot, and they go from there and settle in the land of Haran (not to be confused with Lot's father's name). It was while they were in Ur that they would have served other gods (Joshua 24:2), but it is while in Haran that the LORD in His grace called Abraham to leave that country (2091 B.C.), with all his family, and go to a land that He would show him and so that they could worship Him there. God promised to make Abraham a great nation and that all the families on earth would be blessed in him:

> Now the LORD said to Abram, "Go from your country and your kindred and your father's house to the land that I will show you.

6. By adding up the numbers of the ages from Shem to Terah in the MT (Masoretic Text), when the first son was born, we can establish that Abraham was born 352 years after the Flood (see Genesis 11:10–26). This takes into account that Abraham was born when Terah was 130 years old (not 70). This can be seen from the fact that Abraham was 75 when he left Haran (Genesis 12:4), which took place after Terah had died (Acts 7:4) at the age of 205 (Genesis 11:32). Abraham is not Terah's firstborn son but is mentioned first in Genesis 11:26 because he is most important in the narrative to follow. See Kenneth Mathews, *Genesis 11:27–50:26: An Exegetical and Theological Exposition of Holy Scripture*, The New American Commentary (Nashville, TN: B&H Publishing Group, 2005), 499n34.

And I will make of you a great nation, and I will bless you and make your name great, so that you will be a blessing. I will bless those who bless you, and him who dishonors you I will curse, and in you all the families of the earth shall be blessed (Genesis 12:1–3).

By faith Abraham obeyed God's call and left Haran and took Lot with him and went to live in the land of Canaan (see Galatians 3:8).[7] It was in Canaan, at Shechem by the oak of Moreh, that "the LORD appeared to Abraham and said, 'To your offspring I will give this land' " (Genesis 12:7). After this promise of children and land, Abraham moved and pitched his tent near Bethel, and there he "built an altar to the LORD and called upon the name of the LORD" (Genesis 12:8). Because the land later experienced a famine, Abraham and his family travelled to Egypt for relief (Genesis 12:10). After the famine was over, Abraham returned with great riches (Genesis 12:16) to Bethel, where he had previously made an altar, and there he again called upon the name of the LORD (Genesis 13:4). Notice that worship of the LORD was central to Abraham's life, as the reason God chose him was to "command his children and his household after him to keep the way of the LORD by doing righteousness and justice" (Genesis 18:19). In the context of Genesis 18, this command for Abraham to teach his family about righteousness and justice (ethical demands) is so that they will not end up like the people of Sodom. Abraham was to lead his family in the worship of the LORD, and Lot probably would have been present when Abraham called upon the LORD in worship of Him (cf. Deuteronomy 6:4–7; Joshua 24:15). However, now back in the land of Canaan, Abraham and Lot encounter a problem. Both men have acquired numerous possessions that the land cannot contain, and this results in trouble between the herdsmen of their livestock (Genesis 13:5–7). Because Abraham did not want to have trouble with his nephew Lot, he offers him a choice: "Is not the whole land before you? Separate yourself from me. If you take the left hand, then I will go to the right, or if you take the right hand, then I will go to the left" (Genesis 13:9). This is a key moment in the life of Lot, as the narrative of Genesis explains:

And Lot lifted up his eyes and saw that the Jordan Valley was well watered everywhere like the garden of the LORD, like the land of Egypt, in the direction of Zoar. (This was before the LORD

7. In Galatians 3:8, the Apostle Paul quotes Genesis 12:2 to point to Abraham as the example of faith, as it was by faith he obeyed God.

destroyed Sodom and Gomorrah.) So Lot chose for himself all the Jordan Valley, and Lot journeyed east. Thus they separated from each other. Abram settled in the land of Canaan, while Lot settled among the cities of the valley and moved his tent as far as Sodom (Genesis 13:10–12).

Lot is standing on an elevation close to Bethel (2,800 ft. above sea level) that gave him a magnificent view of the Jordan valley. The well-watered Jordan plain (like the garden in Eden) catches Lot's eye, and based upon this, he makes what he thinks is an appropriate decision to journey east and settle there. As well as being a geographical location, the easterly direction up to now in Genesis has also come to symbolize being outside of God's blessing.[8] By choosing to move outside of the land of Canaan, Lot will be outside the place of blessing (cf. Genesis 10:19). To separate from Abraham was to separate from the person that the LORD had promised to bless. Lot's choice was selfish as he "chose for himself" the best land. His decision was made purely by sight and not by faith (cf. 2 Corinthians 5:7). Lot will, of course, reap the consequences of the decision he made solely on a physical examination of the land later in his life. His decision to move away from Abraham and move his tent as far as Sodom is warned on by the author of Genesis, as the text notes: "Now the men of Sodom were wicked, great sinners against the LORD" (Genesis 13:13).

The notoriety of the men of Sodom is seen in their description as "wicked" and "great sinners." The term "great sinners" is used only here in the Bible and "implies the extreme seriousness of Sodom's sin."[9] The latter term "wicked" (ra') is also used to describe the people at the time of the Flood (Genesis 6:5, 8:21), and indicates that the people of Sodom's "sins deserved the same catastrophic response from God."[10] In reality, these terms underline the folly of Lot's choice to go and live in such a godless place. Lot chose to move near a materially prosperous place that was morally degraded rather than stay near to Abraham, whom God had promised to bless.[11] The influence of the morally corrupt City of Sodom

---

8. The direction "east/eastward" is used throughout the early chapters of Genesis of moving away from the presence/blessing of God: Adam and Eve (Genesis 3:24), Cain (Genesis 4:16), and the Babelites (Genesis 11:2). See Mathews, *Genesis 1–11:26*, 478.

9. Wenham, *Genesis 1–15*, 298.

10. Mathews, *Genesis 11:27–50:26*, 137.

11. Although, even in the bad choice that he had made, Lot still benefitted from the blessings of the promises made to Abraham (Genesis 14:12–16).

seems to have drawn Lot toward them, as we first read that he "moved his tent as far as Sodom" (Genesis 13:12). But what is interesting is that the next time we read of Lot, he is dwelling in Sodom (Genesis 14:12; cf. Psalm 1:1). Lot obviously did not influence Sodom, but rather Sodom influenced Lot.

The Warning of the Coming Destruction of Sodom and Gomorrah

The account of Lot and the coming destruction of Sodom and Gomorrah begins in Genesis 18, although the earlier narrative in Genesis has already prepared the reader for it (Genesis 13:13, 14:12):

> And the LORD appeared to [Abraham] by the oaks of Mamre, as he sat at the door of his tent in the heat of the day. He lifted up his eyes and looked, and behold, three men were standing in front of him. When he saw them, he ran from the tent door to meet them and bowed himself to the earth and said, "O Lord, if I have found favor in your sight, do not pass by your servant" (Genesis 18:1–3).

At the beginning of the chapter, three men appear to Abraham, who shows them tremendous hospitality. What is interesting is that while two of the men are identified as angels (Genesis 19:1), the other is the LORD (Yahweh, Genesis 18:1, 13, 22; cf. 19:24), who appears in human form and speaks, eats, and drinks together with Abraham (cf. Exodus 24:9–11; Judges 6:11–20).[12] This was not the first time that the LORD "appeared" to Abraham (Genesis 12:7, 17:1). On their way to visit Sodom, the LORD confirms His promise of an offspring to Abraham (Genesis 18:14) and then informs him of their mission concerning Sodom:

> Then the LORD said, "Because the outcry against Sodom and Gomorrah is great and their sin is very grave, I will go down to see whether they have done altogether according to the outcry that has come to me. And if not, I will know." So the men turned from there and went toward Sodom, but Abraham still stood before the LORD (Genesis 18:20–22).

---

12. Because the Bible says no one has seen God (the Father, John 1:18), this would be a theophany of the second person of the trinity, the Son (who takes on the name Jesus at His birth in Bethlehem). Likewise, the Apostle John identified Jesus as the person the prophet Isaiah saw in his vision of God (see John 12:41; Isaiah 6:1–3).

The Lord now makes known His decision to destroy Sodom to Abraham, just as ten generations earlier He had spoken to Noah about His plans to destroy the whole earth (Genesis 6:12–13). The reason for the Lord going down to Sodom and Gomorrah is that He had received complaints against them. The word "outcry" (*sĕʿāqâ*) is "a legal/judicial term of a cry for help by someone who is oppressed."[13] Sodom's sins are more than just sexual offences (see below), as their "outcry" reflect the "cry" (*sĕʿāqâ*) from the sojourner (*gēr*) in the land who is being oppressed (see Exodus 22:21–23).[14] The Lord hears the cry of those who have been mistreated, just as He heard the innocent blood of Abel crying out to Him (Genesis 4:10) and the "groaning" (*nĕʾāqâ*) of the people of Israel when they were in slavery in Egypt (Exodus 2:24). The reason for this complaint is that Sodom and Gomorrah's sin is very grave. This was explained earlier in Genesis 13:13: "Now the men of Sodom were wicked, great sinners against the Lord." From the time Lot has lived there, nothing has changed, as the men of Sodom are still acting wickedly. So, the Lord said He would go down to Sodom, for divine investigation (see Genesis 11:5, 7), to see if it is as bad as described.[15] While the two angels go off to Sodom (Genesis 19:1), Abraham stands before the Lord. In this amazing scene (like a courtroom with the Lord as judge), Abraham intercedes for the righteous in Sodom. Doing the work of a prophet (*nābîʾ*, Genesis 20:7), Abraham asks the Lord a series of questions: "Will you indeed sweep away the righteous with the wicked?" (Genesis 18:23). Abraham no doubt has genuine concern for his nephew Lot and his family as he uses the language of faith (righteousness, Genesis 15:6)[16] to plead for the righteous who may be present among the ungodly within Sodom. Abraham continues to approach God with a reverent plea to not destroy Sodom if 50, 45, 40, 30, 20 righteous people can be found there, and then he finally asks:

> "Oh let not the Lord be angry, and I will speak again but this once. Suppose ten are found there." He answered, "For the sake of ten I will not destroy it" (Genesis 18:32).

---

13. Currid, *Genesis 1:1–25:18*, 332.
14. In Genesis 19:9, the men of Sodom identify Lot as a "sojourner/stranger" (*gēr*).
15. This is, of course, anthropomorphic language, as the Lord knows everything (Genesis 45:5; Isaiah 40:14).
16. "And he believed the Lord, and he counted it to him as righteousness" (Genesis 15:6).

The matter was settled; if 10 righteous people can be found there, the LORD would not destroy it. Why 10 people? According to Jewish scholar Nahum Saran: "Ten is a round and complete number that symbolizes totality. Ten persons thus constitute the minimum effective social entity."[17] Perhaps Abraham thought there were ten righteous people in the city: Lot and his wife, two daughters, and two sons-in-law (Genesis 19:12), and possibly some others? The reality was that there were not even ten righteous people in Sodom. Only four people escaped, and even one of them did not survive. Thus, Abraham is proved correct concerning the character of the LORD: "Far be it from you to do such a thing, to put the righteous to death with the wicked, so that the righteous fare as the wicked! Far be that from you! Shall not the Judge of all the earth do what is just?" (Genesis 18:25). The LORD justly judged Sodom and Gomorrah not only because of its wicked behavior but because ten righteous people could not be found there. God does not judge for no purpose, but He always judges justly because His holy law has been broken, which was written on the people of Sodom and Gomorrah's hearts (cf. Romans 2:15). As their Creator, God has every right to judge the people in Sodom and Gomorrah, as they were descendants of Adam ("in Adam") and therefore guilty sinners (cf. 1 Corinthians 15:22).

The Wickedness of Sodom and Gomorrah

From the time that Lot left Abraham and moved his tent near Sodom until we find him living in Sodom, a little over 20 years has passed.[18] Sodom and Gomorrah are probably best known for the description of the immorality that takes place within their walls (cf. Judges 19:16–26):

> The two angels came to Sodom in the evening, and Lot was sitting in the gate of Sodom. When Lot saw them, he rose to meet them and bowed himself with his face to the earth and said, "My lords, please turn aside to your servant's house and spend the night and wash your feet. Then you may rise up early and go on your way." They said, "No; we will spend the night in the town

---

17. Nahum Sarna, *Genesis: The JPS Torah Commentary* (Philadelphia, PA: The Jewish Publication Society, 1989), 134.
18. Using the chronological information in Genesis, it is possible to calculate the 20 years. Abraham was 75 when he left Haran (Genesis 12:4) and was 85 when Ishmael was conceived (Genesis 16:3). Sodom was destroyed at around the time of the conception of Isaac, when Abraham was 99 (Genesis 17:1, 21:5).

THE JUDGMENT OF THE UNGODLY

square." But he pressed them strongly; so they turned aside to him and entered his house. And he made them a feast and baked unleavened bread, and they ate (Genesis 19:1–3).

In the opening verses, the two angels arrive at Sodom (having left Abraham in conversation with the LORD) in the evening and find Lot sitting at the gate of the city (Genesis 19:1). In the ancient world there were no hotels, so the place for visitors to go would be the gate of the city as a way of making known that you need shelter. The subtext of the Sodom account is that it is a wicked city wherein people do pretty much what they want whenever they want to do it. It is not a place where you want to be left unsheltered. Therefore, when Lot sees the visitors at the city gate, he invites them to his home. Lot's presence in the gateway of the city "suggests that he is an integral member of the city, if not a leader in some capacity."[19] Lot has now well and truly settled in life in Sodom, becoming a key member of society, owning a house (Genesis 19:3-4 — Lot had previously lived in a tent Genesis 13:12), and having a family there, unlike Abraham, a sojourner, who is still living in a tent (Genesis 18:1). When the angels arrive there, Lot is hospitable toward his visitors, offering them food and a place to stay for the night (Genesis 19:2–3). Lot's actions importantly show that he has not totally become like the people of Sodom, as they want to treat the visitors (the angels) very differently:

> But before they lay down, the men of the city, the men of Sodom, both young and old, all the people to the last man, surrounded the house. And they called to Lot, "Where are the men who came to you tonight? Bring them out to us, that we may know them." Lot went out to the men at the entrance, shut the door after him, and said, "I beg you, my brothers, do not act so wickedly. Behold, I have two daughters who have not known any man. Let me bring them out to you, and do to them as you please. Only do nothing to these men, for they have come under the shelter of my roof." But they said, "Stand back!" And they said, "This fellow came to sojourn, and he has become the judge! Now we will deal worse with you than with them." Then they pressed

19. Richard P. Belcher, *Genesis: The Beginning of God's Salvation* (Fearn, Ross-Shire: Christian Focus Publications, 2012), 142.

hard against the man Lot, and drew near to break the door down. But the men reached out their hands and brought Lot into the house with them and shut the door. And they struck with blindness the men who were at the entrance of the house, both small and great, so that they wore themselves out groping for the door (Genesis 19:4–11).

Now we see first-hand that the men of Sodom live up to their description of being very wicked. Lot even calls their behavior "wicked," showing that he has not completely lost any notion of right and wrong. Although, in a desperate and somewhat disturbing move to deter the men of Sodom from taking the angels, Lot offers them his two virgin daughters (Genesis 19:8). This is inexplicable behavior from Lot and was forbidden under the law of God (cf. Leviticus 19:29). No doubt he does not want his daughters to experience the sexual abuse that would occur, and so he may be trying to trap the men of Sodom in a legal predicament, as both his daughters are betrothed to men of Sodom (Genesis 19:14).[20] Despite Lot's protest, the inhabitants of Sodom took his suggestion as being judgmental: "This fellow came to sojourn, and he has become the judge!" (Genesis 19:9). In other words, the men of Sodom try and take the moral high ground: "Judge not lest you be judged, Lot!" This wickedness has affected the whole of Sodom, as the words "both young and old, all the people to the last man" show that it is not just a certain wicked part of the city that is known for its corrupt behavior. The purpose of the men of Sodom is that they want to "know" the visitors — in other words, have sexual relations with them (cf. Genesis 4:1). It is no wonder that the sin of Sodom was described as "very grave," as the people had "unnatural desires" (Jude 7) and wanted to commit a shameless act (Romans 1:26–27). In later biblical history, one of the reasons the Canaanites were "vomited out of the land" was because of their sexual immorality — namely homosexual practice (Leviticus 18:22–25).[21] The Bible tells us that there are certain sins that are more heavily weighted than others

20. Currid comments, "According to verse 14, these two daughters are betrothed to Sodomite men, but they are not yet married. They are engaged but still living in their father's house. Throughout the ancient Near East, betrothal was as sacrosanct as marriage. . . . Lot's strategy may be to cause the men to bring down condemnation and judgment on their own heads within the judicial setting of Sodom itself." Currid, *Genesis 1:1–25:18*, 342.

21. Leviticus 18–20 has to do with God's universal moral laws regarding sexual sin and is not speaking about specific ritual prohibitions or dietary laws for the nation of Israel (Leviticus 11:6–10).

(see Leviticus 20; Matthew 23:23; 1 Corinthians 5:1–2, 11). While any sin can exclude you from God's Kingdom, not all sins are the same or as equally abhorrent in the sight of God.[22] There are several reasons why same-sex intercourse is a serious sin, as Dr. Robert Gagnon notes:

1. Homosexual practice, committed or otherwise, is the violation that most clearly and radically offends against God's intentional creation of humans as "male and female" (Genesis 1:27) and definition of marriage as a union between a man and a woman.
2. Every text that treats the issue of homosexual practice in Scripture treats it as a high offense abhorrent to God (Genesis 19:4–11; Leviticus 18:22; Romans 1:24–27).
3. The male-female prerequisite is the foundation or prior analogue for defining other critical sexual norms (Mark 10:6–9; Matthew 19:4–6).[23]

If God judged wicked, immoral pagan nations for these sins in the past, He will certainly judge the world, and His Church if they participate in these sins, today.

Historically, the destruction of Sodom and Gomorrah has been known for God's opposition to homosexuality; however, this interpretation of the sin of the two cities has been challenged in recent decades. Two main arguments against this interpretation have been proposed that the sin of Sodom and Gomorrah was not about homosexuality but about gang rape[24] or inhospitality.[25] Is this true? Was the sin of Sodom and Gomorrah gang rape or inhospitality? With regard to the argument put forth for gang rape, there is an element of truth here, as the men of Sodom were intent on rape, but that is the only element of truth to

22. It is important to keep in mind, however, that nowhere does the Bible say that homosexuality is the worst of all sins, and nowhere does the Bible say practicing homosexuals should be stigmatized. Moreover, the Bible nowhere states that it is unforgivable or unchangeable (see below).
23. See Dr. Robert A.J. Gagnon, "How Bad Is Homosexual Practice According to Scripture and Does Scripture's Indictment Apply to Committed Homosexual Unions?" January 2007, http://robgagnon.net/HowBadIsHomosexualPractice.htm.
24. See Walter Barnett, Homosexuality and the Bible: An Interpretation (Wallingford, PA: Pendle Hill Publications, 1979), 8–9.
25. See Steve Chalke, "A Matter of Integrity (extended) The Church, sexuality, inclusion and an open conversation," 2013, https://www.oasisuk.org/wp-content/uploads/2020/10/A-MATTER-OF-INTEGRITY.pdf.

this argument. The argument for gang rape fails on a number of points. Firstly, to identify the sin of Sodom as heterosexual-orientated rape is questionable, given the fact that in the New Testament, Jude 7 identifies the inhabitants as having "indulged in sexual immorality and pursued unnatural desire." Jude views "unnatural desire" as homosexual activity.[26] The desires of the men of Sodom were not merely uncontrollable urges but unnatural desires in wanting sexual intercourse with other males. In fact, the men of Sodom would have gotten more than they bargained for, as the visitors were angels, something the residents of Sodom did not know. Secondly, the intended gang rape never actually happened. So, if the sin of Sodom was gang rape, this then would make God unjust in His punishment of the city for a sin that never actually happened. What should also be obvious is, how could blind people (Genesis 19:11), who could not even find the door, engage in gang rape?

The argument for inhospitality is probably the more popular interpretation of the sin of Sodom and Gomorrah. The proponents of this view point out that the majority of times the Hebrew word "know" (yāda') is used in the Old Testament, it means "to get acquainted with" rather than "to know." Therefore, when the townspeople turn up at Lot's house and want to get "to know" his guests, they simply want to be "acquainted with" the visitors, since Lot had failed to introduce them properly with the townspeople. While the Hebrew word yāda' can mean "to get acquainted with," the meaning of a word is dependent upon the context it is found in and not upon what it can mean. In the context of Genesis 19:5, the verb yāda'[27] must have sexual connotations, as three verses later the sexual meaning is the only one that makes sense. Otherwise, Lot would be saying that his two daughters, who were engaged to two of the inhabitants of Sodom, had never actually been acquainted with a man! A further reason why the inhospitality view does not make sense is the fact that Lot escapes with his life. However, if Lot was the one who broke the local inhospitality codes, then why are the residents of Sodom and Gomorrah punished for something Lot did, and he is allowed to live? Genesis 18:20 also tells us that the sin of Sodom is "very

---

26. Davids, *2 Peter and Jude*, 51–53.

27. The Hebrew verb *yāda'* is often used in a sexual sense (6 of these times are in Genesis alone 4:1, 17, 25, 19:8, 24:16, 38:26). It is used elsewhere in the Old Testament to describe sexual activity (Numbers 31:17, 18, 35; Judges 11:39, 19:22, 25, 21:11; 1 Samuel 1:19; 1 Kings 1:4).

grave," but this does not really describe inhospitality. It is also pointed out that the sin of Sodom being homosexuality is not the primary issue raised in Ezekiel 16:49–50:

> Behold, this was the guilt of your sister Sodom: she and her daughters had *pride, excess of food*, and *prosperous ease*, but *did not aid the poor and needy*. They were *haughty* and did an *abomination* before me. So I removed them, when I saw it (emphasis mine).

It is important to realize that Sodom was guilty of numerous sins other than homosexuality. In later biblical history, the prophets compared the social injustices committed by God's chosen people Israel/Judah to the people of Sodom: gluttony, prosperous ease, not aiding the poor, haughtiness as well as not administering justice (Isaiah 1:10, 3:9), adultery, lying, and an unwillingness to repent (Jeremiah 23:14). All of these sins say a lot about the state of the Western world today and its rejection of God. The pride, materialism, not helping the poor and the needy, and haughtiness that Ezekiel points to were all part of the sins of Sodom. But this does not mean homosexuality was not. The key word in Ezekiel 16:50 is "abomination," which is the Hebrew word *tôʿēbâ*. Its use in Ezekiel 16:50 ". . . refers to the (attempted) commission of atrocious sexual immorality at Sodom, probably the homosexual intercourse proscribed in Leviticus 18:22; 20:13."[28] Ezekiel 18:12 makes it clear that it is not the exploitation of the poor and needy that is what is meant by committing an abomination, as a very clear distinction is made between oppressing the needy and committing an abomination (singular), as they are separated by several vices.[29] The evidence, then, of Genesis 19 and other passages within Scripture (Jude 7; Ezekiel 16:49–50) is that among the many sins of Sodom and Gomorrah was that of homosexuality. The seriousness of God's judgment upon Sodom was seen in the seriousness of all its sins.

---

28. Robert Gagnon, *The Bible and Homosexual Practice: Texts and Hermeneutics* (Nashville, TN: Abingdon Press, 2001), 83–84.
29. The context of Ezekiel 18 is the consequences of a disobedient son: "If he fathers a son who is violent, a shedder of blood, who does any of these things (though he himself did none of these things), who even eats upon the mountains, defiles his neighbor's wife, *oppresses the poor and needy*, commits robbery, does not restore the pledge, lifts up his eyes to the idols, *commits abomination*, lends at interest, and takes profit; shall he then live? He shall not live. He has done all these abominations; he shall surely die; his blood shall be upon himself" (Ezekiel 18:10–13; emphasis mine).

The same seriousness of homosexuality which now dominates the culture has become an ever-increasing issue for the Church to be accepting of. In fact, the Church today is facing a similar situation to that of the Apostle Paul when he wrote his letter to the Corinthian Church. In 1 Corinthians 5 the Apostle Paul talks about the case of the incestuous man. Paul addresses reports according to which the Corinthians tolerate a case where a man is having sexual relations with his stepmother (1 Corinthians 5:1; cf. Leviticus 18:8). Paul tells the Corinthians not to associate with sexually immoral people (not of the world but in the Church). Such a person the Corinthians are to purge from their midst in the hope of repentance and restoration (1 Corinthians 5:13). The Church at Corinth prided itself in the ability to tolerate what this man was doing and had even become arrogant about it. Paul tells them, however, that they should have mourned over the situation (1 Corinthians. 5:2). Why should they have mourned? Because the life of this individual is at stake and they were doing nothing to rescue him. By the standards of many contemporary churches, we would probably say that the people who tolerated him were the loving ones. But the only one who really loved this man was the Apostle Paul. He was willing to do what needed to be done to recover him for the Kingdom of God. This is why, when Paul moves from the "immoral people" in 1 Corinthians 5:10 to 1 Corinthians 6:9–10, he gives a vice list of groups of offenders not to associate with because they will not inherit the Kingdom of God, of whom belong "men who practice homosexuality."[30]

The biblical opposition to homosexual behavior, as Paul affirms, is founded in the doctrine of creation in Genesis 1–2 (1 Corinthians 6:16; cf. Genesis 2:24). Paul's dealing with a case of a professed Christian and the potential on his part and the part of his communities that approve of what he is doing is that they deceive themselves. Why do they deceive themselves? They deceive themselves by thinking that he could do this action in a serially unrepentant way and get away with it. Paul, however, reminds the Corinthians of the beauty and power of the gospel to transform lives in 1 Corinthians 6:11 (emphasis mine): "And *such were some of you*. But you were washed, you were sanctified, you were justified in the name of the Lord Jesus Christ and by the Spirit of our God." The gospel of Jesus Christ is not affirmational but transformational.

---

30. The Apostle Paul uses two Greek terms in 1 Corinthians 6:9 to describe the active sexual partner (*arsenokoitai*) and to the passive partner (*malakoi*) in a homosexual act (see Leviticus 18:22, 20:13).

Righteous Lot

After Abraham pleaded with the LORD not to destroy the righteous among the wicked, He more than answered Abraham's plea, as He rescued the one person who was righteous, "righteous Lot" (2 Peter 2:7). Peter does say that Lot was "greatly distressed by the sensual conduct of the wicked"; in fact, it tormented "his righteous soul over their lawless deeds that he saw and heard" (2 Peter 2:7–8). But in what way was Lot righteous? Anyone familiar with Genesis may wonder why Lot is called righteous. Already we have seen Lot's selfish motives in moving away from Abraham to go live near the well-watered Jordon valley (Genesis 13:8–12). Then there was his decision to try and give the lusting men of Sodom his two virgin daughters instead of the angels (Genesis 19:6–8). Then, as we will see, on the day Sodom was to be destroyed, he lingered (Genesis 19:16). Even after he escaped the destruction of Sodom, he allowed himself to get drunk and thereby allowed his daughters to take advantage of the situation and have sexual relations with him (Genesis 19:30–35).[31] Yet, even when we consider all these things, the Bible tells us that Lot was a righteous man. How is this so? Well, just as Abraham was counted righteous by faith and yet was by no way free from sin — he sleeps with Hagar because he cannot see how God will provide him with the promised offspring (Genesis 16:1–5) — so the only way Lot can be considered righteous, biblically, would be because of his faith in God (see Romans 4:1–3, 16). In fact, the evidence of Lot's righteousness is shown in several ways in the text of Genesis 19:

- It was only Lot who showed the angels hospitality when they came to the city.

- Lot not only recognized what the men of Sodom wanted to do with the angels was wicked, but he tried to stop them when he could have just let them have them.

- When Lot finally left Sodom, he was obedient in not looking back.

- Lot is seen to be righteous by the fact that he is rescued from Sodom.

---

31. The narrative does point out that Lot "did not know" that his daughters had sexually exploited him (Genesis 19:33–35).

Although Lot is called righteous, he appears to have had little or no effect in Sodom. Theologian Douglas Wilson suggests that "Lot was righteous enough to be distraught at all the wickedness, but not righteous enough to make any kind of difference."[32] The fact that Lot did not make any difference in Sodom can be seen in a number of ways:

- Not even 10 righteous people could be found there (Genesis 18:32).

- No one in Sodom even listened to Lot (Genesis 19:9).

- His sons-in-law appear to scoff at him (Genesis 19:14).

- Lot's wife looked back when commanded not to (Genesis 19:17, 26).

- Lot's daughters tempted their father into getting drunk so that they could have sexual relations with him (Genesis 19:30–36).

- Lot's first daughter bore a son called Moab (from the father), and his second daughter bore a son called Ben-ammi (son of my kins-man). Both the Moabites and Ammonites were idolatrous nations who became the enemies of Israel (Genesis 19:37–38; cf. Judges 3:28, 10:6).[33]

Lot was certainly a righteous man who is held up in Scripture as someone God rescued from among the ungodly, yet his legacy should remind us of the great danger in being a Christian who is spiritually complacent. Lot's selfish choice of living in Sodom ultimately ended with him losing all his possessions (see Genesis 13:5) and having a stained legacy (Genesis 19:30–38). Believers who compromise with the world only have the worst of both worlds as they incur the enmity of the world without living under the blessing of God. Douglas Wilson concludes that "Lot's righteousness was manifested in his distress at the sensual conduct of the wickedness in Sodom; in other words, he was

---

32. See Doug Wilson, "The Offense of the Gospel," Upsetting the World: 2000 National Conference, https://www.ligonier.org/learn/conferences/holiness_00_national/the-offense-of-the-gospel/?.
33. Although the Moabites and Ammonites were enemies of Israel due to their relationship with Lot (and his relationship with Abraham), God granted them land to inhabit (Deuteronomy 2:9, 19).

righteous in what troubled him." It was good that the wickedness of Sodom distressed Lot, but that is not enough. Lot was not a pillar of righteousness in the same way Abraham was. In the Old Testament, the sons of Lot (Moab and Ammon) are those that conspire against the people of God to try and wipe them out (Psalm 83:6–8), whereas in the New Testament, believers are said to be of the same faith as Abraham and told to imitate that faith (see Romans 4:12–13), but we are not told to be like Lot.

The Destruction of Sodom and Gomorrah

After the angels rescued Lot from the men of Sodom by causing them to go blind (Genesis 19:11), they explained to him: ". . . we are about to destroy this place, because the outcry against its people has become great before the LORD, and the LORD has sent us to destroy it" (Genesis 19:13).[34] Lot now knows what Abraham knew — that Sodom is to be destroyed, which took place around 2067 B.C.[35] In the morning, the angels implore Lot to leave because of the coming danger: "Up! Take your wife and your two daughters who are here, lest you be swept away in the punishment of the city" (Genesis 19:15). Despite the fact Lot knows of the coming danger and that God will act according to His word, "he lingered" (Genesis 19:16). The 19th-century Bishop of Liverpool, England, J.C. Ryle, observes of Lot:

> He was slow when he should have been quick, backward when he should have been forward, trifling when he should have been

---

34. In the first century, the Jewish historian Josephus claims to have still been able to see the remains of Sodom: "In fact, vestiges of the divine fire and the faint traces of five cities are still visible. Still, too, may one see ashes reproduced in the fruits, which from their onward appearance would be thought edible, but on being plucked with the hand dissolve into smoke and ashes. So far are the legends about the land of Sodom borne out by ocular evidence." Josephus, *The Wars of the Jews*, 4.4, 84–85.

35. How do we get the date for Sodom and Gomorrah's destruction? Solomon's temple was built in 967 B.C., and the Israelite Exodus from Egypt was 480 years earlier in 1446 B.C. (see 1 Kings 6:1; cf. Judges 11:26). Israel sojourned in Egypt for 430 years (Exodus 12:40–41; cf. Acts 13:17–20), and Jacob was 130 years old when he entered Egypt (Genesis 47:9). Isaac was 60 years old when Jacob was born (Genesis 25:26). Then with 1 year of pregnancy for Sarah with Isaac, the destruction of Sodom and Gomorrah was around 2067. Abraham was 99 when Sodom was destroyed (Genesis 17:1, 21:5), which would place his birth in 2166 B.C. For a defense of these dates, see Simon Turpin, "Biblical Problems with Identifying Tall el-Hammam as Sodom," *Answers Research Journal*, 14 (2021): 45–61, March 10, 2021, https://answersingenesis.org/archaeology/biblical-problems-identifying-tall-el-hammam-sodom/.

hastening, loitering when he should have been hurrying, cold when he should have been hot.[36]

Lot's lingering suggests he could not let go of Sodom and is again another warning to Christians who also "linger" in their Christian lives because they are caught up with the things of this world. Because of his lingering, the angels had to "seize" Lot and set him and his family outside of the city. Apart from this act of mercy from the LORD, they would have faced the same fate as the rest of Sodom (Genesis 19:16). This is a reminder that amid the judgment of Sodom and Gomorrah, God's mercy is evident; He knows how to rescue the godly from their trials (2 Peter 2:9). Warned by the angels not to look back at the coming destruction, Lot and his family go to the city of Zoar. However, only Lot and his two daughters arrive there, as his wife did not heed the warning of the angels and looked back to Sodom and was turned to a pillar of salt (Genesis 19:26). By looking back intently at Sodom, Lot's wife not only disobeyed the angels' warning but showed that she could not let go of living in Sodom.[37] It was on their arrival at Zoar when the LORD destroyed Sodom and Gomorrah:

> The sun had risen on the earth when Lot came to Zoar. Then the LORD rained on Sodom and Gomorrah sulfur and fire from the LORD out of heaven. And he overthrew those cities, and all the valley, and all the inhabitants of the cities, and what grew on the ground (Genesis 19:23–25).

Moses uses the language of the Flood in Genesis 6–7 to describe the destruction of Sodom. Just as the LORD sent the waters of the Flood that "rained" (*mamtîr*, Genesis 7:4) down on the earth in the days of Noah, so He "rained" (*himtîr*) down sulfur and fire on Sodom and Gomorrah in a fiery deluge. The fiery deluge "destroyed" (*šahēt*) Sodom, as the earth was destroyed by water at the time of the Flood (see Genesis 13:10, 19:29; cf. 6:13, 17).[38] The Hebrew word for "sulfur" (*goprît*) is related to an Akkadian word that has to do with oil or petroleum (see Genesis 14:10). It is used elsewhere in the Old Testament of God's judgment of the wicked

---

36. J.C. Ryle, *Holiness* (Durham, England: Evangelical Press, 1879), 147.
37. The Hebrew verb translated "looked back" (*nābat*) can mean "look intently, or to gaze" (see Genesis 15:5).
38. Wenham notes: "שָׁחַת 'destroy': this root, apart from 38:9, is used in Genesis only for the destruction of the flood and of these cities." Wenham, *Genesis 1-15*, 297.

(see Psalm 11:6; Isaiah 34:9; Ezekiel 38:22). The result of the destruction caused the smoke from Sodom to go up like *kĕqîtōr hakkibšān*, "the smoke of a furnace" (Genesis 19:28). The *kibšān* is a kiln that requires intense heat for baking pottery (Exodus 9:8), and the word for smoke (*qîtōr*) is not the word associated with an ordinary fire but an intense thick smoke (i.e., clouds in a thunderstorm; Psalms 119:83, 148:8).

Through the raining down of sulfur and fire, God "overthrew" (*hăpōk*) Sodom, the valley, all the inhabitants, and everything that grew on the ground. Everything was destroyed; it was a total catastrophe. The Greek translation of the Old Testament (LXX) translates the Hebrew word *hăpōk* as *katestrephen*, which is the source for the word catastrophe. The same word is used in the New Testament when Jesus cleanses the temple and "overturned [*katestrephen*] the tables of the money-changers" (Matthew 21:12). The Apostle Peter's description of Sodom's "extinction" (*katastrophe*) fits well with the judgment brought upon the city that turned it to ashes (see 2 Peter 2:6).[39] In the end, what attracted Lot to Sodom (the beautiful land, Genesis 13:10) was all gone. The whole land was burned out so that nothing could grow and no person would live there (see Deuteronomy 29:23; Jeremiah 49:18, 50:40). It is another reminder to Christians that "the world is passing away along with its desires, but whoever does the will of God abides forever" (1 John 2:17). Remember that Lot started out his life living under the blessing of his relative Abraham but then because "he saw" the beautiful Jordan valley, he moved toward Sodom. He later became a resident of the wicked city of Sodom but tragically ended his life by living in a mountain cave like a recluse (Genesis 19:30).

The national catastrophe that came upon Sodom and Gomorrah is used in the New Testament to serve as an example because it anticipates the judgment to come, as can be seen by Jude's comments on the destruction of Sodom and Gomorrah:

> . . . just as Sodom and Gomorrah and the surrounding cities, which likewise indulged in sexual immorality and pursued

---

39. Schreiner comments on whether the word *katastrophe* was original to the text: "I suspect that Metzger's suggestion that some scribes overlooked the word *katastrophe* since the next word 'condemned' (*katekrinen*) begins with the same letters (*kat*) is correct. The inclusion of the word fits with Peter's emphasis on the *results* of the judgment. Perhaps Peter alluded here to the Septuagint, for Gen 19:29 says that God sent Lot away from the middle of 'the destruction' (*tes katastrophes*)." See Thomas Schreiner, *1, 2 Peter, Jude: The New American Commentary* Vol. 37 (Nashville, TN: B&H Publishing Group, 2003), 340.

unnatural desire, serve as an example by undergoing a punishment of eternal fire (Jude 7).

Jude uses Sodom and Gomorrah as an "example" for the punishment of the ungodly, which is characterized as "eternal fire" (*pyros aiōniou*; cf. Matthew 25:46). New Testament scholar Thomas Schreiner notes that the "destruction of Sodom and Gomorrah is not merely a historical curiosity; it functions typologically as a prophecy of what is in store for the rebellious."[40] As was noted at the beginning of the chapter, Jesus said that at His Second Coming the judgment will be just as sudden and devastating as it was at Sodom (Luke 17:29–30). While the destruction of Sodom and Gomorrah was a devastating catastrophe, Jesus' words also seem to indicate the coming future judgment will be even far greater than Sodom's. In preparing His disciples to take the message of the Kingdom out into the towns and streets of Israel, Jesus says of those who reject the message:

> But whenever you enter a town and they do not receive you, go into its streets and say, "Even the dust of your town that clings to our feet we wipe off against you. Nevertheless know this, that the kingdom of God has come near." I tell you, it will be more bearable on that day for Sodom than for that town (Luke 10:10–12).

The final judgment would be far greater for those cities in Jesus' day than for Sodom because of the greater and final revelation that has come to them in the person of Jesus (Luke 12:47–48; cf. Hebrews 1:1–2, 2:1–3). Likewise, those today who hear the gospel and willingly reject it will face a greater judgment than Sodom. This is why the judgment that came upon Sodom and Gomorrah should be a caution against scoffing at God, as it shows that He indeed judges sin justly. It should also cause us to be slow in calling down judgment on people in our society today. The disciples James and John learned this lesson when they wanted God to wipe out the Samaritans (the enemies of Israel) because they did not receive Jesus:

> "Lord, do you want us to tell fire to come down from heaven and consume them?" But he turned and rebuked them. And they went on to another village (Luke 9:54–56).

---

40. Schreiner, *2 Peter, Jude*, 453.

The image of "fire" recalls the destruction of Sodom and Gomorrah. The disciples' zeal for Jesus, however, was misguided and shows their wrong attitude toward the Samaritans. It is our job to preach and warn people, but we should remember that the act of judgment belongs to God alone (Luke 19:24–27). The knowledge that there is a future judgment to come should motivate us to warn those who are still in their sins and are therefore ungodly. As Christians, we should remember that at one time we were once ungodly and "without Christ" and "having no hope and without God in the world" (Ephesians 2:12; NKJV). Therefore, we should not reach out to people in fear or hate but with love and grace, as this is what we have been shown by our Savior (Ephesians 2:5; Titus 3:5). The late 20th-century preacher Martyn Lloyd Jones asked the question of believers:

> Are we like . . . Lot? The world today is amazingly like the world of those days. Is it easy for people to tell that we are Christians? Are we different, do we stand out? Are we, by being what we are, a rebuke to modern society? Above all, are we burdened about it all? Do we grieve for God's honour and God's glory? Do we grieve for the souls of men hurtling themselves thus to destruction? Are we praying about it and doing our utmost to hasten the coming of a true revival and religious awakening? This is the challenge of . . . Lot to the modern Christian.[41]

---

41. Martyn Lloyd Jones, *2 Peter* (Edinburgh: Banner of Truth, 1983), 154.

CHAPTER NINE

THE PATIENCE OF THE LORD

2 Peter 3:10

But do not overlook this one fact, beloved, that with the Lord one day is as a thousand years, and a thousand years as one day. The Lord is not slow to fulfil his promise as some count slowness, but is patient toward you, not wishing that any should perish, but that all should reach repentance (2 Peter 3:8–9).

For hundreds of years the Christian worldview shaped the thinking of the Western world on such issues as science, morality, justice, and truth. Generally, even people who did not identify as Christians would have accepted the fact that there is one God who created all things and had given us His holy law. Today, however, is a different story. Over nearly the last two centuries the effects of the Enlightenment and the Darwinian revolution has helped reshape the Western world in its view on science, morality, justice, and truth. In many ways science has become scientism, morality has become immorality, justice has become injustice, and truth has become relativism. The Western world today has now become a very twisted and corrupt place in which everything seems to be reversed and where people "call evil good and good evil, who put darkness for light and light for darkness, who put bitter for sweet and sweet for bitter!" (Isaiah 5:20). One specific way in which morality has been twisted that is often overlooked is how people are becoming more and more consumed by anger. Whether it be from the common use of foul and abusive language in public and in political discourse or even from physical violent outbursts in public, this outpouring of anger is seen by many as a positive quality rather than a shameful act. It is seen as acceptable because someone has been offended and therefore their anger becomes a justified response. When words break down, people tend toward anger and not civility, but this only makes things worse, not better. This has even led many people today to seek reparation or retaliation rather than reconciliation. Why? Because a secular society that is built upon humanism has no ethical foundation to know what to do with anger.

It is even common today to see a vile hatred of God celebrated in our culture whereby people publicly and unashamedly vent their anger at Him. In an interview on Irish television in 2015, which has been seen by well over 8 million people on the internet, actor and atheist Stephen Fry was asked what he would say if he got to heaven and met God. He said:

> I'll say, bone cancer in children — what's that about? How dare you. How dare you create a world in which there is such misery that is not our fault. It's not right, it's utterly, utterly evil. Why should I respect a capricious, mean minded, stupid God who creates a world which is so full of injustice and pain?

Fry was then asked if he thought he would get into heaven and replied:

> But I wouldn't want to. I wouldn't want to get in on his terms. They are wrong . . . because the God who created this universe, if it was created by God, is quite clearly a maniac, utter maniac, totally selfish. We have to spend our life on our knees thanking him?! What kind of god would do that?[1]

Fry's angry rant is a blasphemous insult of the true character and nature of God and is, in fact, evidence of His mercy toward sinners. As the Psalmist said: "If you, O LORD, should mark iniquities, O Lord, who could stand?" (Psalm 130:3). Sadly, Fry only sees a broken, fallen world and not the reason why it is broken and fallen (Genesis 3). If he had taken the time to read the Bible, he would have seen that God has revealed to us that His original creation, which reflects His character, was declared to

---

1. See "Stephen Fry was asked what he would say to God if they met. His answer is being investigated by police," *The Independent*, May 7, 2015, https://www.independent.co.uk/news/world/europe/stephen-fry-blasphemy-god-ireland-confronted-by-met-a7722191.html.

be "very good" (Genesis 1:31) and did not contain cancer or other infir-mities. No doubt, as an atheist Fry would reject what the Bible says about our fallen world because of his acceptance of evolution as a fact. But what this really shows, however, is that Fry's angry rant is really against the "god" who would use evolution to create the world. This is contrary to the narrative from theistic evolutionists who say that biblical creation is a stumbling block to unbelievers accepting the gospel (cf. 1 Corinthians 1:18–23). Fry's comments show that the opposite is true, as the "god" who would use evolution to create is seen as incompetent, cruel, and unworthy of worship. Nevertheless, as was pointed out in chapter 5, Fry's atheism has no objective foundation to accuse God of being immoral, as atheism cannot account for an objective standard of morality and there-fore cannot accuse anyone of being immoral.

The truth of the matter is that anger, as all sin does, comes from a corrupt reaction of the pride in our sinful natures:

> Now the works of the flesh are evident: sexual immorality, impu-rity, sensuality, idolatry, sorcery, enmity, strife, jealousy, *fits of anger*, rivalries, dissensions, divisions, envy, drunkenness, orgies, and things like these. I warn you, as I warned you before, that those who do such things will not inherit the kingdom of God (Galatians 5:19–21; emphasis mine).

What human anger really demonstrates, though, is how unlike God we truly are. For example, when people get angry, it often leads to a lack of love, compassion, kindness, and mercy, and they are anything but slow to anger on those who have offended them. Forgiveness tends to be difficult if it ever comes at all. This is the very opposite of the true character and nature of God, as revealed in the Bible:

> The Lord is gracious and merciful, slow to anger and abounding in steadfast love (Psalm 145:8).

The prophet Jonah knew this firsthand. Jonah lived in the 8th century under the rule of King Jeroboam II (793–753 B.C.; cf. 2 Kings 14:25). At this time in the history of Israel, God called Jonah to go and preach to their enemies, the people of Nineveh, which was the capital of the Assyr-ian empire. Jonah would have known that the people of Nineveh were well known for their cruelty, as they loved violence and wanted to instill terror into the hearts of their enemies: tearing out the tongues of those who blasphemed their gods, beating people to death with the statues of idols, and feeding their corpses to animals.[2] So, when God told Jonah to go and preach to the people of Nineveh, he refused to go because he knew the true character of God:

> I knew that you are a gracious God and merciful, slow to anger and abounding in steadfast love, and relenting from disaster (Jonah 4:2; cf. Exodus 32:12–14, 34:6).

Jonah did not run away from God because of the responsibility of preaching; he ran away because he knew the history of Israel and what God was really like (e.g., the golden calf incident, see below). Jonah did not want the enemies of Israel to experience God's grace and compassion, but believed they deserved God's anger. This is why after Nineveh received God's mercy, Jonah ended up throwing a temper tantrum and feeling sorrier for himself rather than for the people of Nineveh (Jonah 4:6–9). The reason the Book of Jonah ends with a question (Jonah 4:11) is to force the reader to take sides. Are we going to be like Jonah and show a lack of compassion, or will we show compassion in the situations God has placed them in? People who have a different worldview than we do are not our enemies who need to be destroyed; rather, they are those whose worldview needs to be changed through the transforming power of the gospel (cf. 2 Corinthians 10:4–5).

If we take the time to think about it, what is truly amazing is that even though it is God who is the one offended at every sin all the time (Psalm 7:11–13), He is the one who is slow to anger and patient toward sinners. This is why God's characteristic of patience is something that should be reflected in the life of the believer, as we are called to be like Him (Ephesians 4:2). If we claim to love God, who Himself is patient and is slow to anger toward sinners, then we too must be slow to anger ourselves. This is why the New Testament speaks so much on the issue of anger and why James the half-brother of Jesus said:

> Know this, my beloved brothers: let every person be quick to hear, slow to speak, slow to *anger*; for the *anger* of man does not produce the righteousness of God (James 1:19–20; emphasis mine).

---

2. See Mark F. Rooker, "The Book of Jonah," in *The World and the Word: An Introduction to the Old Testament* (Nashville, TN: B&H Academic, 2011), 450.

Whereas anger is a product of our fallen nature, patience is a fruit of the spirit that must be produced within our life because it reflects the true nature and character of God (Galatians 5:22).

The Lord Is Patient toward You

In the above verses (2 Peter 3:8–9), Peter continues to deal with the scoffing of the false teachers. The false teachers had scoffed at the idea that Jesus would come again and the judgment that comes with it. Peter dealt with these arguments from the scoffers by pointing out that "it escapes their notice . . ." that the events of creation and the Flood are evidence that God has intervened in the world and judged the sinful actions of mankind in the past. Now, however, Peter turns to believers and tells them not to "let this one *fact* escape your notice. . ." (NASB, emphasis added). This may be because the teaching of the scoffers either had caused believers to doubt or because they had their own concerns over the return of the Lord (Jesus, *kyrios*, 3:18; cf. 1:11, 2:20). So, Peter offers them one fact containing two arguments that should not escape their notice: 1) the Lord's timetable is different than ours, and 2) the Lord has a reason for His slowness. It was necessary for Peter to answer these questions as even believers can have a less-than-biblical worldview if they have been influenced by the culture or have questions raised because of the arguments from those who scoff at God's Word.

The first question Peter deals with is the issue of the Lord's timetable (the Father, 3:8–10) as being different to ours, when he states: ". . . that with the Lord one day is as a thousand years, and a thousand years as one day." These words in verse 8 have been misused by many to say that, therefore, the days of creation in Genesis 1 could possibly be referring to long periods of time. However, the context here has nothing to do with the days of creation but with God's patience in the salvation of His people. The context here is eschatological, from the Greek words *eschatos* (last) and *logos* (word), and refers to the "doctrine of the last things." The text says, "with the Lord one day is like a thousand years"; the word "like" is a simile which is used here to teach that God, who inhabits eternity (Isaiah 57:15), is outside of time and does not relate to it the way humans do. Peter tells his readers "do not overlook," and this implies that his readers were meant to recall something, namely Psalm 90:4 (a Psalm of Moses):

> For a thousand years in Your sight
> Are like yesterday when it passes by,
> Or as a watch in the night.

Psalm 90:4 is a case of synonymous parallelism where a long period of a thousand years is contrasted with two short periods: yesterday and a watch in the night. Those who want to interpret the days of creation as 1,000 years should pay attention to the final statement that a thousand years are as a watch in the night, which is 4 hours long. If you use 2 Peter 3:8 to argue that the days of creation are 1,000 years long, then to be consistent you would also have to say they are 4 hours long according to Psalm 90:4. But this is not the point that Peter (or Moses) is making. Peter's argument is that from the divine perspective, time is not the same as from the human perspective. A period that seems long from a human standard is actually brief according to divine calculation. This is the reason for Jesus being slow in His return. Since the Lord does not regard time as we do, then it follows that He is not slow to fulfil His promise. The promise (*epangelia*) is referring back to verse 4, "Where is the promise of his coming?" but it also looks forward to the promise of a new heaven and earth (2 Peter 3:13). The scoffers had a lack of understanding of the ways of God, as they mistook His "slowness" for not fulfilling His promise. This was the mistake of the wicked servant that Jesus referred to in His parable, as he thought he would not be called to account for his actions because: "My master is delayed" (Matthew 24:48). The reason for the Lord's slowness in coming, as Peter explains, is due to His mercy, as He "is patient toward you, not wishing that any should perish, but that all should reach repentance." The fact that Peter is saying the Lord is "not wishing that any should perish" does not mean he believes in universal salvation, as he clearly believes there is a judgment to come (2 Peter 3:7, 10; cf. Acts 10:42). It should be noted that there is debate among Christians as to who the "any" and the "all" specifically refer to, but this is beyond the purpose of this book.[3] Nonetheless, Peter goes on to remind believers that they should "count the patience of our Lord as salvation" (2 Peter 3:15). God's "patience" (*makrothymei*) toward sinners is redemptive, as it speaks to His "long/massive" (*makro*) capacity to contain his "anger" (*thymei*) at sin.

---

3. Christians who are Arminian in their theology understand the "any" and the "all" in 3:9 as referring to God's desire to save every single person alive, whereas Christians who are Calvinistic in their theology generally understand the "any" and the "all" to be an expansion of the "you" in 3:9 and referring to God's desire to save His elect people (3:1; cf. 1 Peter 1:1).

Even though today many who scoff at the Bible see God in the Old Testament as being some sort of tyrant or bully, it is during this period of history that God's patience in judgment is repeatedly seen and most notably after the golden calf incident when the people of Israel committed idolatry (Exodus 32:1–6) and Moses called on God to "Turn from your burning anger and *relent from this disaster* against your people" (Exodus 32:12; emphasis mine; cf. Jonah 4:2). After God relented (Exodus 32:14), He revealed Himself to Moses:

> The LORD passed before him and proclaimed, "The LORD, the LORD, a God merciful and gracious, *slow to anger*, and abounding in steadfast love and faithfulness. . ." (Exodus 34:6; emphasis mine; cf. Numbers 14:18).

One of the five attributes mentioned here that characterize God is that He is "slow to anger" (an idiomatic expression that literally means to be "long nosed"[4]) with the moral failing of His people. Interestingly, in the Greek translation of the Old Testament (LXX), the phrase "slow to anger" (*makrothymos*) has the same Greek root as the word "patience" in 2 Peter 3:9. Not only was God slow to anger when His covenant people (Israel) sinned against Him, but He was also slow to anger when people outside the covenant community sinned against Him. God's patience is especially seen with the wickedness of the Canaanites. The Canaanites were the descendants of Canaan, the grandson of Noah, who had cursed Canaan because of the wicked behavior of his father, Ham (see Genesis 9:20–27, 10:15–19). The Canaanites were well known for their wicked behavior: adultery, bestiality, homosexual acts, and child sacrifice (see Leviticus 18:20–30; Deuteronomy 12:31). Even though God had promised the land of Canaan to Abram (Genesis 12:2–3, 7) He told him that his offspring (Israel) would not yet enter the land of Canaan, as ". . . the iniquity of the Amorites is not yet complete" (Genesis 15:16).[5] God was patient in His judgment of the Canaanites, waiting over 400 years before He judged them, as it was only after Israel's enslavement in Egypt that the time was right for Israel to enter

---

4. "The Hebrew words אֶרֶךְ אַפַּיִם (*'erek 'appayim*) translated 'slow to anger' literally means 'long-nosed,' with its probable origin as an idiomatic expression in the idea of anger being seen in some larger animals by the way they snort." See Douglas Stuart, *Exodus: The New American Commentary* (Nashville, TN: B&H Publishing, 2006), 715.

5. The term *Amorites* is often used to refer to Canaan as a people (Joshua 24:15–18; Judges 6:10).

Canaan. The nation of Israel did not wage war against the Canaanites from a position of moral superiority. In Deuteronomy 9:4–5, God tells Israel:

> Do not say in your heart, after the LORD your God has thrust them out before you, "It is because of my righteousness that the LORD has brought me in to possess this land," whereas it is because of the wickedness of these nations that the LORD is driving them out before you. Not because of your righteousness or the uprightness of your heart are you going in to possess their land, but because of the wickedness of these nations the LORD your God is driving them out from before you, and that he may confirm the word that the LORD swore to your fathers, to Abraham, to Isaac, and to Jacob.

The destruction of the Canaanites was particularized, and it was not just indiscriminate (see Deuteronomy 20:10–14). God ultimately judged the Canaanites not because of their ethnicity but because of their corrupt moral practices, which were bound up in their idolatry (cf. Romans 1:18–32). It has become common for many atheists to use the destruction of the Canaanites to accuse God of having committed "ethnic cleansing." However, ethnic cleansing is fueled by racial hatred, but this was not the reason God told the Israelites to destroy the Canaanites. The issue was idolatry, not ethnicity (see Deuteronomy 12:1–4). In fact, God saved some of the Canaanites because they trusted in Him (see Joshua 6:23, 25; cf. Hebrews 11:31). In the destruction of the Canaanites, God is concerned with sin, not ethnicity. From the beginning, God told Abraham that all the families of the earth would be blessed through him (Genesis 12:3). Ultimately, God's righteous judgment falls on those practicing evil and wickedness — whether people were from the nation of Israel or from the other nations (see Romans 1–3).

When we think about the depths of human sinfulness, it is mystifying that the Lord is patient at all, yet He is. This is because the Lord in His very nature is a saving God: "I, I am the LORD, and besides me there is no savior" (Isaiah 43:11; cf. Titus 3:4, 6). God is patient in containing His divine anger at the sin of humanity, and so He is patient in the sense that He does not give the sinner what he deserves the moment he deserves it. The purpose of the Lord's patience is that people will not perish and face eternal judgment but rather that they would come to repentance. The belief that God is patient so that it will lead people to repentance is also expressed by the Apostle Paul:

> Or do you presume on the riches of his kindness and forbearance and patience, not knowing that God's kindness is meant to lead you to repentance? (Romans 2:4).

It is not uncommon today when hearing preachers and evangelists talk about the gospel that they often leave the message of repentance out of it. But we must remember that some of the first and last words out of the mouth of Jesus when He began and ended His public preaching ministry were about repentance: "Repent, for the kingdom of heaven is at hand" and ". . . repentance for the forgiveness of sins should be proclaimed in his name to all nations. . ." (Matthew 4:17; Luke 24:46–47). This was the same message the Apostle Peter preached to the nation of Israel on the Day of Pentecost: "Repent and be baptized every one of you in the name of Jesus Christ for the forgiveness of your sins, and you will receive the gift of the Holy Spirit" (Acts 2:38). The Apostle Paul also proclaimed a message of repentance in his missionary journeys when he testified "both to Jews and to Greeks of repentance toward God and of faith in our Lord Jesus Christ" (Acts 20:21). The biblical idea of repentance (*metanoia*) is not a simple saying sorry for the "bad things" we have done; rather, it is the forsaking of our sinful actions, turning to God in faith, and producing fruit in keeping with that repentance (Luke 3:8; Acts 26:20; 1 Thessalonians 1:9–10). What is ironic is that the scoffers "use God's patience as an argument against God, when it should lead them to repentance."[6] God's patience toward sinners is a theme that runs throughout Scripture. In fact, in his first letter, the Apostle Peter told us of the patience of God and His saving nature when He waited patiently in the days of Noah:

> For Christ also suffered once for sins, the righteous for the unrighteous, that he might bring us to God, being put to death in the flesh but made alive in the spirit, in which he went and proclaimed to the spirits in prison, because they formerly did not obey, when *God's patience waited in the days of Noah*, while the ark was being prepared, in which a few, that is, eight persons, were brought safely through water (1 Peter 3:18–20; emphasis mine).

6. Schreiner, *1, 2 Peter, Jude*, 381.

While God could have just wiped the entire human race out and simply started out again with Noah, He was patient in his day, indicating He was merciful toward sinners while the Ark was being prepared. In the end, only eight persons — Noah, his wife, his three sons and their wives — were saved from the waters of the Flood (cf. Matthew 7:14). God's patience toward sinners in the account of the Flood is often overlooked, as the Flood has too-often become a sanitized children's story within our churches. It is often seen as a happy tale about Noah and the animals going into the Ark two by two. The reality of the biblical account of the Flood is that it is a horrifying account of judgment but also one of glorifying redemption.

God's Patience in Noah's Day

To appreciate God's patience in the days of Noah, it is necessary to understand what had happened to humanity in those days. Genesis 6:1–4 sets up the background to the Flood:

> When man began to multiply on the face of the land and daughters were born to them, the sons of God saw that the daughters of man were attractive. And they took as their wives any they chose. Then the LORD said, "My Spirit shall not abide in man forever, for he is flesh: his days shall be 120 years." The Nephilim were on the earth in those days, and also afterward, when the sons of God came in to the daughters of man and they bore children to them. These were the mighty men who were of old, the men of renown.

At this time in human history, marriage and procreation were still normative, although the consequence of the actions of the "sons of God"[7] with the "daughters of man" led the LORD to pronounce: "My Spirit shall not abide in man forever, for he is flesh: his days shall be 120 years" (Genesis 6:3). But what is the meaning of the 120 years? There are some commentators who see this as the shortening of human life spans to 120 years, but this view seems to conflict with the life spans of many of the patriarchs who lived after the Flood (Abraham, 175; Isaac, 180; Jacob, 147; Moses, 120; after his restoration, Job lived another 140 years) and even with

---

7. There is a difference of opinion as to the identity of the "sons of God," with commentators on Genesis providing at least four main views as to their identification: 1) angelic beings (Gordon Wenham), 2) godly line of Seth (John Currid), 3) earthly or dynastic kings (Meredith Kline), and 4) demon-possessed kings (Bruce Waltke).

some people living in recent times.[8] It would seem best to understand the 120 years as the time span between the LORD's pronouncement and the Flood (see Genesis 5:32, 7:6), as Hamilton explains:

> Is this an age limit, or is it a period of grace prior to the Flood (i.e., his [remaining] days shall be 120 years)? The first alternative faces the difficulty that most of the people in the rest of Genesis lived well beyond 120 years. It is possible to interpret the longer life spans of the patriarchs as a mitigation or suspension of the divine penalty, just as an earlier announced divine penalty ("on the day you eat of it you shall surely die") was not immediately implemented. But the (imminent) withdrawal of the divine Spirit as a means of lowering the life span of humanity does not make a great deal of sense. Rather, it seems to presage some event that is about to occur. Accordingly, we prefer to see in this phrase a reference to a period of time that prefaces the Flood's beginning. It is parallel to Jon. 4:5, "Yet forty days, and Nineveh shall be overthrown." God's hand of judgment is put on hold.[9]

This period of 120 years is a time of God's patience in which Noah will prepare the Ark.[10] The outcome of the union between "the sons of God" and "the daughters of man" are the "mighty men" described as "men of renown" (Genesis 6:4). These "mighty men"[11] are "the warrior class, men of ignoble reputation whose violent exploits are remembered (cf. Genesis 6:11-13) and whose names strike fear in the hearts of their hearers."[12] These men of renown "seek reputation by their wicked deeds in the way the people of Babel will seek fame through their building enterprise (cf. Genesis 11:4)."[13] Interestingly, before this time the narrative of Genesis has previously focused upon the sins of individuals (Adam, Eve, Cain,

---

8. In recent history, the oldest people ever were Jeanne Calment (1875–1997) of France, who died at the purported age of 122 years, 164 days, and Mbah Ghoto (1870–2019) of Indonesia, who died at 146 years old.
9. See Hamilton, *Genesis 1–17*, 269.
10. This does not mean it took 120 years to build the Ark. Rather, it has been calculated from the chronological data within Genesis 5 and 6 that it took around 55–75 years. See Ham and Hodge, *A Flood of Evidence*, 169–172.
11. The word "mighty" is the Hebrew word *gibbōrîm*, which is used a few chapters later to describe Nimrod, who began to be a "mighty man" on the earth (Genesis 10:8).
12. Mathews, *Genesis 1–11:26*, 338.
13. Ibid., 339. The Hebrew word for "renown," *šēm*, is used in Genesis 11:4 when the people at Babel desire to "make a name (*šēm*) for ourselves."

Lamech), but now the author of Genesis shifts to focus on mankind as a whole to show that God's judgment is not just against certain people but the wickedness of mankind in general. After the events of Genesis 6:1–4, the depths of man's depravity are clearly seen:

> The LORD saw that the wickedness of man was great in the earth, and that every intention of the thoughts of his heart was only evil continually. And the LORD regretted that he had made man on the earth, and it grieved him to his heart. So the LORD said, "I will blot out man whom I have created from the face of the land, man and animals and creeping things and birds of the heavens, for I am sorry that I have made them." . . . Now the earth was corrupt in God's sight, and the earth was filled with violence. And God saw the earth, and behold, it was corrupt, for all flesh had corrupted their way on the earth (Genesis 6:5–7, 11–12).

Since the Fall in Genesis 3, there has been an escalation of human wickedness with murder, pride, anger, vengeance, and polygamy all taking place (see Genesis 4). Genesis 6:5 records the consequences of 6:1–4, as the LORD sees that the wickedness of man has grown to be great in the earth.[14] This is a day when man is graphically described as "wicked" and when "every intent of the thoughts of his heart was only evil continually" (Genesis 6:5). It was because of the great wickedness of man that "the LORD regretted that he had made man on the earth" (Genesis 6:6). Whereas man's heart is only evil continually, God's heart contains "regret" (*nāham*; cf. 1 Samuel 15:11, 35) that He had made mankind. These statements in the Bible such as God "regretting" or "repenting" have been taken by some to mean that God did not know something or, in this case, that His decision to create mankind was a mistake. However, the focus of this passage on God's sorrow is the wickedness of mankind who not only bears His image but was once without sin in His very good creation (Genesis 1:31).[15] This does not mean that the actions or decisions of mankind change the mind of God. Rather, passages such as Genesis 6:6 need to be taken into consideration with Numbers 23:19:

---

14. Jewish scholar Nahum Sarna points out that the words "was great" in 6:5 are: "The use of the same Hebrew stem here as in verse 1 suggests that the measure of evil grows in proportion to the growth in population." Sarna, *Genesis*, 47.
15. This can be seen by the repeated (x4) use of the Hebrew word for mankind, *'ādām*, in Genesis 6:5–7.

God is not man, that he should lie, or a son of man, that he
should change his mind. Has he said, and will he not do it? Or
has he spoken, and will he not fulfill it?

In doing so, we will understand that from our human viewpoint God
seems to change His mind about people, but He is only represented to
us that way that we might relate to our omniscient God (cf. James 1:17).
God's mind doesn't change because it doesn't need to change. He knows
everything, and He knows the end from the beginning (Isaiah 46:10).

The wickedness of man upon the earth has reached such proportions
that the LORD, after viewing the corruption of mankind, decides to blot
them out from the face of the land (Genesis 6:7). The word "blot" (*māhâ*)
at its root has the emphatic meaning "to erase, cancel or obliterate." In
a positive sense it refers to the blotting out of man's transgressions from
his heart (Psalm 51:1). But the Flood is not just about blotting out sin,
but sinners. In a negative sense it is used for blotting out the memory
of Amalek from under heaven because he attacked the faint and weary
among the Israelites after they came out of Egypt (Exodus 17:14; cf. Deuteronomy 25:17–19). This drastic measure is taken because the extent of
sin is not just over all the earth but is in the heart (*lēb*) of man. In Hebrew
anthropology, the heart refers to the center of the will and moral activi-
ties (1 Samuel 16:7; Jeremiah 17:10). Even the devastation caused by the
Flood cannot change the sinful nature of man's heart, as after the Flood
the LORD said: ". . . the intention of man's heart is evil from his youth"
(Genesis 8:21). This is because the reasoning of our hearts depends on
our moral condition (Matthew 12:33–34, 15:19). The only way this can
change is if we are given a new heart by the Spirit of God so that we can
love God aright (Jeremiah 31:33; Hebrews 8:10). It is only God who
can purify our hearts if their intentions have been defiled by sin (Psalm
51:10).

This was also a day when the earth was corrupted and filled with
violence (Genesis 6:11–12). The corruption that has spread all over the
earth is defined by the term "violence" (*hāmās*), a judicial term that has
to do with ". . . the flagrant subversion of the ordered process of law,"[16]
and here it most likely refers ". . . to the arrogant disregard for the sanc-
tity and inviolability of human life."[17] This can be seen in other passages

16. Sarna, *Genesis*, 51.
17. Ibid., 51.

where *hāmās* implies severe treatment of another person (Genesis 16:5) and implies the use of physical violence (Genesis 49:5). Old Testament scholar Kenneth Mathews recognizes that whereas "God has blessed the human family with the power of procreation to fill the earth (1:28; 9:1), these culprits [the mighty men] have 'filled the earth' by procreating 'violence' (cf. v. 13; Ezekiel 8:17; 28:16)."[18] This was ultimately a day when God finally said enough is enough and promised to destroy mankind with the earth (Genesis 6:13). The coming destruction of the world is due to its moral corruption, as is implied by the wordplay of "destroy" (*mašhît*) with "corrupted" (*hišhît*) in Genesis 6:12–13.[19] Jesus also saw the days of Noah as characterizing the days that immediately precede His second coming. Jesus uses several terms to describe the indifference of the people in those days: "eating," "drinking," "marrying" (Matthew 24:37–39). These terms obviously need to be considered with how Genesis describes the people in those days: "wicked," "corrupt," "violent," and "evil hearts." Those words, understood in their proper context, imply that moral corruption extended to the people simply carrying on with life and ultimately being unconcerned about God. What stands out in such a dark world is the contrast between Noah and the wicked people of his generation:

> But Noah found favor in the eyes of the LORD. These are the generations of Noah. Noah was a righteous man, blameless in his generation. Noah walked with God (Genesis 6:8–9).

Noah is in the tenth generation from Adam in the line of Seth (Genesis 5:1–32). His father, Lamech, gave him the name Noah (נֹחַ - *nōah*), which is associated with "rest,"[20] in hope that he would one day bring relief to the ground that was cursed because of Adam's disobedience (Genesis 5:29; cf. Genesis 3:17–19). Perhaps the most significant thing we are told about Noah is that he found favor in the eyes of the LORD (Genesis 6:8). Noah was a recipient of God's favor before God decreed judgment on the wicked generation of Noah's day. The fact that Noah found God's favor, or grace (*hēn*), is interesting, as this is the first time the Hebrew word *hēn* appears in the Bible. This is not to say that there was no one before Noah who did not receive God's grace but that even at the height of human wickedness, God is still gracious to people. It was not that Noah was free from sin and so righteous that God decided to save him and his family. Not at all — Noah was just like the rest of humanity, a descendent of Adam, born in sin, and therefore under the reign of death (Romans 5:17). Rather, Noah received God's grace as a gift, as grace can neither be won nor earned (cf. Romans 3:24; Galatians 2:21). The fact that Noah is described as righteous (*saddîq*) is a further description of a man who has received God's grace. This is why Noah is characterized as a righteous man, blameless in his generation (cf. Job 1:1). When the prophet Ezekiel denounced the wickedness of Jerusalem in his own day, he used Noah as the standard of righteousness: ". . . even if these three men, Noah, Daniel, and Job, were in it, they would deliver but their own lives by their righteousness, declares the Lord GOD" (Ezekiel 14:14). Whereas mankind is wicked, Noah stands out because he is blameless (*tāmîm*, an adjective which conveys the idea of being complete, whole, unmixed, blameless, and impeccable). Again, this does not mean that Noah was sinless but that his behavior was upright (Deuteronomy 18:13; Proverbs 11:5). Noah's blamelessness is evidence of his faith in God. The reason Noah can live such a blameless life is because he is someone who "walked" (*hālak*) with God, just as Enoch did (Genesis 5:22). This ethical language of "walking" is used later in Genesis when, after receiving the covenant of circumcision, the LORD appeared to Abraham and told him to "walk before me, and be blameless. . ." (Genesis 17:1). Likewise, Christians today who follow in the faith of Abraham are told to not "walk as the Gentiles do" but to "walk" in love and wisdom because the days are evil (Ephesians 4:17, 5:2, 15–16). In a day of unrestrained evil, it is Noah who had a right relationship with God that stands out (Genesis 7:1).

Noah: A Herald of Righteousness and Man of Faith

In a day of great wickedness when God waited patiently, Noah was not just described as righteous and blameless. Peter describes him as a herald or preacher (*kēryx*) of righteousness (2 Peter 2:5), and the author of the Book of Hebrews uses him as an example of a man of great faith (*pistis*, Hebrews 11:7). These New Testament authors use Noah as an example in order to encourage and remind believers of how to live out their faith in an unrighteous world. It is important to consider both Noah's preaching and his faith.

In chapter two of his second letter, the Apostle Peter said of Noah:

> . . . if he did not spare the ancient world, but preserved Noah, a herald of righteousness, with seven others, when he brought a flood upon the world of the ungodly . . . (2 Peter 2:5).

Peter speaks of Noah being preserved with seven others through the judgment of the Flood; only eight people were saved by God during the Flood (see 1 Peter 3:20), but it also informs us that Noah was a "herald" or "preacher" of righteousness. In what way was Noah a preacher of righteousness? The Greek word used for "herald" comes from the noun κῆρυξ (kēryx) and is related to the verb "proclaimed" (kēryssō), which is used of "one who makes public declarations of a transcendent nature."[21] Preaching is the means by which God communicates "good news" (euag-gelizō) through His human agents, and this is not just limited to the New Testament (see 1 Peter 1:10–12). But what did Noah preach about? In the New Testament, kēryssō is regularly used for gospel preaching to call people to repentance (Mark 1:4; Luke 24:47; Romans 10:15; 1 Timothy 2:7; 2 Timothy 2:11). It is important to note that neither Genesis 6 nor any passage in the New Testament tells us the extent or specific content of his preaching, which is important to remember, as Noah is often charged with saying things that the text does not even mention. Nevertheless, it does seem safe to assume that he called the wicked people of his day to repentance. This was taught by Jewish tradition at the time of Peter. The Jewish historian Josephus wrote: "But Noah, indignant at their conduct and viewing their counsels with displeasure, urged them to come to a better frame of mind and amend their ways."[22] It is also implicit in him being called "righteous," as New Testament scholar Thomas Schreiner recognizes:

> In emphasizing God's righteous judgment of sinners, Noah also invited the people of his age to repent and to enjoy God's forgive-ness, his saving righteousness. This fits with what Peter said about God's righteousness in 1:1, which is a gift received by believers. Those who enjoy God's saving righteousness repented of their

21. BDAG: *A Greek-English Lexicon of the New Testament*, 543.
22. Josephus, *Antiquity of the Jews*, 1.74

sins and turned to God, acknowledging his righteous judgment against them.[23]

Does this mean that if any of Noah's contemporaries had repented and trusted in God they would have been welcome on the Ark? Again, Genesis and the New Testament are silent on this issue. Genesis 6:18 suggests that the Ark was built for Noah and his family, which seems to be confirmed by the author of Hebrews, who says the Ark was "for the saving of his household" (11:7). This is not to definitively say that God would not have allowed others onto the Ark if they repented. It certainly is possible, but we should be careful not to speculate about what the Bible does not say but rather emphasize what is clear from the text. Despite man's wickedness, God showed Himself to be gracious in saving Noah and his household. Even with the testimony of Noah, a preacher of righteousness, the people went about their daily affairs, unconcerned "until the day when Noah entered the ark, and *they were unaware* until the flood came and swept them all away" (Matthew 24:38–39; emphasis mine). As can be seen from the words of Jesus, the judgment God brought about upon that wicked mankind was sudden and unexpected.

While Peter spoke of Noah as a "preacher of righteousness," the author of Hebrews uses Noah as someone who was faithful in order to encourage his readers to be steadfast in their faith in light of the difficult circumstances they face (Hebrews 10:32–39).

> By faith Noah, being warned by God concerning events as yet unseen, in reverent fear constructed an ark for the saving of his household. By this he condemned the world and became an heir of the righteousness that comes by faith (Hebrews 11:7).

How should we understand the word faith (or trust)? Atheists and skeptics often accuse Christians of believing things or having "faith" without evidence and like to remind them of the old adage: "Faith is believing what you know is not true." In English translations of the New Testament, the most common word for "faith" is the Greek noun πίστις (*pistis*), and "believe" is the Greek verb πιστεύω (*pisteuō*). The leading Greek lexicon today lists a range of meanings for *pistis*, from subjective confidence to an objective basis for confidence, and it shows that it can refer to "that which evokes trust and faith" or a "state of believing based

---

23. Schreiner, *1, 2 Peter, Jude*, 339.

on the reliability of the one trusted, trust, confidence, faith." The word *pisteuō* refers to considering something "to be true and therefore worthy of one's trust" or "to entrust oneself to an entity in complete confidence."[24] In its classical usage, even before the writing of the New Testament, *pistis* referred to "conviction," "certainty," and "proof" that can be relied on.[25] The use of the word *faith* in the New Testament is contrary to atheists and skeptics today who claim that "faith is a belief that is not based on evidence" or "pretending to know what you don't know." The writers of the New Testament never place "faith" (*pistis*) against reason, evidence, or truth, but rather, they use it to refer to a conviction or confidence in something (cf. John 20:28–29; Romans 10:9).

But in what way is Noah an example of faith (or trust)? The writer of Hebrews defines faith as "the substance of things hoped for, the evidence of things not seen" (Hebrews 11:1; NKJV). Faith, in this context, is a settled confidence of something as yet unseen but promised by God. Without faith in the promises of God, it is impossible to please Him (Hebrews 11:6). Noah is a landmark figure in the history of redemption because he was a living example of "the just living by faith" (Hebrews 10:38). This is not "faith" without evidence, as the "faith" of the heroes of faith in Hebrews 11 was based upon knowledge of God's Word. The evidence of Noah's faith is seen in his trusting God, believing in His word, and acting in obedience to God's command to build the Ark (Genesis 6:22, 7:5). When Noah received a "warning," a divine revelation (*chrēmatistheis*, 8:5, 12:25), that a Flood was coming to destroy the earth, he acted on it. Saving faith throughout the Bible is never vague but is always a true response to God's revelation of Himself (Genesis 22:1–2; cf. Hebrews 11:17–19).

What evidence did Noah have to go on when God asked him to build the Ark? Noah had never seen anything resembling a global Flood before. All he had to go on was the truth of the character of God. Noah may have known of God's promise that one day the serpent's head would be crushed (Genesis 3:15) and therefore trusted that God would keep that promise. Noah's faith is illustrated in the fact that, after being warned by God that a great Flood would be coming, he made practical preparations

24. BDAG: *A Greek-English Lexicon of the New Testament*, 816–820.
25. Rudolf Bultmann and Artur Weiser, "πιστεύω, πίστις ..." in the *Theological Dictionary of the New Testament* Volume VI, eds. Gerhard Kittel, Gerhard Friedrich (Grand Rapids, MI: W.B. Eerdmans Publishing Company, 1968), 177.

for something he had "not yet seen." But what motivated Noah to build the Ark? It was his "reverent fear" of God. Noah obeyed God not only because he knew God in a personal way but also because his faith was acting on His word no matter how foolish it may have seemed to the world around him. The "things not yet seen" also bring out a dynamic of the Christian life in that we "walk by faith, not by sight" (2 Corinthians 5:7). The writer to the Hebrews reminds us how those things come together in the believer's life. The believer's righteousness reflected in the world is testifying and witnessing to those unseen realities that are coming. As Christians, we should seek to live our lives in light of a coming judgment and a new heavens and earth (2 Peter 3:11–15). We can't see those things right now, and that faith is seen as foolishness to an unbelieving world.

Noah's faith to take God at His word condemned the faithlessness of the world around him. People may have scoffed at him, called him a fool or insane, but Noah turned out to be the only sane man around. Although Scripture does not specifically say that Noah was scoffed at by the wicked world that he preached to, it is not an unreasonable inference to make. Scoffing is often something people experience for their faith in God (Hebrews 11:36), especially when the truth of God's Word is preached to sinful mankind (e.g., Acts 17:32). It is the essence of sanity to take what God says seriously, whereas it is the insanity of sin to reject the Word of God. The account of Noah and the Flood also teaches us about the reality of alienation from the world and the scoffing that will come from it, for those who side with God. It will cost a person everything for choosing to follow the Lord Jesus in this world, but the reward is priceless (Matthew 13:45–46). It also demonstrates both judgment and salvation. God is a God of righteous judgment who must punish sin, but most wonderfully, He is a God who has provided a way of escape from His judgment. He did this for Noah by way of the Ark. Today, however, Jesus Christ is God's way of escape from His judgment; He is the "Ark" of our salvation, the door by which mankind must enter in to be saved (John 10:9; cf. 14:6), and the only one who can give us rest in a cursed world (Matthew 11:28–29). The Flood is both a horrifying account of judgment but also one of glorifying redemption. Our lives will be characterized by either one of these. Either we will trust in Jesus and be redeemed, or we will face the judgment of God for our sin

(Romans 3:21–26; Acts 17:31).

Noah became an heir of righteousness because of his willingness to believe that which God had promised, and every other heir of righteousness is so only by virtue of having been made one with Christ, the sole heir (Galatians 3:29). Because faith takes us into Christ, who is the heir of all things (Hebrews 1:2), we can only inherit that righteousness by being united with Him. The people that the writer of Hebrews is addressing were under great pressure to give up on Christ and go back to their traditional Jewish belief. But here the writer says to consider Noah, to look at what his faith brought him. Think of what it took for Noah to be righteous in his generation. He constructed an Ark for the saving of his household, and for years he endured a world consumed with wickedness, which required complete faith in God's faithfulness because he knew God was going to destroy the world.

> Therefore we also, since we are surrounded by so great a cloud of witnesses, let us lay aside every weight, and the sin which so easily ensnares us, and let us run with endurance the race that is set before us, looking unto Jesus, the author and finisher of our faith, who for the joy that was set before Him endured the cross, despising the shame, and has sat down at the right hand of the throne of God (Hebrews 12:1–2; NKJV).

We need to remember that just as God judged the whole world in the days of Noah, He has also promised to do so again. Just as in the days of Noah, wickedness still abounds in the hearts of humanity today (Matthew 15:19; Ephesians 2:3). The problem is not merely that as a human race we are sinners, but that we are enemies of God and rightfully under His anger (wrath) and judgment because we are sinful descendants of Adam (Romans 5:10, 12–19). The only solution to this problem is the penal substitutionary atonement of the last Adam, Jesus Christ, as He alone can bear the anger and judgment of God that sinners deserve (1 Peter 1:18–19, 2:24). God's anger can only be propitiated through an atoning sacrifice, and His justice can only be satisfied through the payment of sin's penalty. Both of these standards were met when the Lord Jesus, after being fully obedient to the Father and keeping the law perfectly, freely gave Himself for sinners on the Cross of Calvary. Jesus, in giving His life as an atoning sacrifice, fully satisfied the righteous demands of God.

Therefore, God poured out His wrath upon the innocent Jesus so that guilty sinners who justly deserve God's anger could go free (see Romans 3:23–25; cf. Numbers 8:5–19; Isaiah 53:5–6, 10).[26]

In this sacrificial act of atonement, we see the full measure of God's love for fallen mankind, as the Lord Jesus was sent into the world to save us from our sin (1 John 4:14). Even though it was the Father who sent the Son into the world, Jesus voluntarily laid down His life for us; it was not a decision forced upon Him (John 10:17–18). God's love for a fallen humanity is not because we are so lovable but because He is love (1 John 4:8). Unfortunately, many people tend to think that they can continue in their sin because "God is love, and He is bound to forgive me because that's His job." What this sort of thinking forgets is that God's love is for a world in rebellion against Him. God's love first and foremost deals with sin: "In this is love, not that we have loved God but that he loved us and sent his Son to be the propitiation for our sins" (1 John 4:10). It is often assumed that "world" (*kosmos*) in John 3:16 refers to a very big place, so God's love must be very big because the world is very big. God's love, however, is to be admired not because the world is so big but because the world is so bad (John 3:19), as theologian D.A. Carson points out:

> . . . world in John does not so much refer to bigness as to badness. In John's vocabulary, world is primarily the moral order in wilful and culpable rebellion against God. In John 3:16 God's love in sending the Lord Jesus is to be admired not because it is extended to so big a thing as the world, but to so bad a thing; not to so many people, as to such a wicked people.[27]

The gospel of Jesus Christ does not merely change our status with God, it changes our hearts. As a result, we begin to love that which we did not love and begin to hate what we once loved. The only way for sinners to enjoy God's love is by trusting in what Jesus accomplished for us in His atoning death and His Resurrection from the dead (see John 20:31).

Just as God was patient in the days of Noah, so He is also patient

---

26. In Numbers 8:5–19, the Levites are set apart for service in the sanctuary, as the firstborn of Israel, to make atonement. This is seen in the fact that the people lay their hands on the Levities, and they lay their hands on the animals, and the animals are then sacrificed on their behalf. The Levities were there to make atonement on behalf of the nation of Israel.

27. D.A. Carson, *The Difficult Doctrine of the Love of God* (Nottingham: InterVarsity Press, 2000), 18–19.

today. The fact that Jesus has not already returned means salvation is still available to people (2 Peter 3:15; cf. 2 Corinthians 6:2), which should be a reminder to us as Christians to make the most of every opportunity to witness about our Savior. In the days of Noah, God's patience came to an end when He closed the door of the Ark, as He alone determines when grace is over and the time of judgment begins (see Genesis 7:16). One day in the future, God's patience will run out, and in doing so, it will bring final judgment on the world while sparing the righteous and destroying the unrighteous (2 Peter 2:9).

CHAPTER TEN

THE NEW HEAVENS AND EARTH

2 Peter 3:13

But the day of the Lord will come like a thief, and then the heavens will pass away with a roar, and the heavenly bodies will be burned up and dissolved, and the earth and the works that are done on it will be exposed. Since all these things are thus to be dissolved, what sort of people ought you to be in lives of holiness and godliness, waiting for and hastening the coming of the day of God, because of which the heavens will be set on fire and dissolved, and the heavenly bodies will melt as they burn! But according to his promise we are waiting for new heavens and a new earth in which righteousness dwells (2 Peter 3:10–13).

The doctrine of eschatology (last things), or at least certain aspects of it (the timing and nature of the millennium; is the tribulation past or future, and if it is in the future, will Christians be raptured pre-, mid-, or post-tribulation), is probably one of the most debated and contentious issues within the Church. While these issues are important and may have implications for our ethical and missiological understanding of eschatology, they are not central to the doctrine of eschatology. What is central to the doctrine of eschatology, however, is the biblical teaching that God will one day finally and fully restore this present fallen creation through supernaturally creating a new heavens and earth. Although there are different eschatological perspectives among Christians (Pre-, Post-,

Amillennial), all affirm the presence of a restored new creation that is different to the present creation as important for eschatological hope.[1] The very "promise" Peter mentions to believers that the scoffers doubt (2 Peter 3:4) is not just the removal of sin but of the final and complete restoration of creation, which is the very focal point of the New Testament (cf. Colossians 1:20; Revelation 21–22). It should be of great encouragement to Christians that the climax of eschatology is not only the glorious redemption of believers but also of creation: ". . . that the creation itself will be set free from its bondage to corruption and obtain the freedom of the glory of the children of God" (Romans 8:21).

What may not be known to many Christians, however, is that evolutionists also have a doctrine of eschatology. The idea of evolution and millions of years is not only an account about the origin of the universe, but it is also one about the end of it. If you accept the cosmic evolutionary process of the origin of all things, then to be *consistent* (and thankfully many theistic evolutionists and old-earth creationists are not), you should probably accept the cosmic evolutionary process of the end of all things. These are inseparably tied together. The prolific evolutionary writer and professor of philosophy Michael Ruse, in his book *The Evolution-Creation Struggle*, discusses the antithetical views of both evolution and creation regarding the future:

> . . . in both evolution and creation we have rival religious responses to a crisis of faith — rival stories of origins, rival judgments about the meaning of human life, rival sets of moral dictates, and above all what theologians call rival eschatologies.[2]

---

1. There is a position known as full or hyper-preterism that teaches that the destruction of Jerusalem (A.D. 70) fulfilled all eschatological events, which would include: the resurrection of the dead, the Second Coming of Jesus, the final judgment, and that believers are now enjoying the benefits of the new heavens and earth. According to the New Testament, this is clearly a heretical position on the physical resurrection of the body (see 2 Timothy 2:18). However, theologian Robert Strimple also notes: "In order to maintain their heretical doctrine of the resurrection, the hyper-preterists have devised heretical doctrines of creation, man, sin and its consequences, the person and redemptive work of Christ, and the nature of salvation. Much more than eschatology narrowly defined is at stake in this debate." See Robert Strimple, "Hyper-Preterism on the Resurrection of the Body," in *When Shall These Things Be? A Reformed Response to Hyper-Preterism*, Keith A. Mathison, ed. (Phillipsburg, NJ: Presbyterian and Reformed, 2004), 352.
2. Michael Ruse, *The Evolution-Creation Struggle* (Cambridge, MA: Harvard University Press, 2005), 3.

According to Ruse, evolution and creation are not just rival accounts of origins, the meaning of human life, and morality, but they also contain rival eschatologies. Even though Ruse does believe evolution is a fact, he also recognizes that evolution goes beyond that, because of the moral, epistemological, and ethical questions it asks, to a religious worldview.[3] One of those questions evolutionists ask is: "How will the world end?"

It is becoming increasingly common today to read or hear in the news of evolutionary scientists, politicians, and activist groups warning about apocalyptic end-of-the-world scenarios, urging people to take charge and help save the planet. The reason for this alarmism is because of an evolutionary worldview of the history of the planet. In this worldview, the earth's history spans billions of years and was formed by random, unguided processes, which is why at any point, random processes could make the earth uninhabitable. Therefore, in this worldview, it is up to people to understand it and to fix it. The late evolutionary physicist professor Stephen Hawking commented on the future of humankind:

> It is possible that the human race could become extinct, but it is not inevitable. I think it is almost certain that a disaster such as nuclear war or global warming will befall the Earth within a thousand years. It is essential that we colonize space. I believe that we will eventually establish self-sustaining colonies on Mars and other bodies in the Solar System although probably not within the next 100 years. I am optimistic that progress in science and technology will eventually enable humans to spread beyond the Solar System and out into the far reaches of the Universe.[4]

Hawking's comments are interesting for several reasons. As an atheist, Hawking rejected the fact that the earth was uniquely created and instead chose to believe that it came into existence out of nothing and for no

3. Ruse gives a varied answer to the question, "Is evolution a religion?" He states: "So, what about Darwinism? I don't think believing that Charles Darwin's theory of evolution through natural selection (his version or today's version) commits you to religious belief. I think that if, as I myself would, you extend the scope of the theory to an understanding of knowledge acquisition and justification and the same for morality — evolutionary epistemology and evolutionary ethics — then it can act as a religion substitute or alternative. It gives you a world picture that some people, starting with me, find entirely satisfying." Michael Ruse, "Is Darwinism a Religion?" September 20, 2011, https://www.huffpost.com/entry/is-darwinism-a-religion_b_904828.
4. Stephen Hawking, "Hawking on the future of mankind," January 6, 2012, http://news.bbc.co.uk/today/hi/today/newsid_9672000/9672233.stm.

reason. Yet, he recognizes that if humanity is to go and live on Mars (or other planets), they would have to build "self-sustaining colonies." Why would they need to do this? Because, unlike the earth, Mars is not uniquely designed for life. Mars is too cold for life (in winter, near the poles, temperatures can get down to minus 195 degrees Fahrenheit [125 degrees Celsius]). Its atmosphere is far too thin to support life and is made up of carbon dioxide, so you would not be able to breathe on Mars without a specially made spacesuit. Earth, however, is unique among the planets of the solar system, as it alone is specifically designed to support human life (Isaiah 45:18). Only the earth has the conditions (atmosphere, water, food, etc.) that are necessary to sustain life naturally. In the biblical worldview, there is no need to panic about the future of the planet, as in the Bible, God created the earth a few thousand years ago with a purpose, has promised to keep the earth for life until the consummation of all things (cf. Genesis 8:22), and has shared with us the responsibility for taking care of the earth (Genesis 1:28).

From an atheistic perspective, however, Hawking's plan to escape the coming apocalypse makes sense; if humanity is going to destroy itself on this planet, then in order to survive, they obviously need to find another one. Even this great escape plan will ultimately be futile. Although there are different naturalistic ideas about how the universe will end, most evolutionary scientists agree that the universe will finally come to an end in what they call a "heat death." The evolutionary cosmologist Andrei Linde states,

> In this case, the Universe continues expanding forever. However, in the course of time, galaxies move far away from each other, stars stop burning, and all inhabitants of an open Universe die in the solitude of cold empty space.[5]

In this evolutionary scenario, the time frame for the end of the universe is almost unimaginable; it is thought to take around a thousand billion years for all the stars to use up their energy, as physicist and science writer Robert Matthews explains:

> A mere thousand billion years from now, all the stars will have used up their fuel and fizzled out. There will still be occasional

---

5. Andrei Linde, "Future of the Universe," in *The Origin and Evolution of the Universe*, eds. Ben Zuckerman and Matthew A. Malkin (Sudbury, MA: Jones and Bartlett, 1996), 128.

flashes in the perpetual night: the death throes of stars so large that they have collapsed in on themselves to form black holes. Even these will eventually evaporate in a blast of radiation. For the next 10^{122} years, this Hawking radiation will be the only show in town. By then, even the most massive black holes will evaporate, leaving the universe with nothing to do for an unimaginable 10^{26} years. . . . In the beginning, there may have been light, but in the end, it seems, there will be nothing but darkness.[6]

Even though in the evolutionary worldview the end is a very long, long, long way away, there is no ultimate escape for humanity, as eventually the universe will use up all its energy, and all that will be left is a cold, empty space. It is important to understand that in the naturalistic evolutionary worldview, not only was there was no purpose or reason for the universe to come into existence, but there is also no ultimate purpose or hope for humanity. It is here, however, that evolutionists are inconsistent in how they live out their worldview, as they live as if there is a purpose and hope for humanity. For example, Hawking sees human extinction as a bad thing; however, in an evolutionary worldview, extinction is just a natural part of the evolutionary process of life with no purpose behind it. If you accept evolution, then the human species is just the product of chance random mutations. It then follows that they have no inherent value, meaning, or purpose. For example, atheist and evolutionary biologist Jerry Coyne stated on a BBC documentary: "Evolution . . . says that there is no special purpose for your life because it's a naturalistic philosophy. We have no more extrinsic purpose than a squirrel or an armadillo, and it says that morality does not come from God, it is an evolved phenomenon. . . ."[7] It is no wonder that so many people today have such as skeptical outlook on life and why so many young people believe there is no ultimate purpose to life.

The fact that Hawking and many other evolutionists see human survival as important is ultimately a recognition (whether they accept it or not) of what theologians call the *sensus divinitatis* (a true knowledge of God, Romans 1:18–23). It is to this *sensus* that Christians should appeal

---

6. Robert Matthews, "To Infinity and Beyond," *New Scientist* 158:2129, April 11, 1998, 27–30.

7. See the BBC television documentary entitled *Creationism: Conspiracy Road Trip*. It aired in the UK in October 2012. This quote comes 17 minutes and 47 seconds into the documentary.

in order to show atheists the internal inconsistency of their own world-view. The reason atheists value and seek to preserve human life comes from the fact that knowledge of God gets through to them, not only through His creation but from the fact that they are made in His image (Genesis 1:27).

At the root of this evolutionary interpretation of the end of all things is the influence of the philosophy of naturalism, which is the idea that defines evolution. The philosophy of naturalism, which dominates the sciences today, asserts that all reality can be explained in purely natural categories without any appeal to the supernatural. Naturalism is not only an attack on all things supernatural but also upon science. Over the last several decades, atheists like Stephen Hawking and Richard Dawkins have argued that science, properly understood, renders belief in God untenable. Why? Because unguided, undirected Darwinian mechanisms have produced the appearance of design without itself being guided or directed in any way.[8] Since design is seen as an illusion, the possibility of a designer is also seen as delusional. Why do people like Dawkins believe that complicated things, such as DNA, only appear to be designed? Well, because if it is designed, then the obvious question is, who designed it?

The perspective of today's atheists is directly opposed to the godly men who were responsible for early modern science (i.e., astronomer Nicolaus Copernicus [1473–1543], physicist Isaac Newton [1643–1727], biologist Carl Linnaeus [1707–1778]). Mathematical physicist James Clark Maxwell (1831–1879), who formulated the classical theory of electromagnetic radiation, rejected Darwin's theory of evolution and gave credit to his Creator for his scientific achievements.[9] At Maxwell's instigation, the words of Psalm 111:2 were inscribed (in Latin) above the Cavendish Laboratory in Cambridge University, England:

---

8. Richard Dawkins said: "Biology is the study of complicated things that give the appearance of having been designed for a purpose." Richard Dawkins, *The Blind Watchmaker* (New York: W.W. Norton & Company, 1986), 1.

9. Maxwell strongly opposed Darwin's evolution theory in a paper he presented to the British Association for the Advancement of Science: "No theory of evolution can be formed to account for the similarity of molecules, for evolution necessarily implies continuous change. . . . The exact equality of each molecule to all others of the same kind gives it . . . the essential character of a manufactured article, and precludes the idea of its being eternal and self-existent." J.C. Maxwell, "Discourse on Molecules," a paper presented to the British Association at Bradford in 1873, as cited in: E.L. Williams and G. Mulfinger, *Physical Science for Christian Schools* (Greenville, SC: Bob Jones University Press, 1974), 487.

Great are the works of the Lord, studied by all who delight in them.

Maxwell understood that the right study of God's world begins with a right understanding of who He is (Psalm 111:10). Modern science came about through the working out of a particular worldview, and that worldview was Christianity. Professor of social sciences Rodney Stark, an agnostic, acknowledges this:

> . . . it was not the "wisdom of the east" that gave rise to science, nor did Zen meditation turn people's hearts against slavery . . . science was not the work of Western secularists or even deists; it was entirely the work of devout believers in an active, conscious, creator God. And it was faith in the goodness of this same God and in the mission of Jesus that led other devout Christians to end slavery. . . . Western civilization really was God-given.[10]

The fact of the matter is that in order to do science, you need to *believe* there is law and order in the world before you go out there looking for it. There are certain presuppositions required for science to even work. For example, the belief that the universe is real and intelligible. The belief that the universe is real comes from the fact that God created the universe and therefore matter is real and has a real objective reality. The universe also needs to be orderly for science to even work. But why would the universe be orderly if it is just the result of a naturalistic cosmic accident (or even if the erratic gods of Greece or Rome were in control)? The universe obeys certain laws and is orderly because God is a lawgiver and a God of order. God is relevant to all science, as the very fact we can do science requires God to underpin it. There was a deep-seated conviction among the founders of early modern science that nature (creation) was intelligible because it was made by a rational intellect, namely the God of Scripture. Isaac Newton, quite possibly the greatest scientist of all time, who believed "atheism is so senseless,"[11] in talking about the fine tuning of the planetary systems in his great work *General Scholium to the Principia*, states:

---

10. Rodney Stark, *For the Glory of God: How Monotheism Led to Reformations, Science, Witch-hunts and the End of Slavery* (Princeton, NJ: Princeton University Press, 2003), 376.
11. "A Short Scheme of the True Religion," manuscript quote in *Memoirs of the Life, Writings and Discoveries of Sir Isaac Newton*, by Sir David Brewster, (Edinburgh: Thomas Constable and Co., 1855), 347.

Though these bodies may indeed continue in their orbits by the mere laws of gravity, yet they could by no means have at first derived the regular position of the orbits themselves from those laws. Thus, this most beautiful system of the sun, planets, and comets, could only proceed from the council and dominion of an intelligent and powerful Being.[12]

Newton and many other of these early scientists recognized that because God is rational and has a rational mind and has made humanity in His image such that they also had rationality to "think God's thoughts after him" (Johannes Kepler, astronomer [1571–1630]). The belief that humanity could perceive the rationality, order, and design that has been built into the universe was the very foundation of science itself. If you remove this foundation for science, you will end up with irrationality. It is important to realize that *all* scientists, no matter who they are, have faith; they believe with perfect faith in the rational intelligibility of the universe. However, only those scientists who believe in the triune God of the Bible can give a coherent account for that rationality. This is why it is important to recognize that presuppositions play an important role in any interpretation of the world. The naturalistic evolutionary view of the future of the planet is antithetical to the glorious outlook of the biblical view of the future of the planet.

What is interesting is that there are many Christians who accept the big bang as the explanation for how God created the universe and who also tend to be orthodox in other beliefs (inerrancy of Scripture, virgin birth, miracles, Resurrection of Jesus, etc.) yet are inconsistent in not accepting the evolutionary process of the end of all things. The origin of the universe in the big bang and its end in a "heat death" belong to the same worldview. So, for Christians to accept one and not the other is a sign of inconsistency. It is good that many of those Christians recognize the naturalistic presuppositions of scientists regarding the future of the universe and rightly reject them, yet it is an inconsistency that they do not recognize their naturalistic presuppositions with regard to the origin of the universe and the age of the earth. Just as in Genesis 1 creation

12. Scholium at the end of Sir Isaac Newton's "Mathematical Principles of Natural Philosophy," translated by Andrew Motte, revised by Florian Cajore. Published in *Great Books of the Western World #34*, Robert Maynard Hutchins, editor in chief (Chicago, IL: William Benton, 1952:2), 73–74, http://www.endlesssearch.co.uk/science_newton.htm.

came into existence through the power of God's Word, so the creation of the new heavens and earth will be a supernatural event through the Word of God (3:7; cf. Genesis 1:3; Psalm 33:6). The only difference is that whereas creation in Genesis 1 took six days (Exodus 20:11), as a pattern of the work week for humanity, the new heavens and earth will be a rapid supernatural event (it will not take billions of years for the new heavens and earth to be inaugurated!).

In verses 10–13 the Apostle Peter continues his argument against the scoffers who, like many other philosophical worldviews at that time, rejected the idea of a new world. The Greek Epicurean philosophers (though Peter is probably not arguing against them) were indifferent to the gods because they believed the gods were too removed to be objects of concern; the Epicureans were basically like today's agnostic secularists. They argued that the chief human good was "pleasure" and that the gods did not interfere in human affairs. The Epicureans did not believe in an afterlife but rather believed that at death the body merely returned to its various elements.[13] Unlike the Greek cyclical view of history, the biblical view is finite, linear, and predetermined. Peter is arguing that God has intervened in the past history of the world and will also intervene in the future of the world by creating a new heavens and earth. The new heavens and earth is not a mysterious place but a real physical place where the one true and living God will dwell with His people in a redeemed creation (Revelation 21:3).

The Heavens Will Pass Away, and the Earth Will Be Exposed

Peter did not want his readers to think that the Lord would be "slow" (2 Peter 3:9) in coming, so he reminds them that "the day of the Lord *will come*" (2 Peter 3:10; emphasis mine). The day of the Lord is an eschatological moment in which God will decisively and finally intervene in history to judge His enemies and save His people (Isaiah 13:6, 9; Ezekiel 13:5; 1 Thessalonians 5:2; 2 Thessalonians 2:2), a fact that Peter has already reminded his readers of (see 2 Peter 2:5–9). Peter tells us that the day of the Lord will come like a thief; in other words, it will be sudden and unexpected. This was not a new teaching; Peter was just being consistent with the teaching of Jesus and the Apostle Paul (Peter was familiar with his writings, 2 Peter 3:15–16):

---

13. See Darrell L. Bock, *Acts: Baker Exegetical Commentary on the New Testament* (Grand Rapid, MI: Baker Academic, 2007), 561.

Therefore, stay awake, for you do not know on what day your Lord is coming. But know this, that if the master of the house had known in what part of the night the *thief* was coming, he would have stayed awake and would not have let his house be broken into. Therefore you also must be ready, for the Son of Man is coming at an hour you do not expect (Matthew 24:42–44; emphasis mine).

For you yourselves are fully aware that the day of the Lord will come like a *thief* in the night (1 Thessalonians 5:2; emphasis mine).

The false teachers who scoff at divine intervention in history are challenged by Peter yet again with the sudden arrival of the day of the Lord. The day of the Lord brings with it three specific changes:

1. The heavens will pass away with a roar.
2. The heavenly bodies will be burned up and dissolved.
3. The earth and the works that are done on it will be exposed.

It is important to recognize that each of these points contain differences in translation and interpretation. First, Peter mentions the idea of the passing away of heavens, but again, this was not new to him, as he would have heard Jesus say: "Heaven and earth will pass away, but my words will not pass away" (Matthew 24:35; cf. Isaiah 34:4). Peter's reference to the "heavens" goes back to verses 5 and 7 and refers to the created universe, which God is currently sustaining through His Word. The word "roar" (*rhoizēdon*) is an onomatopoeic word (a word that phonetically is like the sound that it describes) and "refers to a rushing sound, whether the whizzing of an arrow, the rush of wings, or the hissing of snakes."[14] Since fire is prominent in the context (2 Peter 3:7), it probably refers to the "crackling roar" made by a massive fire. In the second point, Peter warns that in this execution of divine judgment on the day of the Lord, the "heavenly bodies" (ESV) or "elements" (KJV; NASB) will be dissolved by burning. But what do the "heavenly bodies" refer to? The Greek word for "heavenly bodies" is *stoicheion*, and commentators offer at least three basic suggestions as to what they could be:

---

14. Schreiner, *1,2 Peter, Jude*, 383.

1. Angelic powers or spirits that rule over the natural world
2. The heavenly bodies, the sun, moon, and stars
3. The four basic elements of the physical universe: earth, air, fire, and water

Since the focus of the passage is on the physical universe, *stoicheion* could either refer to the basic elements of the physical universe or the heavenly bodies, but because verse 12 mentions the "heavens" and the "heavenly bodies/elements," this suggests that the *stoicheion* and the earth are closely related, which favors the basic elements of the physical universe.[15] The consequence of the heavens passing away is that when they are burned up and dissolved, then the earth and the works done on it will be "exposed." Again, there is an interpretive question here, as what does it mean for the earth and the works done in it to be exposed? This question leads to the third point: The verb at the end of verse 10 is one of the most difficult phrases in the New Testament and the focus of enormous textual variation, as is reflected in modern English translations:

"and the earth and its works will be burned up [*katakaēsetai*]" (NASB).

"both the earth and the works that are in it will be burned up [*katakaēsetai*]" (NKJV; cf. KJV).[16]

"and the earth and the works in it will disappear [*aphanisthēsetai*]" (TEV).[17]

"and the earth and everything done in it will be laid bare [*heurethēsetai*]" (NIV).

"and the earth and the works that are done on it will be exposed [*heurethēsetai*]" (ESV).

---

15. See Moo, *2 Peter*, 189–190; Schreiner, *1, 2 Peter, Jude*, 384.
16. The Majority Text (readings from the majority of manuscripts, representing the Byzantine text-type) reads "burned up" and is found in many English translations (NASB; NKJV; KJV) and makes good sense since Peter has been talking about the destruction of the earth by fire. However, if this reading is original, "it is difficult to see how 'will be found [exposed/laid bare]' would have come to be in its place." Schreiner, *1, 2 Peter, Jude*, 385.
17. There is little evidence for the reading that the earth "will disappear" (TEV), and it is most likely scribal conjecture. See Schreiner, *1, 2 Peter, Jude*, 385.

The reading "exposed/laid bare" (ESV; NIV) has the strongest manuscript support,[18] although there are some scholars who argue that *heurethēsetai* "seems to be devoid of meaning in the context."[19] Nevertheless, in his scholarly work *New Testament Text and Translation Commentary*, Philip Comfort argues:

> The awkwardness and opaqueness of the verb εὑρεθήσεται [*heurethēsetai*] can be removed if it is understood as a divine passive: "will be found out by God." As such, the verse speaks of divine judgment (cf. Job 20:27). When all the universe melts away on the final day of judgment (see Rev. 20:11), everything that has been done on earth will be exposed to God's judgment; all will be discovered as to its value (cf. 1 Cor. 3:10–15). This concept suits the context, which speaks of what will occur on the final day of God's judgment (see 3:7).[20]

Despite the difficulties surrounding the end verb in verse 10, many commentators favor the reading that the earth will be "exposed/laid bare" (ESV; NIV) and see it as a reference to the earth being exposed before God in final judgment.[21]

The future judgment of the earth that Peter focused upon is not designed so that people can turn back to their former ways, like the scoffers (2 Peter 2:22). Rather, Peter's words have an ethical basis for how believers should live in light of that future judgment. Peter has continually reminded his readers of these things because the false teaching of the scoffers concerning the future caused them to follow their own sinful desires (2 Peter 3:1–3; cf. 1:12–15). While the scoffers attack the idea of the return of Jesus, Peter gives an eschatological exhortation for believers. In expectation of Jesus' return, Peter urges believers to live holy lives. Why? Because skepticism in the return of Jesus can produce indifference in believers and how they live out their lives in the present. A proper understanding of the future (eschatology) should not cause us to

---

18. It is found in two of the oldest and most complete manuscripts: Codices Sinaiticus & Vaticanus.
19. Bruce M Metzger, *A Textual Commentary on the Greek New Testament* (New York: United Bible Societies, 1971), 706.
20. Philip W. Comfort, *New Testament Text and Translation Commentary: Commentary on the variant readings of the ancient New Testament manuscripts and how they relate to the major English translation* (Carol Stream, IL: Tyndale House Publishers, 2008), 768.
21. See Moo, *2 Peter*, 191; Schreiner, *1, 2 Peter, Jude*, 385–386; Davids, *2 Peter and Jude*, 286.

be skeptical in our thinking or immoral in our conduct but to live holy and godly lives, as Peter says in verse 11: "Since all these things are thus to be dissolved, what sort of people ought you to be in lives of holiness and godliness." In focusing on the future, Peter tells us how to live in the present world. Peter has already stressed that God's "divine power has granted to us all things that pertain to life and godliness" (2 Peter 1:3). He also pointed out that holiness reflects God's own character: "but as he who called you is holy, you also be holy in all your conduct, since it is written, 'You shall be holy, for I am holy' " (1 Peter 1:15–16). So, when Peter says, "what sort of people ought you to be," it is really a rhetorical question. It should be obvious that in looking forward to the return of Jesus, believers should be living holy and godly lives (1 Peter 2:9–12).

The idea that believers can live any way they want is contrary to what Peter has already said in that they should make every effort to supplement their faith with self-control and godliness and to "be all the more diligent to confirm your calling and election. . ." (2 Peter 1:6, 7, 10). In a Western world which is rapidly decaying morally and skeptics scoff at the idea that they will be held accountable for their actions, Christians need to recognize the difference between God's perspective and human perspective.

In verse 12 Peter continues to focus on the fact that living holy and godly lives is founded upon eschatology when he states that we are "waiting for and hastening the coming of the day of God, because of which the heavens will be set on fire and dissolved, and the heavenly bodies will melt as they burn!" A few verses earlier Peter spoke of "the day of the Lord" (3:10), but here he speaks of the "the coming of the day of God." These are not two different events; rather, they "refer to the same eschatological event, which is also spoken of as the 'coming' or 'Parousia' of Christ (2 Peter 1:16; 3:4)."[22] Peter spoke of "hastening [*speudontas*][23] the coming of the day of God." In other words, believers can speed up God's arrival by living holy lives. This does not make God any less sovereign over the world, just as in the same way He uses prayer and the gospel to bring people to salvation. Peter is simply echoing Jesus' teaching, as He taught that prayer plays a part in this:

---

22. Davids, *2 Peter and Jude*, 289.
23. The verb *speudo* has the most natural sense of being able to speed up (Luke 2:16; 19:5, 6; Acts 20:16, 22:18).

Pray then like this: "Our Father in heaven, hallowed be your name. Your kingdom come, your will be done, on earth as it is in heaven" (Matthew 6:9–10).

In the last part of verse 12 Peter describes the cosmic effects of the day of the Lord that the heavens will be destroyed by fire and the elements will melt. Christians, however, do not just "look forward" to the destruction of the heaven and earth, they look forward to the creation of a new heavens and earth in which righteousness will dwell. Living holy and godly lives not only keeps believers from the desires of this decaying world but also prepares us for the "new heavens and a new earth in which *righteousness dwells*" (2 Peter 3:13; emphasis mine; cf. 1:1).

The New Heavens and Earth

This present world will not last forever; it will ultimately pass away, not because the universe will run out of energy or from some human-initiated apocalyptic scenario, but because the God who declares "the end from the beginning" (Isaiah 46:10) has revealed to us that He will one day bring an end to death and suffering by creating a new heavens and a new earth. The belief in a new heavens and earth is not original with Peter but is grounded in the prophetic literature in the Old Testament:

> For behold, I create [*bārā'*] *new heavens* and a *new earth*, and the former things shall not be remembered or come into mind (Isaiah 65:17; emphasis mine).

> For as the *new heavens and* the *new earth* that I make shall remain before me, says the LORD, so shall your offspring and your name remain (Isaiah 66:22; emphasis mine).

The prophet Isaiah, who ministered to the nations of Israel and Judah several centuries before Jesus (~740–690 B.C.), had previously prophesied that in delivering His people Israel out of Babylon, God would be doing a "new thing" that only the Creator of the heavens and earth could do (Isaiah 43:19; cf. 42:9, 48:6). Isaiah acknowledges that God created the world without assistance or counsel, and as the Creator of the entire universe, He acts in history (Isaiah 40:28, 42:5, 44:24, 45:18). In a fallen world where sin dominates, it is only the Creator, who spoke creation into being, who can create a new heavens and earth. These passages in Isaiah that speak of God creating a new heavens and earth are built upon the creation account in the Book of Genesis. In Genesis 1, God created (*bārā'*)[24] the heavens and the earth, and His creation is declared to be "very good" (Genesis 1:31). This is no longer a world that is "very good" but is a world filled with death, suffering, and human rebellion, and many people live in pain, uncertainty, and hopelessness. People naturally ask questions. Can I have hope in a world that seems so uncertain? Will a day ever come when death and suffering will be no more? The prophet Isaiah gave the people of his day (and ours) hope and certainty that one day the LORD "will swallow up death forever; and the Lord God will wipe away tears from all faces, and the reproach of his people he will take away from all the earth" (Isaiah 25:8; cf. 1 Corinthians 15:54). This will happen because of what the suffering servant of the LORD (Jesus) achieved for us through His atoning death and Resurrection from the dead (Isaiah 52:13–53:12; cf. Acts 8:32–33).

The reason we can be confident of a new heavens and earth is that the God who created the heavens alone is in control of world history, and only He can accurately predict the future (Isaiah 41:1–20). Isaiah prophesied that God would use Cyrus, the future king of Persia, to help regather the faithful remnant of Israel back to the land a century and a half before that regathering happened (Isaiah 44:24–28). He identified that future king by name. Isaiah could prophesy this because he served the true God, who has exhaustive foreknowledge of future events (Isaiah 44:6–8). God predicted the future so that when it came about, His people would acknowledge that He, unlike the gods of the nations, is the one true God (Isaiah 41:21–26). God knows the future because He created and oversees all things according to His own wise plan. The purpose of predictive prophecy is to show that God is guiding human history to accomplish His purposes. Because God is all-knowing, we can rest secure in His promise of a new heavens and new earth where there will be no more death and suffering, as there will be a physical restoration of creation to its former Edenic conditions (see below). It is only in the new heavens and earth that the *former* world and all the death, suffering, and corruption in it will be no longer remembered.

There is another important issue to deal with which scholars are divided over: Does Peter teach that the new heavens and earth will replace

---

24. In Genesis 1, God is the subject of the verb *bārā*, and the material out of which something is created is never mentioned (Genesis 1:21, 1:27 x3). These verses designate God bringing something new and unique into existence.

the current material universe? Or does he envision a transformation of the existing world? What makes this issue complicated is that there are other passages in the New Testament that seem to suggest both these things. Those who believe in the replacement of this earth with a new one point to passages that suggest a complete replacement of the entire creation: Psalm 102:25–26; Isaiah 51:6; Matthew 24:35; 1 Corinthians 7:31; Revelation 21:1. Those who hold to this position argue that the word *parerchomai* (pass away) means "to come to an end and so no longer be there."[25] On the other hand, there are also passages that suggest the transformation of creation: Matthew 19:28; Acts 3:21; Romans 8:21; Revelation 21:5. Those who hold to this position argue that the word *kainos* (new) is not contrasting something that is new as opposed to old and is done away with, but something that is new in its quality "in the sense that what is old has become obsolete, and should be replaced by what is new."[26] Although there is merit in both positions, and while it is difficult to be absolutely sure, it seems the transformation of creation is what Peter has in mind in chapter 3. Peter's point is not that the earth will be replaced but that everything that has gone on in it will be exposed through judgment, presumably bringing damage to the earth. Keep in mind that Peter has already shown his readers what he means by the destruction of the earth. Only a few verses earlier, Peter paralleled the destruction of the earth in the time of Noah, through the global Flood, with the coming judgment of the earth by fire (2 Peter 3:6–7). The global Flood was cataclysmic, but it did not totally destroy the earth so that it no longer existed. Rather, after the Flood had purged the old world of sin, Noah and his family were ready to start again by being fruitful and multiplying in the "new earth" (Genesis 9:1). The restoration of creation implies that the future creation will resemble the pre-Fall creation, when man and animals were herbivores and sin and death were not there (Genesis 1:29–31). The plan of God in Scripture speaks about a restoration of creation in the future because of the Curse brought on it through Adam's rebellion (cf. Romans 8:19–22). This would also be consistent with Peter's statement about the Messiah (Jesus) in Acts 3:21:

> . . . whom heaven must receive until the time for restoring all the things about which God spoke by the mouth of his holy prophets long ago.

---

25. See BDAG: *A Greek-English Lexicon of the New Testament*, 776.
26. Ibid, 497.

In context, Peter's sermon to the Jewish people comes after the healing of the blind beggar (Acts 3:7–10). The Apostle Peter speaks of a future "restoration of all things," and the genitive neuter construction *panton* ("of all things") indicates that he is referring to all of creation, not just people. The translation "restoration" (*apokatastasis*) is correct, as it is from the same root word for "restore" in Acts 1:6. The restoration of which Peter speaks is "of that more perfect state of (even physical) things which existed before the Fall."[27] The restoration of all things is about transformation, not destruction. Christians who believe in the idea that the world is millions of years old (i.e., theistic evolutionists and old-earth creationists) must be able to explain what creation will be restored to. Will it be restored to a state of death, suffering, and natural disasters? These things have always existed in a theistic evolutionary and old-earth view of creation.

But why does Peter speak of a new earth? This is often surprising for Christians, as there are many books, Bible studies, and sermons on heaven, but they often mention nothing about the new earth. Christians often talk about living with God in heaven when they die, but the Bible tells us there is more than that. As theologian Anthony Hoekema explains,

> Since God will make the new earth his dwelling place, and since where God dwells there heaven is, we shall then continue to be in heaven while we are on the new earth. For heaven and earth will then no longer be separated as they are now, but will be one. But to leave the new earth out of the consideration when we think of the final state of believers is greatly to impoverish biblical teaching about the life to come.[28]

The destiny of the redeemed is not an ethereal existence in God's abode in heaven, the place where He is worshiped and that is full of His blessing. Rather, heaven will one day come down and meet earth, and those who have been redeemed out of every tribe, tongue, and nation will live in the new heavens and earth (Revelation 5:9, 21:2). To properly understand the need of a new earth, it is necessary to go back to the Book of Genesis were God created the first earth. In Genesis 1 when God created

---

27. See Thayer, *Greek-English Lexicon of the New Testament*, 63.
28. Anthony Hoekema, *The Bible and the Future* (Grand Rapids: Eerdmans, 1979), 274.

the physical universe, it was created not only to declare His glory but also for mankind to inhabit (Psalm 19:1; Isaiah 45:18). The pinnacle of His creation is when He uniquely created mankind in His image:

> Then God said, "Let us make man in our image, after our likeness. And let them have dominion over the fish of the sea and over the birds of the heavens and over the livestock and over all the earth and over every creeping thing that creeps on the earth." So God created man in his own image, in the image of God he created him; male and female he created them. And God blessed them. And God said to them, "Be fruitful and multiply and fill the earth and subdue it, and have dominion over the fish of the sea and over the birds of the heavens and over every living thing that moves on the earth" (Genesis 1:26–28).

In Genesis 1:26, God creates mankind to be His viceroys (royal figures), who would represent Him by having "dominion" or "rule" (rādâ)[29] over His creation (see Psalm 8:4–8, 72:8; 1 Kings 4:33).[30] God then blesses and commands[31] His image-bearers (Adam and Eve) to be fruitful and multiply and fill the earth, subdue it, and have rule over it.[32] Mankind was specifically endowed with and given responsibility for subduing and ruling over God's creation. This is even reiterated after the global Flood of Noah's day (Genesis 9:2–3). The distinction between mankind and the animals is clear, as His image-bearers are called to rule over the earth, which the animals are part of (Genesis 1:28; cf. 9:2–3). Mankind is unique; they are not animals, as they are given certain communicable divine attributes: reason, personality, and morality. Not only that, but mankind was originally endowed with holiness and righteousness (cf. Ecclesiastes 7:29; Ephesians 4:24). In the context of God's creation and

---

29. The word rādâ is often used of royal dominion (1 Kings 4:24; Psalm 110:2; Isaiah 14:2).
30. In Psalm 8 David sees his role as king in reference to Adam (mankind) in ruling the earth. While in 1 Kings 4:33, King Solomon exercises his wisdom over "trees, from the cedar that is in Lebanon to the hyssop that grows out of the wall. He spoke also of beasts, and of birds, and of reptiles, and of fish." These are the same categories of animals that Adam had dominion over (Genesis 1:26–28).
31. The language of Genesis 1:26–28 clearly indicates that this was a command given to mankind. See Andrew Kulikovsky, "Is There a Dominion Mandate? Discussion: In Defense of Human Dominion," May 1, 2013, https://answersingenesis.org/environmental-science/stewardship/is-there-a-dominion-mandate-discussion-in-defense-of-human-dominion/.
32. To be blessed in the Old Testament is directly tied to reproduction (Genesis 9:1; 17:16, 20; 22:17; 24:60; 28:3), which is something only a male and female can naturally do.

blessing of mankind, it is important to understand God's command to Adam in the Garden in Eden:

> And the Lord God planted *a garden in Eden*, in the east, and there he put the man whom he had formed. . . .

> The LORD God took the man and put him in the garden of Eden to *work* it and *keep* it. And the LORD God commanded the man, saying, "You may surely eat of every tree of the garden, but of the tree of the knowledge of good and evil you shall not eat, for in the day that you eat of it you shall surely die" (Genesis 2:8, 15–17; emphasis mine).

Notice that the garden is not Eden, but it is toward the east *in* Eden; Eden is a much larger geographical location. It is in that Garden that God places Adam and commands him how he is to work in the Garden and to regulate how he was to act before Him. The Hebrew words in Genesis 2:15 for "work" (*'aḇaḏ*) and "keep" (*šāmar*) are used elsewhere of the work of the priestly duties at the tabernacle (Numbers 1:53, 3:7–10, 18:5), man's worship of God (Exodus 8:1, 20; 9:1, 13), and of his obedience to God's Word (Genesis 17:9, 18:19). The two words also appear together in Deuteronomy 10:12–13 in the context of worshiping God. Adam, therefore, was put in the Garden to worship God by "working" and "keeping" it. The Garden in Eden was a unique and special place that God created for Adam to function as a priest in His "tabernacle." It was also a place where the LORD God came on a regular basis to have fellowship with Adam and Eve when He "walked"[33] (*mithallēk*) with them in the Garden (Genesis 3:8), just as He often "walked" in the sanctuary and camp when He dwelt among His people Israel to fellowship with them (Leviticus 26:12; Deuteronomy 23:14). Adam was blessed and commanded by God to rule over the entire creation and to worship Him in the Garden in Eden. In this role, Adam's "kingly and priestly activity in the garden was to be a beginning fulfilment of the commission in 1:28 and was not limited to the garden's original earthly boundaries but was to be extended over the whole world."[34] Adam's task, then, was to spread the goodness of the Garden in

33. The *hitpael* verb form "walking" (*mithallēk*) in Genesis 3:8 implies this, as it stresses habitual aspects of action. See Hamilton, Genesis 1-17, 192. In the context of Genesis 3:8, however, the LORD God comes (in a theophany) to Adam and Eve in judgment.

34. G.K. Beale, *The Temple and the Church's Mission: A Biblical Theology of the Dwelling Place of God, New Studies in Biblical Theology 17* (Downers Grove, IL: InterVarsity, 2004), 68.

Eden over the entire earth. Adam, however, did not "keep" (guard) the Garden as he was commanded. Instead of guarding the Garden from the serpent (Satan) and driving him out if it, through temptation he lost his rule over creation and instead was driven out of the Garden (Genesis 3:24; cf. 4:14). In order to prevent entrance back into the Garden, God places the cherubim (plural) to guard its entrance in the east (cf. Genesis 4:14, 11:2). Along with the cherubim, God places a flaming sword to guard the tree of life. The sword is independent of the cherubim, as it "turned every way" to "guard" (*šāmar*) the way to the tree of life. It is a sad reflection on Adam, who was created to "guard" (*šāmar*) the Garden, but it is now he who is guarded from it. Adam lost his rule over the earth, and Satan began to rule over it (John 12:31, 14:30, 16:11; cf. 1 John 5:19).[35] The image that mankind was originally made in was now defaced but not totally lost (Genesis 9:6; James 3:9; cf. Acts 17:28).[36] Whereas before Adam had disobeyed God's command there was only blessing in creation (Genesis 1:22, 28; 2:3), now because of his disobedience God curses the ground:

> And to Adam he said, "Because you have listened to the voice of your wife and have eaten of the tree of which I commanded you, 'You shall not eat of it,' *cursed is the ground* because of you; in pain you shall eat of it all the days of your life. . ." (Genesis 3:17; emphasis mine; cf. 5:29, 8:21).

This was not just the ground in the Garden in Eden, as God said of the ground "thorns and thistles it shall bring forth for you" and Adam was sent "out from the garden of Eden to work the ground from which he was taken" (Genesis 3:18, 23). From the moment Adam disobeyed God in the Garden in Eden, sin has reigned, and the whole of creation now groans under the weight of sin (Romans 5:17, 8:22).

---

35. The title "prince" or "ruler" (*archon*), as well as other titles in the New Testament — "the father of lies" (John 8:44), "the god of this world" (2 Corinthians 4:4), "prince of the power of the air" (Ephesians 2:2) — are used to refer to Satan (the serpent). Satan's creaturely "rule" over the world was defeated at the Cross, he is now a defeated foe who is in his last act of rebellion (cf. Acts 26:18; Colossians 1:13).
36. Even after the Fall in Genesis 3, the image of God is not erased. In the context of Genesis 9:6, God is speaking to Noah after the Flood and is declaring that man's life, even though it is fallen, is sacred because he is created in the image of God. In the context of James 3:9, James has already alluded to the creation account (3:7; Genesis 1:26) to show the various creatures that are under man's dominion, and in 3:9 he reminds believers of the fact that they should not curse people because they bear the image of God (Genesis 1:27).

In the midst of His judgment, God graciously gave a promise of redemption concerning the offspring of the woman: "I will put enmity between you and the woman, and between your offspring and her offspring; he shall bruise your head, and you shall bruise his heel" (Genesis 3:15). The hope of the appointed offspring is unveiled progressively through the birth to Eve of Seth (Genesis 4:26, 5:1–32), Noah's offspring (Genesis 9:9), and the offspring of Abraham (Genesis 12:1–3, 7). The promised "offspring" finds its fulfilment in the Lord Jesus, the last Adam, whom the Apostle Paul identifies as the "offspring" of Abraham (Galatians 3:16). The promised offspring came to crush the head of the serpent: "Whoever makes a practice of sinning is of the devil, for the devil has been sinning from the beginning. The reason the Son of God appeared was to destroy the works of the devil" (1 John 3:8). It was by Jesus' victorious death on the Cross that He disarmed the rule and authority of Satan and brought about the reconciliation of all creation:

> For in him all the fullness of God was pleased to dwell, and through him to reconcile to himself all things, whether on earth or in heaven, making peace by the blood of his cross (Colossians 1:19–20).

> He disarmed the rulers and authorities and put them to open shame, by triumphing over them in him (Colossians 2:15).[37]

The reconciliation that Jesus' death brought about is clearly cosmic in scope, as the phrase "all things" (*ta panta*) occurs five times in the context and refers to the created universe (Colossians 1:16 [x2], 17, 18, 20). The reconciliation of the world is as wide as the scope of the Curse. The Greek word translated "reconcile" is *apokatallossō*, which presumes that a state of hostility exists, as it refers to restoration of fellowship (see Romans 5:10; 2 Corinthians 5:18–20).[38] It is contrasted here with blood, which implies violence and death. However, this surely makes no sense in an old-earth creation or theistic evolutionary worldview where violence and death have been around from the beginning. How would Jesus' death on the Cross reconcile creation if bloodshed has always been a part of it? To

---

37. The "rulers" and "authorities" that Paul refers to are the spiritual powers that Christ is head over (see Colossians 2:10; cf. 1:16; Ephesians 6:11–12).

38. In Romans 5:10 and 2 Corinthians 5:18, 19, 20, the reconciliation is between God and humans. However, in the context of Colossians 1:20, the reconciliation Paul is talking about is not limited to humans, as it makes clear the entire creation is in view.

accept millions of years of human and animal death before the creation and Fall of man undermines the teaching about the full redemptive work of Christ. This reconciliation of all things (on earth and in heaven) comes about because of Christ's work on the Cross, which has brought peace (*shalom* — wholeness), bringing an end to the hostility that exists in creation. The reversal of the Curse is what is promised to us in the ministry of Jesus and is the fulfilment of His atoning work. Paul also connects Christ's restoring work to the image of God, as one of the things God does in our redemption is gradually renew that image: ". . . put on the new self, which is being renewed in knowledge after the image of its creator" (Colossians 3:10).

God's original plan for creation in Genesis comes to fulfilment in the Book of Revelation where the pre-Fall conditions in the Garden in Eden are restored for the people of God in eternity (see Revelation 2:7; 22:2, 14, 19). The Eden in the new creation is not just a part of the earth, but it extends throughout the whole earth.

Genesis 1–2	Genesis 3–Revelation 20	Revelation 21–22
Original very good earth	Fallen earth	New redeemed earth
Universal blessing	Blessing selectively given	Fulfilled blessing
No Curse	Cursed earth	Curse removed
Mankind is unashamed	Mankind is shamed	Mankind has no shame or potential for it
No sin	Sin corrupts	Sin removed
First Adam created to reign	First Adam falls from grace; Last Adam comes to redeem	Last Adam reigns along with his co-heirs, a redeemed humanity
Tree of life in Eden (humanity can eat from)	Tree of life in paradise (humanity cut off from)	Tree of life in New Jerusalem (humanity can eat from forever)
Serpent (Satan) on earth	Serpent (Satan) cursed but still present on earth	Serpent (Satan) removed from the earth and thrown into the lake of fire

Mankind is in fellowship with God	Mankind cut off from fellowship with God	Mankind now dwells face-to-face with God
Mankind created from the earth	Mankind dies and returns to the earth	Redeemed mankind resurrected from the earth to live on the new earth
Edenic paradise	Edenic paradise lost	Edenic paradise regained[39]

Heaven is not about floating on clouds playing harps, as it is pictured in many medieval paintings in museums, but it is about having dominion over a global Eden in which we will rule and enjoy it as it was originally intended (cf. Revelation 3:21). The new heavens and earth will be vividly different to the present fallen earth that we now live upon. Our finite minds are not able to comprehend or imagine what the new heavens and earth will be like, even though we often wonder what it will be like, but consider some of the things that we are told will not be there:[40]

1. No more sea (Revelation 21:1)
2. No more separation between God and man (Revelation 21:2–3)
3. No more tears (Revelation 21:4)
4. No more mourning (Revelation 21:4)
5. No more crying (Revelation 21:4)
6. No more pain or suffering (or disease) (Revelation 21:4)
7. No more death (Revelation 21:4)
8. No more sinners: the cowardly, the faithless, the detestable, murderers, the sexually immoral, sorcerers, idolaters (Revelation 21:8)
9. No temple (Revelation 21:22)
10. No more closing of the city gates (Revelation 21:25)

---

39. This is a shortened list from Randy Alcorn's book *Heaven* (Carol Stream, IL: Tyndale House Publishers, 2004), 82–85.
40. It is important to keep in mind that Christians disagree over the meaning of many of the symbols in Revelation. For example, does the lack of the sea refer to: 1) the origin of evil (Revelation 12:18, 13:1); 2) the nations that persecute the saints (Revelation 12:18, 13:1, 17:1–6); 3) the place of the dead (Revelation 20:13); 4) the location of the world's idolatrous trade activity (Revelation 18:10–19); or 5) a body of water, part of this world (Revelation 5:13, 7:1–4, 8:8–9, 10:2, 5–6, 8, 14:7, 16:3). See Grant R. Osborne, *Revelation: Baker Exegetical Commentary on the New Testament* (Grand Rapids, MI: Baker Academic, 2002), 730–731.

11. No sun, moon, or night because God gives it light (Revelation 21:23–25)
12. Nothing unclean (Revelation 21:27)
13. No more Curse (Revelation 22:3)

Because such things as tears, crying, pain, death, murder, sexual immorality, and idolatry are part and parcel of this fallen world, it is hard to imagine what it will be like to live in a world without them, but the God who created the world has promised that He will do away with them. The things of this world that cause us pain and heartache will one day be no more. The one thing to look forward to most about the new heavens and earth is the absence of sin and all the devastation it has brought about. When that day finally arrives and we are in the new heavens and earth in our fully redeemed bodies, we will finally be free from sin and even the ability to sin, as then we will possess glorified minds, as our bodies will be redeemed (cf. Romans 8:23, 30). In our glorified state in the new heavens and earth, believers will not be able to sin, as we will be perfectly sanctified (glorified). This does not mean we will no longer be human, but rather, as God's creatures in our union with Him, we will finally be perfected. In this sense, the eternal state will be even better than Eden, as the possibility to fall into corruption will be completely absent. With our redeemed minds, our thoughts will be pure and holy, as we are free from the "body of death" (Romans 7:24) to truly love God with all our mind, heart, soul, and strength.

The Bible describes the end of all things in term of its beginning, as a renewal of paradise. This does not mean that the new heavens and earth is just about going back to Eden's original paradise when history and culture were just starting out. Just as there was direct continuity from the pre-Fall to post-Fall world, so there will be with this world to the new world. The physical creation will be renewed, and we will continue to live and act in it, enjoying the blessing of the new earth. In the new earth, our resurrection bodies will be part of the new creation, which will never grow old or be weak or ill. In 1 Corinthians 15, the Apostle Paul points out that our new bodies will have a glory that our present ones do not have (1 Corinthians 15:42–44). The reason we need new bodies is the result of the corruption[41] brought about through Adam's disobedience

---

41. The Greek word for corruption, *phthora* (1 Corinthians 15:42), is the same word used in Romans 8:21 where Paul refers to the creation's bondage to decay.

(Genesis 3:19). Unlike the Greek philosophical view of the afterlife, Paul does not teach that our future bodies will be made from spirit. In order to make his point about the nature of the body, in typical form, Paul makes his appeal to Scripture. Paul quotes from Genesis 2:7 where God made Adam from the dust of the ground and gave him a soul, making him a living being:

> And so it is written, "The first man Adam became a living being." The last Adam became a life-giving spirit. However, the spiritual is not first, but the natural, and afterward the spiritual. The first man was of the earth, made of dust; the second Man is the Lord from heaven. As was the man of dust, so also are those who are made of dust; and as is the heavenly Man, so also are those who are heavenly. And as we have borne the image of the man of dust, we shall also bear the image of the heavenly Man (1 Corinthians 15:45–49; NKJV).

Paul uses the word "first" before "man" in order to draw the contrast between Adam and Christ. There is a difference between our present bodies and our resurrection bodies. Paul's reference to "the natural" is referring to Adam, while "the spiritual" refers to Christ. The parallel Paul uses is that of Adam's bodily existence and Christ's resurrected body. In verse 47, Paul moves from the contrast between "natural" and "spiritual" to that between the "earthly" and "heavenly." This helps define what he meant by "natural" and "spiritual" by stressing the origins of the two men. Just as the first Adam was of the earth and therefore the originator of humanity, so Jesus Christ, the Last Adam, is the originator of a new humanity. Our resurrection bodies will be just like Jesus' body after His Resurrection (1 Corinthians 15:51–54; cf. Luke 24:36–40). This will be a physical body able to enjoy food, drink, and fellowship with others (Isaiah 25:6; Luke 14:15; 22:18, 29–30; cf. John 21:12–14).

The new heavens and earth will be anything but boring (as some people seem to think) but will be a place of joy and blessing. As King David wrote, "You make known to me the path of life; in your presence there is fullness of joy; at your right hand are pleasures forevermore" (Psalm 16:11). The New Testament pictures the future of Christians as a future lived not just in heaven but in a renewed and restored earth in resurrected material bodies where we will enjoy, worship, and glorify the triune God forever. The new heavens and earth is a glorious future that Christians have to look forward to where sin and death and the enemies of God have been defeated and in which the triune God will be gloriously present with His people (Revelation: the Father [21:22, 22:3]; Jesus, the Lamb [21:22, 22:3]; and the Holy Spirit [22:17]).

In the beginning God "walked" (dwelt) with man in the Garden to fellowship with him. After man sinned against Him, God graciously came again and "walked" (dwelt) with man on the earth to redeem him from his sin. Finally, in the end when sin and death has been done away with, God will once again "walk" (dwell) with man in the new heavens and earth where we will enjoy His fellowship forever.

> He who testifies to these things says, "Surely I am coming soon." Amen. Come, Lord Jesus! The grace of the Lord Jesus be with all. Amen (Revelation 22:20–21).

APPENDIX

HONORING CHRIST AS LORD

1 Peter 3:15

As we think about Peter's second letter and the coming scoffers, it is important to know what Peter has already said to the believers. In 1 Peter 3:15, Peter is writing about defending their faith in a culture that is hostile to the truth of the Christian faith. When it comes to apologetics, 1 Peter 3:15 is probably the most well-known passage in the Bible. Yet, when we consider the immediate and wider context of this verse, there is a lot more to it than we may have seen at first. This appendix will briefly seek to unpack 1 Peter 3:15 and its application for us as Christians today and the way in which we should engage those who malign the faith of Christians (cf. 1 Peter 4:4).

There is a danger of becoming so familiar with the biblical text that we conclude we know what it is saying without really knowing everything about it. For example, every apologist knows 1 Peter 3:15 because it is a foundational verse for apologetics, yet often the middle of the verse is emphasized ("always being prepared to make a defense") without an understanding of its context of enduring suffering for doing good:

> Finally, all of you, have unity of mind, sympathy, brotherly love, a tender heart, and a humble mind. Do not repay evil for evil or reviling for reviling, but on the contrary, bless, for to this you were called, that you may obtain a blessing. For "Whoever desires to love life and see good days, let him keep his tongue from evil

and his lips from speaking deceit; let him turn away from evil and do good; let him seek peace and pursue it. For the eyes of the Lord are on the righteous, and his ears are open to their prayer. But the face of the Lord is against those who do evil." Now who is there to harm you if you are zealous for what is good? But even if you should suffer for righteousness' sake, you will be blessed. Have no fear of them, nor be troubled, but in your hearts honor Christ the Lord as holy, always being prepared to make a defense to anyone who asks you for a reason for the hope that is in you; yet do it with gentleness and respect (1 Peter 3:8–15).

Many Christians also mistakenly believe that apologetics can be practiced only by the pastor or leader in the church or even by those who are more academically inclined. Peter, however, tells us that apologetics is not just for some Christians but for all believers (Peter was a fisherman). Peter not only tells us that apologetics is for all believers, but also that it involves four things:

- The precondition of apologetics is "in your hearts honor Christ the Lord as holy."

- Believers should always be prepared; in other words, we need to know Scripture.

- Believers should give a reasoned defense of the faith to those who ask from us (it is not "I am going to prove it to you").

- Apologetics is to be done with gentleness and respect.

We need to keep these four things in mind when we are asked to give a defense of our faith by those who do not yet know Christ.

Suffering and Defending the Faith

In his letter, Peter has already told believers that they are "a chosen race, a royal priesthood, a holy nation" (1 Peter 2:9). As a "holy nation," believers are set apart to be different from the world. In a world where we should be seen as different, our lives of faith will usually lead to suffering, whether that may be persecution from the government (1 Peter 2:13–18, 4:15–16) or from unjust masters (1 Peter 2:18–19). Peter is reminding his readers to expect suffering as Christians. Just as Christ suffered for us as our example of gentleness and suffering for righteousness, He is also an example of hope (1 Peter 1:21, 2:21–23). It is in the context of enduring suffering for righteousness' sake (1 Peter 3:14) that believers are to honor Christ the Lord as holy and be prepared to give a reason for their hope. In writing to Christians about defending their faith while suffering for it, Peter is not just talking about something he has no experience of, as he suffered on numerous occasions for his faith (see Acts 4:1–22, 12:1–19). His readers can know that he has lived what he is writing about.

Honoring Christ the Lord

In a world where we fear suffering, Peter reminds us that our focus should be on honoring Christ the Lord. What does it mean to honor Christ the Lord? The word for honor (*hagiazo*) here has the sense of "treat as holy, regard reverently" Christ as Lord. In other words, we are to treat Christ with a special status (see Hebrews 9:13–14). This is not an option but rather a command to all believers, and the desire of our hearts should always be to understand and obey the commands of our Lord (John 14:15, 23; 15:10).

Our holiness will ultimately come from our devotion to Christ, and personal holiness in a culture of opposition usually leads to suffering. To treat Christ as holy also means that we do not see ourselves as the center of our being or purpose; rather, it means we see ourselves as those who are redeemed sinners (1 Peter 1:16, 18–19). Moreover, what you treat as holy in your heart will have an impact on the rest of your life: morality, understanding of life and death, ethical decisions, priorities, and so on.

Apologetics begins by honoring Christ the Lord, not by temporally setting Him aside so that we can engage in a rational discussion. Apologetics applies Scripture to the unbelief of unbelievers and even the unbelief of believers ("help my unbelief"; Mark 9:24). Honoring Christ as Lord means that He 1) has control over all things, 2) speaks with supreme authority, and 3) is present with us (for the purpose of blessing and judgment). Therefore, to honor Christ as Lord is to know that He is in control over our defense of the faith.

Who Is Christ the Lord?

We need to keep in mind that Peter is writing to Greek-speaking people outside of Palestine (1 Peter 1:1), and the vast majority of New Testament references to the Old Testament come from the Greek Septuagint (LXX)

— the Bible of the Early Church. The phrase "honor Christ the Lord" is an adaptation from the Old Testament in Isaiah 8:13. The majority of the time in the LXX, the Hebrew name for God (Yahweh) is translated as *kurios* (Lord).

Isaiah 8:13		1 Peter 3:15a	
ESV	LXX	ESV	NA28
But the Lord of hosts, him you shall honor as holy. Let him be your fear, and let him be your dread.	*Kyrion auton hagiasate kai autos estai sou phobos*	but in your hearts honor Christ the Lord as holy	*kyrion de ton Christon hagias-ate en tais kardi-ais humon*

The term "Lord" in the LXX of Isaiah 8:13 refers directly to the "Lord of Hosts." In Peter's use of the LXX, he inserts "Christ" (Messiah), asserting that we should honor Him as Lord.

In context of Isaiah 8, the nation of Judah is about to face an imminent Assyrian invasion. Isaiah is saying to the people of God that they should not fear the Assyrians but fear "the Lord of hosts." The contrast is between fearing man or fearing the Lord. In the midst of your suffering, do not fear those who are bringing about your suffering, but fear God. Do not allow your attention to be drawn away in an attempt to appease them, but instead hold firm and endure what you have to endure because your goal is to honor Christ the Lord. To honor Christ as Lord in our hearts is to remember that not only is He sovereign over our lives, but also, because of His work on the Cross and His Resurrection from the dead, He is now at the right hand of God where all things are subject to Him (1 Peter 3:22; cf. Romans 8:34; Ephesians 1:20–21). Christ's suffering on the Cross should be a reminder to us that triumph can often come out of suffering since that is what brought us to God (1 Peter 3:18).

We often practice apologetics, hoping that people will think well of us, but it is not about the approval of others — it is about honoring Christ the Lord. Modern apologetics can often leave out sin and repentance because it is seen to be about winning philosophical arguments rather than a willingness to be identified with Christ to the degree that it will cost us. Apologetics cannot be man-centered but must center upon our risen Lord (Acts 17:30–31).

If Christ is rightly honored in the hearts of His people, they will fear Him and not the world. But notice that "always being prepared to make a defense" flows from the obedience to the first part of the text, that is, the obedience to honoring Christ the Lord as holy in our hearts. It is because we are a royal priesthood and a chosen people that we are commanded to give a reason for the hope in us.

The Hope in You

Peter tells us that our personal holiness will require an explanation because it sets us apart as sojourners and exiles (1 Peter 2:11). Those to whom we give an answer are "anyone who asks you for a reason for the hope that is in you." The "you" here is in the plural form. In other words, it is addressed to all believers. Every believer is being commanded to honor Christ the Lord as holy in their hearts and to give a reason for the hope they have. To reason (*apologia*) almost always means to give a defense (see Acts 22:1, 25:16; Philippians 1:7, 16), and this can often come in hostile and unexpected circumstances (Acts 24:10–24, 26:1–23).

The questioning is concerning the hope within us, which means that the hope of the Christian causes the unbelieving questioner to ask why the Christian is different (cf. 1 Peter 4:4). What is the hope in the face of a Christian's suffering? It is a living hope, the hope of a life to come, as Peter had earlier reminded his readers:

> Blessed be the God and Father of our Lord Jesus Christ! According to his great mercy, he has caused us to be born again to a living hope through the resurrection of Jesus Christ from the dead, to an inheritance that is imperishable, undefiled, and unfading, kept in heaven for you. . . (1 Peter 1:3–4).

However, if we don't live in such a way as to honor Christ — if we dress, talk, think, and react like the world — then who is going to ask us about the hope that we have? There must be something about our lives that results in us acting differently from the world. Sometimes people don't hear our words until they see our deeds (1 Peter 2:12). This is not to say that what we do is more important than what we say but that our words must be consistent with our testimony. Remember it was not until Christ died that the Roman centurion recognized who He truly was (Mark 15:39). Most of all, we must not forget to explain the reason for our hope in gentleness and respect. If we suffer, it should be because we have honored Jesus as Lord, not because we have dishonored Him in conduct or speech.

In a world where we face suffering and scoffing for our faith, our apologetic efforts to unbelievers must begin by honoring Christ as Lord in our hearts.

A Library of Answers for Families and Churches

Over 100 faith-affirming answers to some of the most-questioned topics about faith, science, & the Bible.

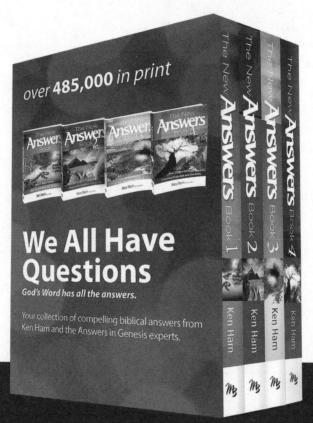

over **485,000** *in print*

We All Have Questions

God's Word has all the answers.

Your collection of compelling biblical answers from Ken Ham and the Answers in Genesis experts.

Also available in digital format.